Financing China Trade and Investment

FINANCING CHINA TRADE AND INVESTMENT

Edited by KUI-WAI LI

Foreword by EDGARDO BARANDIARAN

Westport, Connecticut
London

Library of Congress Cataloging-in-Publication Data

Financing China trade and investment / edited by Kui-Wai Li ; foreword by
    Edgardo Barandiaran
          p.   cm.
      Includes bibliographical references and index.
      ISBN 0–275–95115–4 (alk. paper)
          1. Investments, Foreign—China.   2. Foreign exchange market—
      China.   3. Stock-exchanges—China.   4. China—Foreign economic
      relations.   I. Li, Kui-Wai.
      HG5782.F56   1997
      332.6′73′0951—dc20   96–20691

British Library Cataloguing in Publication Data is available.

Library of Congress Catalog Card Number: 96–20691
ISBN: 0–275–95115–4

First published in 1997

Praeger Publishers, 88 Post Road West, Westport, CT 06881
An imprint of Greenwood Publishing Group, Inc.

Printed in the United States of America

The paper used in this book complies with the
Permanent Paper Standard issued by the National
Information Standards Organization (Z39.48–1984).

10 9 8 7 6 5 4 3 2 1

Contents

Tables and Figures

TABLES

FIGURES

Foreword

For decades to come, historians and social scientists will argue about China's extraordinary economic transformation because it challenges dominant visions and theories and also promotes many new ideas, most of which will be discarded somewhere in the long process of producing authenticated knowledge. The process has started indeed: ongoing analysis of the Chinese experience is already generating the ideas that future historians and social scientists will use to revise and update old visions and theories or to develop new ones.

This book presents the ideas of a distinguished group of researchers about the role of capital accumulation in China's economic transformation. Economists have started to debate the relative importance of resource accumulation and productivity gains in accounting for the high growth of the last seventeen years. For the time being, the prevalent view is that China's growth, as compared to that of most East Asian countries, is the result of a huge accumulation of physical capital and labor, with gains in total factor productivity accounting for (perhaps much) less than thirty percent of the increased output. According to this view, China will be able to maintain high growth rates only if productivity gains increase substantially, which is possible only if further reforms are undertaken rapidly.

Indeed the accumulation of physical capital in the last seventeen years has been extraordinary. It has taken place in many labor-intensive activities, especially agriculture and manufacturing, creating employment for more than one hundred million people; in capital-intensive utilities, by building the infrastructure for transportation, communication, electricity, and water supply; and to a much lesser extent in capital-intensive activities, which provide consumption goods and services for the increasing number of middle- and high-income families. More importantly, it has taken place in many enterprises in which for several reasons the government had invested heavily in the 1950s and 1960s, and in which large investment is needed now if these enterprises' retired and current workers are to enjoy the standard of living to which they claim to be entitled.

Since 1978, the stock of physical capital has been growing at a compound rate close to ten percent per year, with an average gross investment in fixed assets of over thirty percent of Gross Domestic Product (GDP). Since mid-1993, as part of its stabilization drive, the government has succeeded in reducing the growth rate of this investment and changing its composition somewhat, with a higher share of investments in labor-intensive activities and infrastructure. Although at constant prices the level of gross investment in fixed assets will hardly decline, as a percentage of GDP it is likely to decline for several years because of the expected high growth rate of GDP (in turn the result of the large capital accumulation of the last five years). By the end of the century, the stock of physical capital may be eight to ten times higher than it was at the beginning of economic reform in 1978, with a population that will have grown only fifty to sixty percent.

Contrary to the experience of many developing countries, national savings have not been a binding constraint to capital accumulation. Independent of the key role played by foreign capital in facilitating this accumulation, at the macroeconomic level it may be argued that the large inflow of capital has been offset by the accumulation of both international reserves and assets abroad. Furthermore, national savings has been great enough to accumulate large inventories of all kinds of goods, albeit some of little economic value. Although assessments are still tentative because of the deficiencies of the national accounts and other statistics, the savings of both households and the state sector (inclusive of government and enterprises) and the willingness of overseas Chinese to invest in China provide a sound foundation for sustaining a high level of capital accumulation.

Since 1985, when the first phase of economic reform was complete, household savings have been growing at high rates, whereas the savings of the state sector have stagnated and perhaps declined somewhat relative to the GDP. Conclusions of ongoing research on household savings behavior are still tentative because the implications of radical changes in underlying institutions—reforms aimed essentially at transferring the responsibilities for insurance and intertemporal allocation of income from the state to households—have yet to be identified. For example, the ongoing reform of the social security system may have had little effect on household savings so far, but upon its completion the impact may be significant. Similarly, radical changes in the institutions of the state sector have yet to lead to new behavioral patterns in the sector's investments and savings. Given the importance of national savings for sustaining high growth rates, research on savings behavior is a high priority in the agenda of state agencies and universities.

At the end of 1995, the accumulated inflow of overseas Chinese capital (close to 100 billion U.S. dollars) accounted for over forty percent of the accumulated inflow of total foreign capital, and for over seventy percent of total foreign direct investment. Ethnic groups that succeeded in accumulating wealth outside their original countries have often shown a willingness to invest heavily in their homeland, with the actual levels depending much on political and economic circumstances. As is increasingly recognized, the great success of ethnic Chinese in East Asia is an essential part of the economic miracle of the region, and their expansion to China should be seen as a natural response to the open door policy. Not surprisingly, the contribution of overseas Chinese to the transformation of their homeland is not limited to capital but also includes new organizational forms and managerial practices that are spreading on the coastal provinces. Indeed it is tempting to speculate that both the combination of these organizational forms with those inherited from the centralized economy of the 1970s and the tensions of different managerial practices will lead eventually to new forms of practices with survival value in China's emerging market economy.

Foreign capital other than that of overseas Chinese has also been flowing in significant amounts, and at the end of 1995, the accumulated inflow was expected to be as high as 140 to 160 billion U.S. dollars, or around twenty to twenty-five percent of China's 1995 GDP. Most of this capital has been borrowed by the state sector from a variety of sources at commercial and concessional terms, with portfolio and foreign direct investments financing mainly nonstate enterprises. This foreign capital has been important to finance large physical infrastructure projects and social services, as well as to support the transfer of foreign technology and the introduction of new organizational forms.

Whereas overseas Chinese capital has been flowing directly to a variety of nonstate enterprises, most household savings and some foreign loans are channeled to state and nonstate enterprises through the state system of financial intermediation. The system has been changing gradually since the division of the People's Bank of China in 1984, but it is still a system very much based on four big state banks and controlled by the central bank (the People's Bank of China) and other government agencies. Only in the last two years has a plan been emerging to slowly transform this system into one dominated by profit-motivated banks and nonbank financial institutions. The four big state banks are expected to become commercial entities, albeit with a special governance structure reflecting state ownership, and subject to the competition of other intermediaries, including foreign ones. The pace of the process is conditioned by the development of an effective legal order supportive of market financial transactions and the investment in human resources, as well as by the redefinition (perhaps the severance) of the special relationship between the state enterprises and the state banks. The successful reform of the central bank in the last two years—including a new internal organization and a redefinition of its role in financing the government, which have allowed the control of its domestic credit and monetary liabilities—is indicative of the government's commitment to reform the banking system.

By 1993, experiments with the corporatization of state enterprises, the issue of several types of marketable bonds and stocks, and the establishment of exchanges in Shenzhen and Shanghai had led to the expectation that securities markets would rapidly be a main source of capital for enterprises. Now it is clear that in the next few years securities markets will be important only for placing government bonds. It seems that the high expectation in 1993 was based on the illusion that the issue and exchange of securities other than government bonds would be possible just by enacting special rules enforced by a specialized agency but lacking the support of an effective legal order. This has not been the experience of other countries, however; this experience suggests that markets for private securities became important only after a strong financial intermediation system had emerged, mainly because private securities assume a very effective and sophisticated order of property rights and contracts. For example, the disclosure of relevant information is now recognized to be a serious issue in all financial transactions, especially in those involving securities issued by enterprises because they lack a state guarantee, but the ineffectiveness of rules governing the disclosure of information is a direct consequence of the weaknesses of the legal order.

The limited development of a market-oriented financial system is well reflected in the allocation of credit risk, and therefore in its pricing. There may be no legal basis to say that the government assumes the credit risk of all loans granted by banks and nonbank financial institutions, or, alternatively, that their domestic and foreign liabilities are guaranteed by the government. It would be difficult, however, to argue with depositors and foreign creditors that such is not the case. The line dividing liabilities with and without a state guarantee is indeed blurred; there has been little progress in drawing it, although foreign lenders now recognize that they must demand explicit guarantees. It is often said that final borrowers, especially the state enterprises, pay subsidized interest rates, but this argument fails to acknowledge that the government may have assumed the credit risk of their operations. Actually, a major barrier to transform the system into a market-oriented one is the lack of a capacity to assess credit risk, an unnecessary task when someone else is assuming this risk unconditionally.

Increasing regional disparities in output and income growth underlie the concern for the regional distribution of investment in physical capital. This distribution is the result of substantial regional differences in investment opportunities, and therefore in the regional demand for credit, rather than of weaknesses of the financial system. Actually, persistent barriers to the domestic mobility of capital have prevented a large flow of capital from low- to high-growth provinces, especially to the coastal provinces. The government may encourage investment in low-growth regions by increasing the prospective return of investments there, particularly of investments in infrastructure, but it should be reassured that the financial system has not been blocking the flow of capital. Although the limited domestic mobility of capital leads to distortions in capital allocation, the main weakness of China's state system of financial intermediation is the little weight attached to the economic benefits and risks in the allocation of banks' loanable funds.

In the next fifteen years, the Chinese economy is expected to grow at high annual rates, between six and ten percent. Capital accumulation will continue to play a critical role in determining the growth rate of output, and a market-oriented financial system is likely to facilitate it by enhancing the efficiency of capital mobilization and allocation. National savings are expected to be complemented by the inflow of foreign capital, although the latter may take new forms to safeguard effectively foreigners' capital. As outlined above, China's economic prospects are impressive, but to realize them a good understanding of its recent transformation and performance is essential.

Edgardo Barandiaran
Senior Economist
Resident Mission in China
The World Bank, Washington D.C.

Preface

Studies on the experience of China's economic reform have been either superficial or extreme. One extreme is to express the success of China's economic reform, while the other extreme is to criticize it. There is no doubt that China's economic reform has changed the livelihood of the Chinese people. But it would be naïve just to be pleased with one's success. On the contrary, criticisms are often regarded as piercing words. For those who concern themselves with China's future, the appropriate attitude is not just to feel pleased with her success nor to restrict criticisms to be discussed, but to evaluate the criticisms positively as challenges that require further action and attention. There are always criticisms, but if the problems can be solved gradually, then such criticisms in fact act primarily as incentives or stimulants for the society to change and move forward.

The publication of this book has been encouraged by the lack of economic and business-related studies on the Chinese economy, and this book raises important issues which have often been overlooked in the existing literature. In the area of capital accumulation, or simply the availability of financial capital, one has to accept that there has been an adequate supply of financial capital in China's economic reform so far. There are four sources of capital: state budget, bank loans, foreign direct investment, and equities. The first principle in economics tells us that there is always scarcity, and capital is a good subject about which no one would dare to say "enough." Emphasis has often been given to the "quantity" question of capital. The theoretical base is that a higher level of capital leads to a higher level of investment, which in turn generates output and income. Less emphasis, however, is given to the quality, efficiency, or productivity of investment. Such a measurement is often difficult to make and can only be done indirectly. This book suggests that the efficiency of capital is equally important. Economic problems, such as inflation, emerge if a large amount of capital is used inefficiently. On the contrary, real economic growth will take place if the amount of capital, however small, is used efficiently.

By looking at the trade and investment aspects of China's economic reform, I hope to bring out the "efficiency" question as an equally important issue in capital accumulation. Government officials, policy makers, and investors in general should ensure that each capital unit invested must bring the highest possible return, however it is measured. This book concentrates on four sources of capital: banking, foreign direct investment and trade, official flows, and equities. The analysis concentrates on the various economic mechanisms, instruments, and environments that could yield a higher degree of efficiency.

I would like to thank the authors for their contributions. It has been unkind of me to set the tight deadlines. I am indebted to Dr. Edgardo Barandiaran for the foreword and his various suggestions when reading the chapters. A word of gratitude should also be given to my employer, the City University of Hong Kong, for the time and use of various facilities. I am grateful to my wife and my family for their high degree of patience and support. Finally, I would like to thank Marcy Weiner and James Ice of Greenwood Publishing Group who have at various stages contributed to the publication of this book.

Overview

INTRODUCTION

The objective of this book is to examine the various sources and performance of investment capital in China's economic reform. These sources include bank credits, foreign direct investment and trade, official flows, and equity markets. Economic reform in China began in 1978 when Deng Xiao-ping made his famous analogy that "it does not matter whether the cat is black or white provided it catches mice." This was interpreted to mean economic growth is the ultimate target of the society. The introduction of the "family responsibility system" in the rural areas was considered to be the realistic target by the central authority. Since 1978, the Chinese economy has grown considerably. According to official statistics, China's nominal Gross National Product has increased from Rmb 358.8 billion in 1978 to Rmb 3,134.2 billion in 1993, an increase of 773.5 percent. The overall price indexes have grown by 254.9 percent in the same period. Total investment in fixed assets has increased from Rmb 91,090 million in 1980 to Rmb 1,245,788 million in 1993, an increase of 1,268 percent. The Chinese economy experienced three distinct periods of income growth between the end of the 1970s and the decade of the 1980s. The first period was short and ended in 1980. Between 1981 and 1985, nominal income growth accelerated by 22.9 percent. A high growth rate was also experienced in 1988. In the Eighth Five-Year Plan (1990–1995), the economy experienced an average growth rate of 11.7 percent. The State Statistics Bureau estimated that between 1991 and 1995, China invested a total of Rmb 3,890 billion in fixed assets, giving an annual growth rate of 17.9 percent.[1]

There have been numerous theories and arguments outlining China's success and failure in economic reform. China's state sector is concentrated in the industries. Economic reform that began in the agricultural sector had permitted the nonstate sector to function more effectively.[2] The Hong Kong connection as well as overseas Chinese has been active in supplying foreign funds to China.[3] The "push and pull" argument is common among survey studies suggesting that China's low cost of land and labor has been the "pull" factor, while the high and rising labor cost in Hong Kong, Japan, Taiwan, and other Asian countries was the "push" factor.[4] The establishment of Special Economic Zones along the coastal region as "experiments" of market economies has been successful and has further stimulated the interior region to open up.[5] Sectoral and country studies have also been conducted regularly by the World Bank and other international agencies to look at China's reform process.

The problems arising from economic reform have often been discussed. The high inflation and the various economic bottlenecks, for example, reflected the rigid economic structure. The exercise of a tight monetary control at different times has imposed quantitative restriction temporarily but has had little effect on the monetary structure or the operation of banks. Disparity in income between the coastal and interior regions has also been widened. The lack of infrastructure development and corruption are additional problems.

Taking into consideration all the positive and negative aspects of the reform, it would be fair to say that the reform has done more good than harm to the Chinese economy. Other than the quantifiable factors, theories explaining the economic reform in China have extended to the conceptual level. For example, the theories of property right, transaction cost, liberalization, marketization, and privatization have been discussed in the context of reform and transitional economies.[6] However, the sequence of economic reform and the "lead-led" relationship in the various aspects of reform has been overlooked in many analyses.

The availability of natural endowment cannot contribute to development if there is a lack of suitable investment, or financial capital. Education and a skilled labor force can be sustained only if there is sufficient financial capital to finance the various programs. The supply of investment often is the major obstacle in development. Typically, investment is financed by four sources: bank loans, foreign investments, exports, and the security market. Experience suggests that emphasis has often been given to the availability of investment or financial capital, while the efficiency or the productivity of investment has been ignored.

FINANCING INVESTMENT

Financial resources ultimately mobilize other resources. The availability and efficiency of financial capital determine to a large extent the pace of transforming other resources into material output. Drake (1980, p. 27) considers the role of financial resources in economic development as a process of expansion and elaboration of the financial structure, which is composed of financial institutions, financial instruments, and financial activities.

There are three groups of theories explaining the role of financial resources in economic development.[7] They are the structuralist theory, the financial repression theory, and the financial market theory. The structuralist theory contains three basic elements (FitzGerald and Vos, 1989, p. 27): (1) analysis goes beyond the operation of economic agents, and looks into their behavior in the institutional and organizational context; (2) analysis takes into account market rigidities for reasons of different institutional behavior, market power, transaction costs, and agency problems; and (3) analysis takes into account endogenous structural rigidities and the process that drives institutional change. The structural theory was first advocated in the "two-gap" analysis proposed by Chenery and Bruno (1962) and Chenery and Strout (1966). Thirlwall (1978, p. 295) points out that sustained growth can occur if two conditions are satisfied: a rising marginal savings rate and a marginal rate of export rising faster than the marginal rate of import. Taylor (1983) states that three adjustment mechanisms that can be exercised when saving is not equal to investment are the expansion of output, price changes, and demand variation. A major problem of the structuralist theory is its high level of complexity.

The financial repression theory considers the institutional aspect and believes that financial resources are the most powerful form of resources. McKinnon (1973) defines financial repression as a situation in which investment opportunities are lost as a result of a weak and inefficient financial sector. Shaw (1973) postulates a "shallow" economy in which there is distortion of financial prices, commonly through a government-imposed interest ceiling below the market equilibrium rate. The financial repression module, as summarized in Fry (1988), is a useful framework in that it links up financial policies with the institutional structure and produces a more applicable and realistic analysis. The theory concentrates on a few macroeconomic variables and studies the implications of their movements. It assumes that money is a "conduit" through which capital is channeled to productive activities. Money and capital are complementary in the early stage of economic development. Li (1994) applies the financial repression theory to the first decade of China's economic reform (1978–1989) and argues that although economic growth had accelerated, the rate of output growth was lower than the rate of growth of fixed-asset investments, bank loans, and the money supply, suggesting that financial capital or investment in general could have been used more efficiently. Li (1994) suggests that the reform of the interest rate could be the single most effective economic instrument that should act as the "thin end of a wedge" in the selection of productve investment projects, in acceleration of total output, and eventually in the increase of national income.

The financial market theory looks at the development of the stock market in raising capital for development. The financial and the real side of the economy, as Tobin (1969, p. 16) argues, must be consistent because financial inputs injected into the real side must reproduce the equivalent value of the real inputs to the financial side. Similarly, Goldsmith (1969, p. 4) considers the role and impact of the private equity market and believes that a country's financial superstructure grows more rapidly than the infrastructure of national product and wealth. Patrick (1966) identifies two causality relationship between financial development and economic growth. One is the "demand-following" phenomenon, the other is "supply-leading" phenomenon. Typically, the former phenomenon dominates in the initial process of growth. However, Dickie (1981) finds that there are obstacles in establishing equity markets in developing countries. Obstacles appear in both the supply and demand sides.

INVESTMENT CAPITAL IN CHINA

There are four major sources of investment in China: bank loans, equity market, foreign investment and trade, and official flows from international institutions. The value of total investment in fixed assets increased from Rmb 91,090 million in 1980 to Rmb 1,245,788 million in 1993. As far as the ownership pattern is concerned, the share of state-owned units continues to decline, while the reverse is true in the case of collective ownership. Individual ownership has expanded though the percentage share since 1992 has dropped considerably.[8] Among the various sources of finance, domestic loans and self-raised funds have become dominant, while state appropriation has declined in importance, reflecting the rising expectation from the nonstate sector. In the use of funds, construction is still the largest item of expenditure, reflecting the authority's emphasis on infrastructure development since the early 1990s, though the percentage shares have fallen slightly since 1990.

Total bank loans have exceeded total deposits in most years since 1990. The three largest loan items are: industrial production enterprises loans, commercial enterprises loans, and fixed-asset loans. The extent of loans given out by national banks depends largely on the banking structure in China.

The major conflict in loan deployment lies in the debate on the extent of assisting loss-making SOEs. To maintain a better monetary and macroeconomic control, the central authority wants to limit the amount of loans given out readily to SOEs with financial problems. A considerable amount of bank loans are not geared to investment purposes, but rather they are used to pay off previous debts, workers' wages, and other non-output-related activities. It was reported that SOEs owe a total of Rmb 2.5 trillion in assets, Rmb 800 million of which represents net assets; the rest is debt. Another report says that 41.4 percent of SOEs in China were in the red in the first eleven months of 1994, though this was an improvement from 46.6 percent in March 1994.[9] It was also reported that bad and overdue debts of SOEs comprise about twenty percent of the banks' portfolios. The new debt enterprises incurred in 1994 amounted to Rmb 500 billion. By September 1995, the so-called "triangular" debts amounted to Rmb 700 billion. The reason given for such a disproportionately high level of bad bank loans was policy loans on political directives.[10]

The banking law passed in March 1995 separated all national banks into a three-tier structure: the central bank, policy banks, and state-owned commercial banks. The three policy banks fund all the policy-related activities that may not be commercially sound. These are likely to be construction and infrastructural works which require a large amount of fixed capital. State-owned commercial banks must make their credits and loans on a commercial basis, so that borrowing institutions will have the ability to repay the loans.

The banking law passed in early 1995 was heading the right direction, but much effort needed to be committed and changes to be introduced if bad debts from state-owned enterprises were to be eradicated. Another area of focus is the method in which loans are given out. People close to the banking circle in China believe that the "net present value" formula has been used in loan applications. There are still a number of issues unknown to the outside world. Issues such as risk, project viability, and payback calculations are standard questions a bank has to address when it makes a loan. It has often been said that loans are given out on a political basis rather than on the basis of economic rules. The interest rate, for example, does not function as an economic instrument in directing investment. Institutional reform in the banking structure is only one element of reform. Banking operation is another element of reform which should be introduced gradually. The idea is to make banks a truly financial intermediary between borrowers and lenders. A recent report suggests that China's central bank is to implement a scheme to be carried out in stages beginning in 1996 to tighten bank lending to state enterprises in order to cut unprofitable loans. Under the scheme, each enterprise will be granted a loan license by the central bank, which must be presented to the four state-owned commercial banks when they borrow. The license will show the enterprise's debt situation and financial ability in the repayment of loans.[11]

Both foreign direct investment (FDI) and foreign trade provide an external source of capital. Despite the small percentage share in total fixed-asset investments, FDIs are considered a vital source of capital not only in the absorption of external resources, but as a pillar in the export market. However, it is only in recent years that the trade balance has been helpful as a source of foreign income. The reason is the large import bill, especially in the mid-1980s. A trade surplus was experienced in the three-year period between 1990 and 1992, but the situation reversed drastically in 1993 just before the unification of China's foreign exchange rate. After the unification of the official exchange rate in 1994, however, the Renminbi devalued considerably. This effectively lowered the price of China's exports, resulting in a handsome trade surplus in 1994 and 1995.

Most trading nations would expect China to take a more significant role in world trade, mainly because China can be a large supplier of exports, on the one hand, and provide a large world market for overseas suppliers, on the other. There have been, however, a number of issues that attracted the world's attention in recent years. China's admission to both the General Agreement on Trade and Tariff (GATT) and the World Trade Organization (WTO) has invited debates which basically concentrate on two issues. One is that China should accept the international practices of free trade. This will involve considerable changes to be introduced domestically, such as the eradication of companies violating copy rights. The second issue is that China's domestic market should be made more open so that major trading partners, such as the United States, would not experience a huge trade deficit that favors China only. The United States obviously is aware of its trade deficit with Japan in the 1970s, and a repetition of such an experience would not be desirable.[12] Whether China should be admitted as a "developing" country has also been debated heatedly.

The Chinese government responded by stating her principles. First, China would not accept the status of a "developed" economy if admitted to any world trade institutions. Second, time is required to address the various domestic problems. Despite the heated debates, there is agreement that the negotiating parties have shown their good will. President Clinton's delinking of the human rights issue from the trade issue in 1994 had effectively removed a major political obstacle in the Sino-U.S. trade negotiations. Further liberalization on currency convertibility was expected to take place in 1996.[13]

Official flows to China are another important source of foreign capital. Indeed, official flows often stimulate other foreign investments and act as a symbol of security and acceptance of the recipient's overall economic standard by the World Bank.

Self-raised funds, funds raised by enterprises themselves through the issue of shares, stocks, and bonds, constitute the largest source of funds. On December 9, 1990, the Shanghai Stock Exchange was set up. This was followed by the establishment of the Shenzhen Stock Market on July 3, 1991. There are two related issues in the discussion of the equity market as a source of capital in China. One is the quantity issue, while the other is the question of quality.

Reformists who believe in the importance of "quantity" argue that economic growth in China requires as much capital funds as possible. Borrowing from world financial institutions and governments, and foreign direct investments are the additional channels through which additional capital is raised. The conventional channels of state funding through the fiscal framework and loans from national banks are thought to be inadequate in supplying capital funds. The development of the equity market is considered to be an additional channel through which funds are obtained from the market. Since the establishment of the stock markets in Shanghai and Shenzhen, different types of shares have been promoted (A-shares for Chinese nationals, B-shares for foreigners). Subsequently, capital has also been raised from the Hong Kong Stock Market (H-shares) and from the New York Stock Exchange (N-shares).

The argument of the "quantity" reformists is that China needs as much capital as possible. The larger the quantity of capital, the greater the level of growth in output and income. Other issues, such as structural rigidity and sectoral imbalances, are secondary. On the contrary, the "quality" reformists point out the importance of qualitative improvements in capital utilization. A large quantity of capital has to be assisted by suitable economic structure and instruments. Otherwise the inefficient use of capital would generate problems for the economy. These problems include a rapid rate of inflation, industrial bottlenecks, structural constraints, corruption, and a lack of economic disciplines.

The heavy speculative element in the equity markets is seen to have provided wrong signals to the user of capital. The "easy money" nature of the equity market may lack a monitoring device on the use of capital so raised. On the contrary, reform should focus more on improvments in economic instruments. Li (1994) suggests a greater use of the interest rate as an opportunity cost mechanism in the allocation of capital. Wu Jinglian, a professor from the State Council's "think tank," remarked that there was no shortage of credit in China, but the problems rested in the distribution and allocation of the resource. Wu also suggested greater use of the interest rate to channel the flow of capital.[14]

EFFICIENCY OF INVESTMENT

There are three problems in capital efficiency. A measurement problem arises if intermediate outputs are used as inputs. The second problem is the time lag in the yield of output. It is common to take an one-year lag in the yield of investment. In reality, this varies between industries. A related problem is the flow of yield. Investment made today will give a flow of output in future years. Investment in infrastructure, for example, tends to generate a flow of income lasting a number of years.

These various problems would impose difficulties in making a judgment on investment efficiency. Indeed, macroeconomic evidence of the capital efficiency of investment in China is not readily available. What is available, however, is a number of sectoral or industrial studies which, in most cases, documented the growth in output and income in different industries and sectors.[15] At the aggregate level, Li (1994, p. 131) uses a simple Least Square Estimation method and quarterly data between 1982 and 1989. Industrial output is regressed on state budget allocation, bank loans for circulating funds, foreign direct investment, bank loans for fixed assets, and self-raised funds. The coefficients of these estimates can be regarded as the efficiency ratios of these capital resources. The empirical results show that the capital coefficient estimate for bank loans for circulating funds is highest, followed by foreign direct investment, and self-raised funds. The coefficient estimates for both banks loans for fixed assets and state budget allocations are negative, implying that their marginal productivity is negative. A drop in these capital resources could generate a positive impact on total industrial output. Bank loans for circulating funds performed best.

Alternatively, one can also look for simpler productivity results as "guidelines." Various ratios can be calculated as macro indicators of investment performance. The following three ratios (based on nominal figures) are calculated as efficiency indicators, assuming a time lag of one year, (t-1), occurs between the amount invested and their outcome:

1. The income/investment ratio = Gross National Product$_{(t)}$/Value of Fixed Asset Investment$_{(t-1)}$

2. The output/investment ratio = Total Industrial Output$_{(t)}$/Value of Fixed Asset Investment$_{(t-1)}$

3. The export/foreign investment ratio = Total Export$_{(t)}$/Foreign Direct Investment$_{(t-1)}$

The income/investment ratio indicates the extent of income generated from investment activities. The ratio is an aggregate figure. If the productivity of investment increases, the ratio will rise over the years. The industry output/investment ratio carries a similar interpretation except that it shows the influence of investment on industrial output. A rising productivity of investment will give a rising ratio as time passes. If investment rises at a faster rate than either income or industrial output, these ratios will fall. The export/FDI ratio gives a similar measurement on the external sector of the Chinese economy. Foreign direct investment has mainly been concentrated in industries that are geared to the export market. This ratio indicates the extent of exports generated from FDI.

Table O.1 reports these ratios. The first two ratios show a similar trend, though the second ratio is consistently higher than the first ratio. In both cases, they show a declining trend in the mid-1980s, but the ratios increased again from 1990 onward. The fall in the ratios in the mid-1980s was the direct result of a rise in fixed-asset investment relatively faster than the increase in both GNP and industrial output. On the other hand, the rise in these two ratios in the late 1980s was due to the slower rise in fixed-asset investment, particularly in 1989. Furthermore, these ratios show little changes throughout the period between 1981 and 1994.

The export/FDI ratios are much larger than the other two ratios. On the surface, this seems to suggest that foreign direct investments have a strong impact on the export market. One should be aware, however, that FDI remained relatively small during the entire 1980s. The large ratio actually reflected a low level of FDI instead. Indeed, FDI increased drastically after 1989, corresponding to a gradual fall in the export/FDI ratio. By 1993, the large FDI had reduced the ratio to a single-digit figure.

Table O.1
Macroeconomic Ratios

	GNP$_t$/FIX$_{t-1}$	IO$_t$/FIX$_{t-1}$	EX$_t$/FDI$_{t-1}$
1981	5.24	5.93	
1982	5.40	6.05	
1983	4.72	5.25	
1984	4.87	5.33	
1985	4.67	5.30	21.74
1986	3.81	4.40	18.63
1987	3.74	4.57	21.05
1988	3.85	5.01	20.54
1989	3.58	4.95	16.45
1990	4.27	5.78	18.30
1991	4.55	6.35	20.60
1992	4.43	6.73	19.45
1993	3.99	6.71	8.29
1994	3.61	6.17	4.40

Notes: GNP = Gross National Product; FIX = total value of fixed asset investment; IO = total value of industrial output; EX = total exports; FDI = value of foreign direct investment used; t = current year.
Source: China Statistical Yearbook, Beijing, 1994 and 1995.

THE LAYOUT OF CHAPTERS

In China, the major sources of financial capital are bank credits, the stock markets, foreign direct investment, trade, and official flows. Each of these investment sources is faced with a different degree of success and problems. The rest of this book can conveniently be grouped into four sections:

1. Money and banking (Chapters One and Two)—Chapter One provides a detailed analysis of China's monetary framework and policy, as well as recent developments in the banking structure. It has been pointed out that the granting of loans has never been publicized. Chapter Two looks at the experience of foreign banks in granting loans to Chinese industries. It introduces various criteria used to examine issues such as risk and the ability to repay.

2. Foreign direct investment and trade (Chapters Three, Four, Five, and Six)—The first two chapters in this section look at the experiences of trade and foreign direct investment and their impact on economic growth. The latter two chapters examine mainland China's trade relationship with Japan and Taiwan.

3. Foreign exchange market and official flows (Chapters Seven, and Eight)—While official flows from world institutions provide an effective source of investment, the foreign exchange market studies the relative price of China's exports in the world market.

4. Equity markets (Chapters Nine, Ten, and Eleven)—These three chapters look at different aspects of the equity markets. The futures market is presented first, while the last two chapters examine the historical development and performance of the two stock markets.

NOTES

1. *China News Digest*, August 18, 1995, and Li (1994, p. 25).

2. This point was made by Professor Jeffrey Sachs in a conference speech in December 1994 in Hong Kong.

3. See, for example, Sung (1991).

4. See, for example, the various investment survey reports conducted by the Federation of Hong Kong Industries, Hong Kong.

5. See, for example, Y. C. Jao and C. K. Leung, eds. (1986).

6. See, for example, Perkins (1994), Hsu (1990).

7. For a more detailed discussion of the theories, see Li (1994, Chapter 1).

8. For a discussion in the 1980s, see Li (1994, p. 56).

9. *China News Digest*, January 12 and June 4, 1995.

10. *South China Morning Post*, November 2, 1995.

11. *South China Morning Post*, November 2, 1995.

12. Ambassador Charlene Barshefsky remarked at a luncheon in Hong Kong after her trip to Beijing that 40 percent of China's export went to the United States, while China accounted for only 2 percent of U.S. exports. U.S.'s trade deficit with China increases by 25 percent annually. U.S. trade imbalance with China is expected to top 38 billion U.S. dollars in 1996. U.S. investment in China has amounted to 10 billion U.S. dollars. *Hong Kong Economic Times* and *South China Morning Post*, November 14, 1995.

13. *South China Morning Post*, November 14, 1995.

14. *South China Morning Post* and *Hong Kong Economic Times*, October 25, 1995.

15. In the case of agriculture, see, for example, Lin (1992). In the case of industries, see, for example, Jefferson and Rawski (1994).

REFERENCES

Chenery, Hollis B. and Bruno, M., 1962, "Development Alternatives in an Open Economy: the Case of Israel," *Economic Journal*, 72 March: 79–103.

Chenery, Hollis and Strout, A.M., 1966, "Foreign Assistance and Economic Development," *American Economic Review*, 56(4) September: 679–733.

Dickie, Robert B., 1981, "Development of Third World Securities Markets," *Law and Policy in International Business*, (13): 177–222.

Drake, Peter J., 1980, *Money, Finance and Development*, London: John Wiley & Sons.

FitzGerald, E.V.K., and Vos, Rob, 1989, *Financial Economic Development: A Structural Approach to Monetary Policy*, Aldershot: Gower.

Fry, Maxwell, 1988, *Money, Interest and Banking in Economic Development*, Baltimore: Johns Hopkins University Press.

Goldsmith, Raymond W., 1969, *Financial Structure and Development*, New Haven: Yale University Press.

Hsu, John C., 1990, *China's Foreign Trade Reform*, London: Cambridge University Press.

Jao, Yu C. and Leung, Chi K. (ed), 1986, *China's Special Economic Zones*, Hong Kong: Oxford University Press.

Jefferson, Gary H. and Rawski, Thomas G., 1994, "Enterprise Reform in Chinese Industry," *Journal of Economic Perspectives*, 8(2) Spring: 47–70.

Li, Kui-Wai, 1994, *Financial Repression and Economic Reform in China*, Westport: Praeger Publishers.

Lin, Justin Y., 1992, "Rural Reform and Agricultural Growth in China," *American Economic Review*, 82(1) March: 34–51.

McKinnon, Ronald I., 1973, *Money and Capital in Economic Development*, Washington: Brookings Institution.

Patrick, Hugh T., 1966, "Financial Development and Economic Growth in Underdeveloped Countries," *Economic Development and Cultural Change*, January: 174–189.

Perkins, Dwight, 1994, "Completing China's Move to the Market," *Journal of Economic Perspectives*, 8(2) Spring: 23–46.

Shaw, Edward S., 1973, *Financial Deepening and Economic Development*, New York: Oxford University Press.

Sung, Yun-Wing, 1991, *The China-Hong Kong Connection*, Cambridge: Cambridge University Press.

Taylor, Lance, 1983, *Structuralist Macroeconomics: Applicable Models for the Third World*, New York: Basic Books.

Thirlwall, A.P., 1978, *Growth and Development*, 2nd Edition, London: Macmillan.

Tobin, James, 1969, "A General Equilibrium Approach to Monetary Theory," *Journal of Money, Credit and Banking*, 7(1): 15–29.

Tobin, James, 1978, "Monetary Policy and the Economy: The Transmission Mechanism," *Southern Economic Journal*, 44(3) January: 421–431.

1
Money and Banking in China

XU TANG and KUI-WAI LI

DEFINITION OF MONEY

Cash circulation, which accounted for twenty percent of total deposits, was the only form of money controlled by the People's Bank of China (PBC) in the prereform years. Three currency indices were then used to monitor the quantity of money: 1) a 1:8 cash circulation to total retail sales ratio was normally considered; 2) a 1:4 cash circulation to total farm and sideline products purchased by the government ratio was normally considered; and 3) a 1:5 cash circulation to total goods in stock ratio. Both bank deposits and credits, however, expanded rapidly in the postreform years, suggesting that money supply could not be monitored by cash alone. Similarly, the three conventional indices could not explain monetary movements any more. For example, the ratio of cash to total deposits increased from 10.4 percent to 18.6 percent between 1992 and 1993, and the ratio of cash circulation to total retail sales was 1:6 in 1981 and 1982.

Beginning from 1992, the People's Bank of China defined money as follows:[1]

M0 = cash;

M1 = M0 + demand deposits of enterprise and rural collectives and other institutions;

M2 = M1 + time deposits of enterprises + deposits of self-financed funds of capital construction + household savings deposits + other deposits.

Although M0 is still the most important monetary aggregate, M1 is becoming the major indicator of money supply, while M2 is becoming an important indicator for the central bank. Table 1.1 shows the percentage growth rates of the three definitions of money for the period from 1985 to 1994. M0 tended to grow faster than other monetary aggregates, especially in 1988, 1992, and 1993.

TARGETS AND INSTRUMENTS OF MONETARY POLICY

In the past, the money supply process was based on the credits given to the enterprises. At that time, money was supplied as long as the enterprises needed loans. Loans granted by the PBC to banks are called reloans, which could be considered as the base money. Cash in China is backed up neither by foreign exchange reserve nor by securities. The PBC determines the money and credit growth rates. After the reform, the central bank attempted to exercise an independent monetary policy, but realized that there were conflicts between growth and stability. There are four policy targets: mone-

Table 1.1
Money Growth Rates, 1985–1994 (percentages)

Year	M0	M1	M2
1985	24.7	5.8	17.0
1986	23.3	28.1	29.3
1987	19.4	16.2	24.2
1988	46.7	22.5	22.4
1989	9.8	6.3	18.3
1990	12.8	20.2	28.0
1991	20.2	23.2	26.5
1992	36.5	35.7	31.3
1993	35.3	21.0	24.0
1994	26.4	32.5	37.1

Note: The 1994 figures included the first three quarters only.
Source: China Financial Outlook 1994, Beijing: China Financial Publishing House, 1994, p. 23.

tary stability, economic growth, full employment, and international payment balance.

Monetary stability is considered a prerequisite to economic growth. The government states that "the final target of monetary policy is to keep money stable and therefore promote economic growth."[2] One concern is the relationship between money supply and inflation. Another concern is the time lag in the implementation of the policy. Intermediate targets, such as the credit aggregate, are often used. With the expansion of credit channels, however, credit aggregate can no longer reflect the real financial situation any more. In the first half of 1993, for example, when the economy was overheated, total credit of specialized banks was not allowed to exceed their credit aggregate, and banks could not lend their money to nonbank financial institutions.

Total assets and total liabilities of the People's Bank of China for 1987 and 1993 increased by 248.8 percent and 239.9 percent respectively. Total loans had risen by 252.6 percent, while budget lending had increased by 207.2 percent. The former showed the active supply of bank credits, while the latter showed the various subsidies supported by the budget. Liabilities to financial institutions have increased by 362.6 percent. Currency issue has risen by 310.4 percent.

The asset of PBC is determined by three factors. The first factor is reloan, which includes all kinds of special loans and loans to banks and other financial institutions. By the end of 1993, this reached Rmb 1,058.08 billion, and accounted for seventy-nine percent of PBC's total assets.[3] The second factor is gold and foreign exchange assets in international financial institutions. This reached Rmb 87.55 billion by the end of 1993, accounting for 6.5 percent of total assets. The third factor is fiscal loans, which include treasury overdraft and lending. This amounted to Rmb 158.21 billion by the end of 1993, accounting for 11.8 percent of total assets.

The more common monetary policy instruments are:

1. Credit ceiling—The PBC allocates approved credits to the specialized banks, depending on the banks' deposits.

2. Reloan—Credits of the specialized banks accounted for roughly seventy-five percent of total credits, the balance was made up by the reloan executed by PBC. In 1986, according to data in Table 1.2 for example, the highest loan/deposit ratio of the specialized bank was 149 percent. This implies that about one-third (forty-nine percent) of the specialized banks' loans was provided by the PBC. And despite the decrease in the loan/deposit ratio (from 141 in 1986 to 121 in 1993), there was still a great need for central bank loans. The total amount of reloan made by PBC to specialized

Table 1.2
The Loan/Deposit Ratio of Major Banks (percentage)

Year	ICBC	ABC	PCBC	BOC	BOCo	Aver
1986	149	168	113	88	-	141
1987	139	156	120	83	71	138
1988	139	149	125	90	95	142
1989	139	143	130	90	106	137
1990	132	143	122	85	88	130
1991	124	143	123	79	88	121
1992	117	132	107	81	79	114
1993	113	128	99	-	81	121

Notes: ICBC = Industrial and Commercial Bank of China; ABC = Agricultural Bank of China; PCBC = People's Construction Bank of China; BOC = Bank of China; BOCo = Bank of Communications; Aver = average.
Source: Almanac of China's Financial and Banking, 1992-1993, Beijing, p. 397-402.

banks increased from Rmb 338.8 billion in 1988 to Rmb 962.6 billion in 1993.

3. Required reserve ratio—The reserves submitted to PBC in 1984 were based on three kinds of deposits: enterprise deposits (twenty percent), savings deposits (forty percent), and rural deposits (twenty percent).[4] In 1985, the required reserve rate was set at ten percent across all deposits. The current required reserve rate is thirteen percent. The required reserve changes the money supply through the money multiplier, which is about 2 to 2.5 at present.[5] In 1993, the total required reserve of all banks reached Rmb 288.5 billion, while the total deposits of the specialized banks was Rmb 2,140 billion.[6] A simple calculation suggests that if there was a one percent increase in the required reserve rate, an amount of Rmb 21.4 billion would have to be submitted by the specialized banks.

4. Standby reserve rate—Each bank deposits part of its assets in cash or in PBC's settlement account. The function of standby reserve is to meet the withdrawal by depositors from banks and transfer from banks to PBC's settlement account. The PBC determines the lowest standby reserve rate. At a time when credit demand is high, banks keep a very low level of standby reserve and maintain an overdraft in the settlement account with the PBC. Beginning from July 1993, PBC has instructed banks to keep the ratio of standby reserve against total deposits at five percent, thus tightening the amount of credits. By 1994, the standby reserve rates of most banks have been kept at nearly ten percent, indicating a tight credit situation.

5. Rediscount rate—Commercial paper is considered an instrument of credit after a trial experience was carried out in Shanghai and Chongqing

in 1984. The Shanghai branch of the PBC began to rediscount commercial papers in 1986. The rediscount rate is usually lower than the loan rate, and the amount discounted is small. Owing to a lack of laws governing disputes, the discounting of bills of exchange was stopped temporarily between 1991 and 1993. In May 1994, PBC promulgated the "Management Methods of Commercial Bill of Exchange" and drafted the Bill Law of the People's Republic of China.

6. Interest rate—China has a dual interest rate system. One is the official rate, which includes the deposit rate and the loan rate of national banks and the savings deposit rate of other depositary financial institutions. The other is the market rate, which includes the interbank and loan rates of some financial institutions. The PBC alone decides and changes the official interest rate.

The illegal fund-raising activities and the rapid development of the financial market had led to a drop in deposits, especially in savings deposits in specialized banks in the first half of 1993.[7] The annual growth rate of deposits in the first quarter of 1993 decreased from 26.7 percent to 22.9 percent, much lower than the average annual growth rate of 33.6 percent between 1979 and 1991. As a result, the deposit rate was increased twice in May and July 1993.[8] For example, beginning from May 15, 1993, the household demand deposit rate was raised from 1.80 percent to 2.16 percent, and from July 11, 1993, the rate was raised again to 3.15 percent. It was only then that deposits began to pick up.

There are two kinds of market interest rates. One is the floating rate. According to the regulations of the PBC, a margin (ranging from twenty to sixty percent) can be imposed on the authorized rate when banks, trust and investment companies (twenty percent), and urban credit cooperatives (thirty percent) extend their working capital loans. The rural credit cooperatives can add a margin (sixty percent) on the current capital loan rates and fixed-assets loan rate.[9] The second kind is the interbank rate, which differs in areas and in maturity. For example, in Shanghai in February 1993, the longest maturity of interbank fund was 120 days and the shortest was ten days. And the highest monthly interbank rate was 7.92 percent and the lowest was 6.60 percent.[10]

The interest rate structure is very complicated. The deposit and loan rates are divided into many types, and there are three kinds of prime rates: 1) purchase of farm and sideline products and shipbuilding industrial loans (which is five percent lower than the working capital loan); 2) capital construction, electrical machinery industries (which is 0.9 percent lower than working capital loan and two percent lower than capital construction loan); and 3) poverty-releasing loan (which is two to three percent lower than working capital loan).[11] Loans determined by commercial banks are not included in the loans of the PBC.

The Chinese economy has often experienced a negative interest rate. In 1993, for example, the highest rate was 13.86 percent (on five-year or longer fixed-asset loans), while the retail price index was 13.2 percent, and it increased to 21.7 percent in 1994.[12] As a result, enterprises can make profit through interest rate margins. The difficulty is that if the PBC imposes a positive interest rate, it will impose a huge repayment pressure on state-owned enterprises. Nearly eighty percent of large and medium state-owned enterprises' working capital and one-third of their total fixed-assets investment are funded by bank loans. An increase in the interest rate means they have to face a high cost. Furthermore, state-owned enterprises form the major productive sector, and they employ a large number of workers. Bankruptcy in state-owned enterprises means a rise in unemployment, which will cause social problems for the state.

The market interest rate is gradually playing a more important role. Except for the interbank rate, the price of treasury bonds in the secondary market is already determined by the bid and offer price. As the PBC exercises open market operations, the interest rate of treasury bonds will become the indicator of market interest rate. Furthermore, as the nonstate sector is becoming more important, commercial banks will tend not to lend to nonprofitable projects.

7. Open market operation—The amount of treasury bills issued in China is limited. By 1993, the average issue per year was thirty to forty billion Renminbi, and the total amount of bonds issued by specialized banks was below ten billion Renminbi, equivalent to 4.2 percent of the total deposits of specialized banks.[13] In 1994, the quantity of treasury bills increased by thirty to forty billion Renminbi annually to Rmb 100 billion.[14] The PBC began to issue central bank financing notes in May 1993 with the intention of preparing the conditions to implement open market operation, and to collect funds from financial institutions in economically richer areas. The face amounts of the notes are one hundred thousand, five hundred thousand, one million, and five million. The maturity periods of the notes are three, six, and nine months. These notes can be transferred among licensed financial institutions and can be used as mortgage when they borrow from PBC. China's poor financial structure, such as the lack of a sound clearing and settlement system to meet the large amount of fund transaction, has prevented the full implementation of open market operations. Open market operations, however, are expected to be implemented soon in Shanghai because it has been chosen to be the trading center of treasury securities, and primary dealers have been identified.

8. Foreign exchange operations—The management of foreign exchange is based on a double-track system. Foreign exchange earned by all units and individuals should be sold to the state, but they can exchange the currency in the foreign exchange swap market at a higher rate. For example, in 1993, the official rate of U.S. dollars to Rmb was 1:5.7, but the swap market rate was around 1:8. Although the demand and supply of foreign exchange are reflected in the swap market, the central bank intervenes to stabilize the foreign exchange rate, for example, from July 1993 onward, by buying and selling foreign exchange to regulate the market rate.

The foreign exchange system was unified on January 1, 1994. The previous foreign exchange retention system was replaced by the managed floating rate system based on the demand and supply of the market. The foreign exchange earned by enterprises is sold to the central bank, and when enterprises need foreign exchange for their import, they can purchase from the central bank. The unification resulted in an increase in foreign exchange reserve. The first three quarters of 1994 showed that reserve has doubled from seventeen billion U.S. dollars to thirty billion U.S. dollars. Given a U.S. dollar/Rmb exchange rate of 1:8.6, China's base money had increased by Rmb 150 billion. This increased the pressure on inflation. One solution is to allow the Renminbi to appreciate, and consequently the US$/Rmb exchange rate decreased from 1:8.7 to 1:8.55 in the second half of 1994.

MONETARY POLICY: 1985–1989 AND 1990–1994

Monetary policy in the 1985–1989 period was characterized by a "stop-go" nature. The overheated economy in 1984 caused increases in major monetary variables. Bank loans increased by 32.7 percent to Rmb 117.6 billion. Currency supply increased by Rmb 26.23 billion, equivalent to 2.9 times the size of the increase between 1983 and 1984. By the end of 1984, currency in circulation increased by 49.9 percent.[15] A tight monetary policy was implemented in 1985, and five measures were adopted (Liu, 1991, pp. 226–253): 1) specialized banks were allowed to make loans to the extent of their own deposits; 2) a strict credit control policy was instituted; 3) the deposit and loan rates increased twice; 4) the credit funds of People's Construction Bank of China (PCBC) were incorporated into the credit management of PBC; and 5) the Renminbi was devaluated. The exchange rate of U.S. dollars to Rmb was adjusted from 1:2.80 to 1:3.20 in December 1985.

These measures succeeded in reducing the rapid growth of credit and money. The growth rates of bank loans and currency supply dropped to 23.9

percent and 24.7 percent, respectively, in 1985. By 1986, however, economic activities had cooled down considerably, but the growth of industrial production fell from 5.6 percent in January to 0.9 percent in February. Subsequently, three measures were applied to relax the tight monetary policy: 1) the PBC increased the amount of reloan by five billion Renminbi in order to clear up the enterprise debts; 2) it canceled the directory credit plan imposed on the specialized banks; and 3) temporary loans were granted to the specialized banks. The industrial production growth rate increased from 3.9 percent to 17.3 percent between April and December, but the growth rate of money also accelerated.

To cope with the overheated economy in 1987, the PBC formulated a moderately tight monetary policy. Measures included: 1) specialized banks were asked to be "self-balanced"; 2) no distinction was made between approved and nonapproved loans; 3) the deposit reserve rate was increased to twelve percent in December, while the annual loan rate was increased to 7.2 percent and the short-term loan rate to 7.2 percent; and 4) rural credit cooperatives were required to submit Rmb 5 billion of special deposits. The Agricultural Bank of China (ABC) was asked to cut the loans to township enterprises. Loans, currency circulation, and M1 increased only by eighteen percent, 19.4 percent, and 16.22 percent, respectively, the lowest growth rates since 1986. The annual growth rate of industrial production was 14.6 percent.

A "stop-go" monetary policy, characterized by "quantity control and structural readjustment," was applied again in 1988.[16] Measures included: 1) credit aggregates were restricted; 2) the long-term (three years) interest rate was increased and all short-term loans were recalled; 3) the required reserve rate was raised to thirteen percent, the annual reloan rate to 8.28 percent, and short-term reloan rate to 7.56 percent; 4) financial institutions were asked to submit special deposits; and 5) strong administrative measures were applied.

Price reform and liberalization had caused inflation, and consumption rose. In August 1988, saving deposits decreased unprecedentedly by Rmb 2.68 billion, showing signs of a tight monetary policy. Beginning from September 1988, the loan growth rate declined to seventeen percent only, while the annual growth rates of M0, M1, and M2 were 46.72 percent, 22.48 percent, and 22.38 percent, respectively.[17] The tight monetary policy continued through 1989. A national credit aggregate system was set up by the PBC to oversee the national banks and nonbank financial institutions. Credit ceilings were imposed. If branches/head office of specialized banks exceeded the quarterly credit plan, approval from their head office/PBC was needed. Industrial output subsequently decreased from 20.79 percent to

8.54 percent between 1988 and 1989, while the growth rates of M0, M1, and M2 decreased to 9.84 percent, 6.31 percent, and 18.32 percent, respectively.[18] The retail price dropped to 17.8 percent, 0.7 percent less than the previous year.

A loose monetary policy was implemented from 1990 until the middle of 1993. From October 1989, the Chinese economy experienced negative growth in income for several months, mainly caused by the triangular-debt problem among different enterprises. In 1990, the State Council relaxed the tight monetary policy. Major measures include (Zhou, 1993, pp. 115–127): 1) a reloan readjustment plan increased credits from thirty billion to sixty billion Renminbi; 2) PBC increased its technology reconstruction loans to enterprises and loans were granted to solve the triangular-debt problem; 3) banks' deposit and loan rates were lowered by an average of 1.26 percent; and 4) a favorable interest rate was granted to import and export enterprises.

The economy picked up at the end of the third quarter in 1990. The industrial growth rate increased by an average of fourteen percent between October and December. Bank loans increased by 22.2 percent. However, economic acceleration soon led the State Council to introduce a tight monetary policy again in 1991. Due to various unforeseeable factors, the result of the monetary policy in 1991 was very different from what was planned originally. In the original plan, total loans and M0 in 1991 were to increase by Rmb 210 billion and fifty billion Renminbi, respectively. However, the actual loans extended by PBC amounted to thirty billion Renminbi, mainly for the payment of triangular debt. Another ten billion Renminbi was extended for disaster relief. And due to a poor harvest, the purchasing fund was increased by fifteen to twenty billion Renminbi. As a result, the increase in loans and M0 approved by the State Council was Rmb 283 billion and fifty-five billion Renminbi, representing an increase of 18.97 percent and 20.17 percent, respectively.

The PBC faced a dilemma when Deng Xiaoping toured southern China and called for further reform in February 1992. Monetary policy has to be used to stabilize the economy and to promote further reform at the same time. In mid-1992, the State Council estimated that the GNP growth rate would reach nine percent and the price would increase by six percent, and subsequently adjusted the credit aggregate to Rmb 350 billion and the growth of M0 to ninety billion Renminbi. Again, the high demand for loans had led to a sharp increase in credits. Total loans between 1991 and 1992 increased by 19.79 percent (Rmb 357 billion), while M0 and M1 increased by 36.45 percent (Rmb 115.8 billion) and 35.73 percent, respectively, exceeding the growth rate of GNP (12.8 percent) and price (5.4 percent).[19]

As the demand for loans remained high, various illegal fund-raising activities appeared. Enterprises issued bonds and stocks without prior approval, and their interest rate ranged from fifteen percent to forty percent, much higher than that offered by banks. According to the Agricultural Bank of China's (ABC) statistics based on twenty-six provinces and provincial cities, the amount of agricultural funds illegally channeled to bonds and stocks reached Rmb 52.8 billion in the first quarter, equivalent to 1.9 times of ABC's incremental loans and rural cooperative credits to these provinces and cities in the same period.

Illegal interbank borrowing and lending deteriorated rapidly, resulted in large amounts of funds channeled to the real estate and stock markets, promoting a "bubble" economy. The estimated total amount of illegal interbank borrowing and lending in the first half of the year was about Rmb 100 billion. Annual GNP grew by 13.1 percent in the first half of the year. Household income also increased rapidly. For example, salaries paid through enterprises' deposits in banks increased by 36.7 percent. M1 and M2 began to drop from March, while M0 grew by 31.3 percent in January, hitting 54.1 percent in June 1993.[20]

A decline in the growth rate of money supply would have indicated a tight money and credit situation, but the decrease in the growth rate of deposits and a rapid increase in cash were the major features of financial deterioration. Subsequently in June 1993, the State Council issued a document, popularly known as the Austerity Plan, to strengthen macro control. The major features of the 1993 Austerity Plan are: 1) a strict control was imposed on currency issue; 2) all forms of illegal interbank borrowing and lending were stopped; 3) the savings deposit rate was increased; 4) all illegal fund-raising activities were stopped and disorganized investments cleared; 5) the five percent standard ratio on the excess reserve of specialized banks was applied rigidly; 6) from the branches of all PBC the authority to grant reloan was withdrawn; 7) financial institutions were told to purchase all treasury bonds and the administration and trading of securities were improved; 8) the management of the real estate market was strengthened and speculative activities were stopped; and 9) a strict control was imposed on capital construction.

Instruments implemented in the middle of 1993 were in fact a combination of economic and administrative measures. From the third quarter of 1993, a reversal in the financial situation emerged. Savings deposits rose rapidly. Illegal fund-raising activities were kept under control, seventy percent of the Rmb 100 billion illegal interbank lending was returned. The excess reserve ratio of specialized banks reached five percent, and some even reached ten percent.[21]

New problems, however, emerged. The tight monetary policy hurt the economy badly. First, industrial growth rate dropped to 3.6 percent in October (the cumulative industrial growth rate in the first three quarters was 24.1 percent); the triangular debt reappeared, and some enterprises could not even pay their workers; the real estate market was in deep depression. For a long while most banks could not make new loans because of the limit on the excess reserve ratio. Under these circumstances, the State Council and PBC loosened the monetary policy. The PBC increased credit and eased the tight supply of funds and prevented the economy from sliding further in 1994.

One can identify a monetary pattern in 1993. Money supply first increased in January and February (with a growth rate of M1 and M2 at 37.1 percent and 32.3 percent, respectively, in January and 42.8 percent and 32.6 percent, respectively, in February). Industrial production also accelerated until July when industrial production fell. The industrial growth rate decreased from 6.8 percent in September to 3.6 percent in October 1993. A time lag of three months can be identified between a tight M1 supply and the decline in industrial production. When the PBC decided to loosen money in October by adjusting upward the annual loan aggregates from Rmb 380 billion to Rmb 450 billion, the economy edged upward in November. The growth rate of state-owned industry increased from 3.6 percent to 5.6 percent, and finally to 13.9 percent between October and December. The lag in the effect of a loose monetary policy on industrial production is about two months, shorter than the reverse situation. There is also a time lag between the growth of money supply and the increase in price. The annual data of M1 and retailed price index suggest that changes in price occurred one year after the increase of M1.

Although M0 has been the monetary target in China, it often is not controllable. This is because banks do not control the payment of salary and sales of goods. Cash is circulated outside the banking system. The planned supply of M0 is always different from the actual amount circulated. In the case of M1 and M2, there are also some factors that PBC cannot control. For example, if credits are supplied automatically, it is natural for problematic enterprises to seek help from the banks. It is, therefore, very difficult for PBC to control money supply.

THE STRUCTURE OF BANKS AND NONBANK INSTITUTIONS

The Chinese banking system consisted of money and exchange shops before 1840. Foreign banks, which first appeared during the Opium War, monopolized Chinese banking for about fifty years. In 1897, the first commercial bank, known as the Imperial Bank of China, was set up when the Qing Government realized the outflow of silver. By 1927, there were 203 Chinese banks, consisting of official banks, private commercial banks, and money shops. In 1946, the four official banks (Zhong Yang Bank, Bank of China, Bank of Communications, and China Farmers Bank), together with the Central Trust Bureau, Postal Saving and Exchange House, and Central Cooperative Funds, controlled the major commercial banking activities and monopolized the credit business. In June 1947, the deposits of these institutions accounted for 91.7 percent of national deposits, and 93.3 percent of the total loans.[22]

Over a period of six years in the 1950s, the People's Bank of China (PBC) expropriated, amalgamated, and centralized all banks. With branches being set up all over China, PBC had became an instrument in the implementation of a highly centralized and planned economic administrative system. Funds were controlled by the head office and could flow only vertically. Currency issue coexisted with commercial banking business, and since both the bank and the enterprises were state-owned, currency issue could not be controlled.

Since the late 1970s, several steps were taken. The Agricultural Bank of China (ABC) was reestablished in 1979. The Bank of China (BOC) was separated from PBC, became the international department dealing with foreign exchange business, and has become one of the four specialized banks. The People's Construction Bank of China (PCBC) was separated from the Ministry of Finance (MOF). It mainly deals with the loans related to capital construction allocated by the MOF. In the meantime, the People's Insurance Company of China (PICC) was set up to develop domestic insurance, while the China International Trust and Investment Company (CITIC) was set up to develop the trust and investment business. The China Investment Company (CIC), accountable to PCBC, was set up in 1981 to engage in foreign fund raising and administration of international loans.[23]

A new banking structure emerged with PBC being the central bank and the four state-owned specialized banks (ABC, BOC, PCBC, and CIC) concentrated on different economic sectors. PBC was both a central bank and a specialized bank that dealt specially with urban credit business. The PBC's function of administering other specialized banks often conflicted with its commercial banking activities. PBC began to function as a central bank from 1984 and would not deal with commercial banking business any longer. Meanwhile, the Industrial and Commercial Bank of China (ICBC) was set up to deal with industrial and commercial deposits and loans which were originally handled by the PBC. Between 1984 and 1993, China's banking sector changed drastically. Regional commercial banks appeared.

For example, the Shenzhen Development Bank and the Guangdong Development Bank played a very important role in developing the local economy. Commercial banks owned by large corporations, such as CITIC Industrial Bank, Everbright Bank, and Hua Xia Bank, also appeared. A considerable number of trust and investment companies, financial companies, securities companies, and urban credit cooperatives developed in a short period.

These new financial institutions challenged the activities of the four specialized banks, which have to deal with commercial banks and handle other policy-related banking business at the same time. Very often, the specialized banks use their funds first on commercial loans in order to make a profit, but the unprofitable, policy-related loans were left to the PBC. In order to operate according to commercial principles, the specialized banks are transformed into commercial banks, while the policy banks are restricted from commercial banking business. The Chinese authority set up three non-profit-making policy banks: the State Development Bank (SDB), the Agriculture Development Bank of China (ADBC), and the Import and Export Bank of China (IEBC).

Figure 1.1 shows the current banking and financial structure in China. Other than the PBC, which is the central bank, the banking system is composed of four types of banks: state-owned commercial banks (previously the specialized banks), commercial banks, policy banks, and branches of foreign banks. There are seven types of nonbank financial institutions: trust and investment companies, insurance companies, finance companies, financial leasing companies, urban credit cooperatives, rural credit cooperatives, and securities companies.

The People's Bank of China (PBC)

China's central bank, the People's Bank of China (PBC), was founded on December 1, 1948, but incorporated other banks in the 1950s. On January 1, 1984, the State Council passed a resolution proposing the People's Bank of China to be the Central Bank. The Council of PBC is the decision-making body; there is no restriction on the number of council members. The governor and executive vice-governor of PBC are the president and vice-president of the Council, respectively. Council members are key officials from the State Planning Commission (SPC), Ministry of Finance (MOF), State Foreign Exchange Administrative Bureau (SFEAB), state-owned commercial (specialized) banks, and People's Insurance Company of China (PICC). The main responsibilities of the council are to: a) examine monetary policy; b) examine national credit plan, cash plan, and foreign exchange revenue and expenditure

Figure 1.1
Bank and Nonbank Structure in China

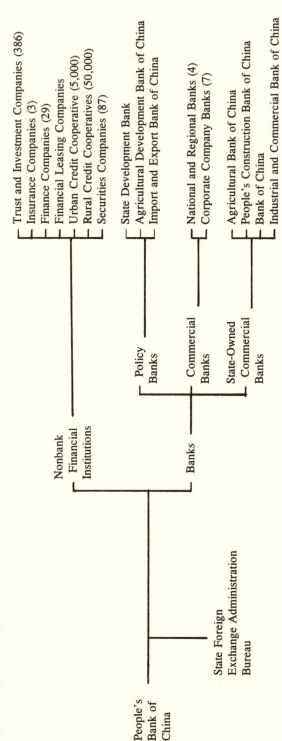

Note: ( ) = number of banks as of the end of 1994.
Source: China Financial Outlook 1994, People's Bank of China, pp. 74-75.

plans; d) establish or merge national commercial banks and other financial institutions; and e) research on other relevant issues.

In fact, most important financial decisions are made by the State Council. It appoints the governor of the central bank and presidents of the state-owned commercial banks, and formulates the national credit and cash plans. Since the executive vice premier of the State Council is concurrently the governor of the central bank, major financial policies are determined in State Council meetings.

Major functions of the central bank include (*Law of the People's Bank of China*, Article 4, People's Republic of China, 1995): 1) fiduciary issue; 2) lender of last resort; 3) act as the government's treasury; 4) bank clearing; 5) manage foreign exchange; 6) represent the government in international financial areas; 7) promulgate the Regulations and Acts Involving Finance and Banking; 8) establish and supervise financial institutions and banks; and 9) execute monetary policy.

The three organizational levels of PBC are: head office, branches, and subbranches. State-owned commercial banks are supposed to assist the PBC to implement the monetary policy, but branches of PBC find it difficult to resist the pressure of lending to local governments. The establishment, merger, and dismissal of financial institutions have to be approved by PBC. Regional financial institutions are approved by local branches of PBC. Each financial institution opens different accounts in PBC. For example, banks open reserve accounts, deposit accounts, settlement accounts, loan accounts, government securities accounts, and foreign exchange accounts. Financial institutions submit required reserves and standby reserves to PBC through these accounts.

As the lender of last resort, PBC provides two kinds of services to financial institutions. One is reloan and rediscount. The second is the clearance facility. Larger banks have their own clearing system; transfer and settlement of funds can be done within themselves, but transfer and settlement of funds with a different bank have to be done through the clearing system of PBC. By 1993, PBC has opened 201 satellite stations and clearance can be done in 300 cities. The accounts can be settled within twenty-four hours. In 1993, Rmb 1,780 billion was settled through this network.[24]

An inner-city bill exchange business is also arranged by PBC. Financial institutions can send their settlement bills to the bill exchange center and the accounts can be settled within twenty-four hours, the longest settlement would not exceed forty-eight hours. Through a telecommunication network, PBC provides an interbank market service to financial institutions. Trust and investment companies depend a lot on the interbank market, and they often borrow from this market.

The independent status of the central bank was given a considerable amount of attention and discussion in the National People's Congress (NPC) meeting held in March 1995. The NPC was asked to vote on a new law paving the way for the establishment of an independent banking system. The new Law of the People's Bank of China is divided into eight chapters with forty-eight articles. The Law covers the role of the central bank, its composition, business areas, and supervisory functions over other financial institutions. By spelling out the accounting principles and legal obligations of the central bank, it is thought that the law could help to maintain a "stable and healthy" operation of the Chinese financial market. Under the new law, the central bank comes under the leadership of the State Council only. This would avoid regional governments putting pressure on the central bank for loans. Monetary policy tools include: a) setting a deposits reserve for all financial institutions; b) setting the lending rate; c) working as a discount window for other financial institutions; d) providing loans for commercial banks; and e) conducting bonds and foreign exchange in the open market. Other measures could only be decided by the State Council. The new law would restrict the central bank in the subscription and underwriting of government bonds and bills.[25] In the closing session of the NPC meeting, however, only 66.5 percent of the 2,678 deputies agreed to pass the new law on the central bank. This relatively low percentage reflected opposition from regions against supervision of the central bank by the State Council alone.[26] Nonetheless, the central bank began to strengthen its loan monitoring in 1995. It will focus on fixed-asset investment loans, credit quality, and securities repurchases. One thousand lending institutions will be targeted for scrutiny.[27]

State-Owned Commercial Banks

State-owned commercial banks, which were specialized banks before the separation of policy banks, are: Industrial and Commercial Bank of China (ICBC), Agriculture Bank of China (ABC), People's Construction Bank of China (PCBC), and Bank of China (BOC). Together, these four banks hold seventy-five percent of total financial business in China, and have strong monopoly over special areas in banking activities.

Founded in 1984, the Industrial and Commercial Bank of China (ICBC) is the largest bank dealing with urban business. The total asset reached Rmb 1,433.6 billion at the end of 1992.[28] The Agricultural Bank of China (ABC) resumed its business in 1979 and deals mainly with rural business and handles deposits and loans of township enterprises and rural households. ABC managed the rural credit cooperatives on behalf of PBC for a long time, and the deposits of these cooperatives became the bank's major source of funds.

The People's Construction Bank of China (PCBC) is a specialized bank under the administration of PBC. Its business has extended to commercial banking activities in recent years, and its asset is over Rmb 1,000 billion at the end of 1993.[29] The Bank of China (BOC) has achieved certain international reputation, and it has stopped its domestic business since 1979. BOC mainly deals with international financial business, such as settlement in international trade, international borrowing and foreign exchange trade. The total assets of BOC are the smallest compared with the other three state-owned banks. In recent years, it has set up branches and subbranches in many cities to deal with foreign exchange business.

Competition among state-owned commercial banks is increasing. The PCBC, ABC, and BOC are competing with ICBC for urban financial business by opening up more and more subbranches in cities. The ICBC, ABC, and PCBC are developing overseas business and opening branches abroad, competing with BOC and foreign banks in international finance. The total number of branches and subbranches of the state-owned commercial banks has exceeded 120,000 and the total staff had reached 1.6 million by the end of 1992.[30] In 1993, the ICBC held 34.4 percent of the total assets of all financial institutions, ABC held 17.21 percent, PCBC held 13.23 percent, while BOC held only 8.26 percent, and other commercial banks and nonbank financial institutions held 4.1 percent and 22.84 percent, respectively.

Policy Banks

The three policy banks, which deal with policy-related banking activities, were founded in 1994. They are the State Development Bank (SDB), the Agricultural Development Bank of China (ADBC), and the Export and Import Bank of China (IEBC). Their capital comes from three channels: allocation from MOF; issue of bonds to financial institutions; and bank deposits. The SDB and IEBC have no branches but set up representative offices in a few cities. ADBC is the only bank that has set up branches and subbranches in many cities, especially in strong agriculture-based provinces and districts. Policy loans are approved by policy banks, while the extension and management of these loans are administered by PCBC and BOC.

Commercial Banks

Commercial banks include the Bank of Communications, CITIC Industrial Bank, Everbright Bank, and Huaxia Bank. The Bank of Communications is the only share-holding bank, and the other three banks are owned by large enterprise groups. Founded in 1987, the Bank of Communications is a share-holding company and has set up branches in the capitals of most provinces. The initial Rmb 1 billion capital was cofunded by PBC, four specialized banks, and PICC, while the equities of branches and subbranches were funded by local government and enterprises. In 1993, the Bank of Communications reformed its equity structure by combining the equities of the head office, branches, and subbranches. Its business expanded rapidly, with total assets of Rmb 157 billion in 1993.

The CITIC Industrial Bank was founded in the eighties and is solely owned by CITIC. It has branches and subbranches in some cities. Its total assets were Rmb 33.59 billion in 1992. Both Everbright Bank and Hua Xia Bank were founded in the early 1990s. Everbright Bank is solely owned by the Everbright International Trust and Investment Company, while Hua Xia Bank is solely owned by the Shou Gang Company. The assets of Everbright Bank and Hua Xia Bank were nearly Rmb 2.7 billion and Rmb 1 billion, respectively, in 1992.[31]

Regional commercial banks include Guangdong Development Bank, Shenzhen Development Bank, Pudong Development Bank, Fujian Industrial Bank, Yantai House Saving Bank, and Benbu House Saving Bank. The business range of these banks is broad, but they can only do business in a certain region. PBC has approved the Merchant Bank of Shenzhen to set up branches outside Shenzhen and it is becoming a national commercial bank. Most of these banks are share-holding banks. For example, the Shenzhen Development Bank is listed in the Shenzhen Stock Exchange. Some of the banks are owned by enterprise groups: for example, Merchant Bank of Shenzhen is controlled by the Merchant Group of Shenzhen and Shekou. The activities of regional commercial banks are restricted to certain regions. Since most of these banks are located in special economic zones or developed areas and since they do not have the burden of catering to poorly developed areas, they make a handsome level of profit.

Commercial banks and regional commercial banks can be distinguished from the regional names attached to the banks. Assets of these two kinds of commercial banks accounted for only 4.1 percent of the total assets of financial institutions at the end of 1993, but their growth rate is the fastest.[32] Deposits of commercial banks mainly come from enterprises, individuals, and rural deposits. As of 1993, fifty-seven percent of their deposits came from enterprises, fourteen percent from private individuals. In the case of state-owned commercial banks, the proportions were thirty-five percent and fifty-one percent, respectively. On the contrary, forty-three percent of their loans were given to industrial and commercial enterprises. Commercial banks do not lend to policy-related projects or projects that require a long payback time. However, forty-seven percent of the loans went to "other" items. This was considered to be out of proportion too.[33]

China's first private bank, the Minsheng Bank, was approved by Beijing in early 1995.[34] The Minsheng Bank, registered with a capital of fifty-three billion Renminbi, serves mainly small businesses which are short of capital.

Foreign Banks

There are not many branches of foreign banks in China; the total number is only seventy-four, while the representative office of foreign financial institutions has reached 225. The business of foreign banks is restricted to foreign currency only and deals mainly with international settlement. As the assets of these banks are small, their direct effect on the Chinese economy is limited, though their influence can be profound and lasting.

In general, a foreign bank has to have a minimum of two years' business record in China before it can apply for a license or establish a branch. Japanese banks form the largest group of foreign banks. As of June 1993, there were fifty-five Japanese foreign banks, equivalent to thirty-two percent of the total. French banks are the next largest group with a total of sixteen banks, followed by Hong Kong and the United States; both have a total of twelve banks. Beijing has the largest number of foreign banks (a total of 129, equivalent to seventy-five percent of the total), followed by Shanghai (thirty-four), and Guangzhou (eighteen). Large cities in China tend to be the favorite sites for foreign banks.

Foreign banks wanting to establish branches in China have to undergo a strict application process. As of June 1993, a total of seventy-four branches belonged to twenty-nine foreign banks. Hong Kong–based banks have a total of twenty-one branches, followed by Japanese foreign banks with a total of fifteen branches and British banks with a total of twelve branches. One British bank, the Standard Chartered Bank, has the largest number of branches (seven). Among the twenty-eight foreign banks with branches in China, fifteen of which have branches in Shenzhen, thirteen have branches in Shanghai. Beijing does not allow foreign banks to open branches.[35] Foreign banks in Shanghai, however, can serve as agents in handling the Renminbi at the automatic teller machines (ATMs). Shanghai intends to set up an interbank foreign exchange borrowing and lending market and float foreign currency bonds in order to absorb the twenty billion dollars in private savings.[36]

The existence of foreign banks imposes potential competition to domestic banks. The modern operation and management of foreign banks have a great impact on domestic banks, and their link with the world community can help Chinese banks to gain information on international finance.

Nonbank Financial Institutions

By 1994, the total number has reached 57,000 and their assets accounted for twenty-two percent of all financial institutions. Most nonbank financial institutions have only one head office. Trust and investment companies are the most important nonbank financial institutions; their total assets reached Rmb 245.8 billion in 1993.[37] They cannot accept deposits from enterprises and households, and their funds come mainly from long-term borrowing from other banks and from the interbank market, while their assets are mainly trust loans and lending in the interbank market, including ten percent fixed-assets loans.

Trust and investment companies are the most active participants in the interbank market. In 1993, fourteen percent and 21.6 percent of their total assets and liabilities, respectively, were engaged in the interbank market. They often come under the control of the government. For example, in order to prevent them from using the interbank market funds in fixed-asset investment, the State Council decided in 1993 that state-owned commercial banks could not lend money to trust and investment companies in the interbank market. In the 1980s, when the economy was overheated on various occasions, these companies were ordered to stop operation temporarily and some were even closed. The trust and investment companies had increased to 745 in 1988, but by 1992, the number was halved to 386.

Urban credit cooperatives began to develop in the mid-1980s and 1990s. By 1994, there were more than 5,000 urban credit cooperatives. Their assets reached Rmb 187.9 billion in 1993, equivalent to 5.5 percent of state-owned commercial banks' assets or the total assets of the Bank of Communications.

Urban credit cooperatives could take deposits from households, collective enterprises, and institutions, but not deposits of state-owned enterprises and institutions. Their business strategy tends to be more conservative than that of banks. About forty-one percent of their asset are loans; this is also equivalent to fifty-eight percent of their total deposits. When compared to state-owned commercial banks, whose asset portfolio is composed seventy-five percent of loans and whose ratio of loan against deposit is 120 percent, urban credit cooperatives are considered units with excess funds.

There are about 50,000 rural credit cooperatives. They mainly take deposits from farmers and rural units and extend loans to farmers and township enterprises. It is difficult for them to operate effectively as most of them are faced with a large number of poor farmers. Their assets are too small to undertake risk. Consequently, they transfer most of their deposits to ABC. In 1993, the total assets of rural credit cooperatives were Rmb 452 billion, seventy percent of which were in the form of loans equivalent to seventy-three percent of total deposits.

Finance companies were founded only in recent years. In 1994, there were altogether twenty-nine domestic finance companies and four foreign finance companies, commonly known as joint venture finance companies (they are Zhengda Financial Company, Shanghai United Financial Company, Shanghai International Financial Company, and China International Financial Company). According to current financial laws and regulations, a finance company is mostly owned by large enterprise groups or corporations; their main business includes managing the funds of the group, taking deposits of, and extending loans to enterprises. Finance companies can conduct business in the interbank market as well as issuing bonds in the financial market. By 1993, total assets of finance companies reached Rmb 20.1 billion, while their total loans reached Rmb 15.5 billion.

There are now three insurance companies in China—People's Insurance Company of China (PICC), Pacific Insurance Company, and Pinan Insurance Company. Foreign insurance companies are developing their business in Shanghai, Shenzhen, and Haikou. PICC is the oldest insurance company, though in the 1960s and 1970s, it conducted only international insurance business. In 1979, PICC resumed domestic insurance business and now it has set up branches and subbranches in many major cities. The total staff of PICC reached 100 thousand and its total assets reached forty-eight billion Renminbi in 1992.

The Pacific Insurance Company is solely owned by the Bank of Communications. It conducts business in only a few major cities, and its operation is very active and competitive. Pinan Insurance Company is a regional company whose business scope is within Shenzhen only. With the opening up of the financial market and the establishment of a modern social security system, insurance companies in China are expected to develop quickly and more foreign insurance companies are expected to invest in China. Finally, securities companies are active financial institutions which have developed rapidly in recent years. There are now eighty-seven securities companies in China and they play a very important role in the capital market.

BANK CREDIT MANAGEMENT

Policy Banks

The State Development Bank (SDB) extends loans to major construction projects and is involved in the planning of major construction projects. Most policy loans are extended to promote energy, communication, and raw materials production.

Loans of the Import and Export Bank of China (IEBC) are intended to promote the export and import of large equipment with a long productive life span and require a considerable amount of funding support in the beginning. The IEBC also deals with other business such as discount loans and export credit guaranty.

Most of the loans given by the Agricultural Development Bank of China (ADBC) are used for the purchase of grain, cotton, oil, and other sideline products by state farms. ADBC also extends loans to water conservancy construction and acts as the agent of the MOF in the allocation of farm-supporting funds.

State-Owned Commercial and Commercial Banks

The functions of both state-owned and non-state-owned commercial banks are similar. In the past, only working capital loans, and not fixed asset loans, were extended to productive enterprises. However, many enterprises require investment funds for the replacement of productive machinery in the reform period. While the treasury could not support all the requirements for technical transformation of enterprises, banks began to extend loans for the purpose of technical transformation and, later, fixed-asset loans.

The extension of working-capital loans is based on either the "credit-balance" method or the "entire-credit" method. According to the former, the working capital of an enterprise is divided into quota capital, which is provided by the treasury, and nonquota capital, which comes from bank loans. The "entire-credit" method means that banks fund the entire working capital of the enterprises. In the past, the working capital of new enterprises was allocated by the treasury. More recently, banks are increasingly under pressure to supply working capital to enterprises, reaching Rmb 2,586.97 billion in 1993, equivalent to eighty-two percent of total bank loans, double the 1989 amount. Most credits were extended to the state-owned sector. Loans to the nonstate sector were Rmb 300 billion, accounting for only ten percent of total loans.[38]

Fixed-asset loans, the most important part in banks' assets, had increased from Rmb 792 million in 1980 to Rmb 517 billion in 1993, equivalent to 19.5 percent of total credit balance of state banks. In 1993, fixed asset investment was Rmb 1,182.9 billion, thirty percent of which was provided by the banks.[39] Fixed-asset loans of banks could be divided into two types: capital construction loans and technical innovation loans. The former is used to construct new projects, while the latter is used to replace old equipment or to renovate old enterprises.

As a commercial bank, the ratio of loans against deposits must not exceed seventy-five percent. However, since state-owned commercial banks are faced with many bad debts, the seventy-five percent ratio can only be applied to new loans. The other twenty-five percent is composed of required reserves submitted to the central bank (thirteen percent), excess reserves (seven percent), and deposits kept within the bank (five percent).

Most bank loans are either long- or medium-term fixed-asset loans. Banks must balance these loans with long- and medium-term funds. Normally, current capital loans are short term, but since these loans are recycled within the enterprise, they cannot be recovered by the bank. In order to diversify the banks' risks, loans made to a certain borrower must not exceed ten percent of its total capital.

Enterprises wanting to obtain loans from the bank must comply with one of the following three conditions: 1) it is a medium to large state-owned enterprise; 2) it has a good relationship with the bank; 3) it holds mortgages. Banks extend most of their fixed asset loans to energy construction, communications, and raw materials projects according to the national industrial development plan, and extend most of their working-capital loans to support large- and medium-sized state-owned enterprises. Loans to collective and individual enterprises are extended by credit cooperatives and other financial institutions. Joint-venture companies can seek foreign loans.

Interbank Market

The original intention of the interbank market is to provide financial institutions with a place to raise short-term funds. In practice, however, these funds are used in fixed-asset investment and in the speculation of the real-estate and securities markets. This caused confusion in the real estate market and fraudulence of funds flourished in the securities market, especially in the coastal areas. In 1993, PBC strengthened the administration of the interbank market, and financial institutions have to comply with the following rules:

1. Banks cannot use the reloan from PBC and funds of affiliated banks in the interbank market. If the excess reserve ratio of the bank is below five percent or the bank has not returned the reloan of PBC in time, such funds cannot be used in the interbank market.
2. Banks shall not extend loans and invest in the real estate market using funds borrowed in the interbank market, and similarly, banks cannot use funds borrowed in the interbank market to purchase securities or speculate in the real estate market.
3. The funds borrowed from the interbank market must not exceed five percent of its deposits in the same period. For urban credit cooperatives, their borrowed funds must not exceed twice their own capital. For other financial institutions, the borrowed funds must not exceed their own capital.
4. Funds borrowed from the interbank market have to be repaid either within seven days or in less than four months.
5. Interbank borrowing and lending are conducted through PBC.

Financing centers supported by PBC are set up in provinces, national autonomous regions, municipalities, and cities. Interbank markets are divided into different strata. Interbank borrowing and lending among financial institutions in provinces, national autonomic regions, and municipalities must make up for the shortage of their funds from the central bank. Funds within state-owned commercial banks must be dealt with through their own branches or PBC financing centers. Interbank borrowing and lending of the credit cooperatives, trust and investment companies, finance companies, leasing companies, and insurance companies must be conducted through PBC financing centers.

Commercial papers discounting developed slowly. By the end of 1993, the discount loan balance was three billion Renminbi. Commercial paper is a certificate of claim and obligation in a transaction. Most discounted notes are commercial bills, which are called bank acceptance bills. A negotiable commercial bill has to show a good credit history; its maturity ranges from three to six months and the longest shall not exceed nine months.

The 1994 Regulations on Commercial Bill of Exchange passed the following rules:

1. The user of commercial bills must be a legal person who has a bank account. Transactions among state-owned enterprises, share-holding companies, collective industrial enterprises, supply and marketing cooperatives, and joint ventures can use commercial bills.
2. The issuance, acceptance, and discount of commercial bills must undergo legal transactions.

3. All the commercial bills are registered and are negotiable unless stated otherwise on the reverse side of the bill.

4. The discounting must be carried out by national banks. Non-bank financial institutions cannot discount bills.

5. Commercial acceptance bills and bank acceptance bills must be printed by the PBC head office.

These regulations have promoted and standardized the development of commercial bills. However, since commercial credits are not frequently used in China, default of debt and violation of contract are frequently found.

BANKS' DEPOSIT AND LOAN POLICY

For a long time, banks in China have depended on the reloans of PBC to expand credit, but with the transition to commercial banks, credit expansion has become more and more dependent on deposits. There are two kinds of deposits: enterprise and institution deposits, and household savings deposits. Deposits of enterprises and institutions can be divided into demand deposits and time deposits. Time deposits usually have a higher interest rate. Demand deposits can use checks, and interest is paid to the balance of demand deposits. The ratio of demand deposit to time deposit is about six to one. Checks are not available to household current or time deposits.

Certificates of deposits (CDs), which were first issued in 1987 by BOC to raise funds for purchasing export products, are also issued to institutions and individuals. By the end of 1993, the total CD amounted to ninety billion Renminbi.

The level of saving deposits is closely connected to the income of individuals. Between 1988 and 1993, income of urban households doubled from Rmb 119.2 billion to Rmb 258.3 billion, while the annual net income per capita in rural areas increased from Rmb 545 to Rmb 922.[40] The level of savings deposits is also connected to various financial innovations; such as BOC's Great Wall Card, which began in 1985, ABC's Golden Grain Card, PCBC's VISA and Dragon Cards, and ICBC's Peony Card. The number of Peony Cards reached five million by the end of 1994.

Before 1988, individuals' saving deposits were lower than enterprise deposits. In recent years, savings deposits have increased at a faster pace than enterprise deposits. By 1993, saving deposits had reached Rmb 1,520 billion, while enterprise deposits were only Rmb 861 billion. Other deposits include deposits of institutions and foreign exchange.[41] A sharp fall in savings deposits could imply a "bubble" economy characterized by a high rate of inflation, as experienced in 1988 and 1993.

In China, it is possible that a fall in savings deposits leads to a rise in enterprise deposits, as a result of a transfer of funds from households' consumption to enterprise deposits. On the contrary, it is equally likely that a decrease in enterprise deposits leads to an increase in saving deposits. For example, before the Austerity Plan in 1993, many enterprises raised funds directly in order to expand output. A large amount of saving deposits was channeled to the capital market and enterprise deposits increased. Under the Plan, enterprises' deposits declined, while savings deposits experienced a rapid rate of growth in the third quarter of 1994.

Generally speaking, the credit policy of state banks is determined by the industrial policy. Commercial banks are rarely asked by the state to extend favorable loans to certain industries and projects. All state banks are obliged to extend loans, since they can get reloans from PBC as funds to support projects and industries selected by the state. This credit policy is mandatory for state banks but is voluntary for commercial banks.

RECENT REFORM IN CHINA'S BANKING SYSTEM

Many problems arise during the transition from a planned economy to a market economy. First, reforming the commercial banks will take a long time. In 1994, policy banks were separated from specialized banks, but specialized banks still cannot operate according to commercial rules. So long as loss-making enterprises can get loans from banks, banks are faced with strong pressure of social instability if they stop extending loans. Specialized banks cannot transform into real commercial banks if the structure of state enterprises remains unchanged.

The central government has emphasized that local governments must provide services for the local economy. Local officials can get promotion as long as a high local economic growth rate is achieved. This is done by asking banks to extend as many loans as possible to promote the local economy. Banks can no longer operate according to economic rules. The transformation of specialized banks into commercial banks will take a long time, depending largely on the transformation of state enterprises and local governments.

Second, the lack of propriety rights in banks has affected their operation. State-owned banks occupy about seventy-five percent of total banking business.[42] These banks have no managers. No one is responsible for the security and asset values. Some economists proposed that these banks be transformed into share-holding companies, with a board of directors making important decisions while a board of supervisors supervises the operation of the bank.

Third, the specialized banks were faced with a huge amount of bad debt when they were transformed into commercial banks. Currently, one-third of state-owned enterprises are in deficit, and loans to these enterprises cannot be recovered. Originally these loans were extended to solve state-related problems, and it is unreasonable for the commercial banks to undertake all the bad debt. Some economists propose that the treasury share the burden of bad debt, while deficit enterprises can cover their debts with bonds.

Bank innovations were suggested as a solution. At the end of 1993, the ratio of total state-owned bank assets to total GNP was one to one. This is considered to be very high. In the coming years, the following reform measures will be adopted:

1. Regional banks—In the past, there was resistance to establishing regional banks. The fear was that regional banks would become a small treasury for the local government and the main source of the local economic expansion. However, the experiences of regional banks like the Shenzhen Development Bank and Guangdong Development Bank have shown that regional banks behave more like commercial banks than specialized banks.

2. Urban and rural credit cooperative banks—Both urban and rural credit cooperative banks cannot establish branches and usually are very small; they cannot survive with a large amount of bad debt. Urban cooperative banks will be set up in large and medium-sized cities from the equity of different urban credit cooperatives, while rural credit cooperative banks will be set up in rural areas.

3. Strengthen the management of state-owned banks—PBC will formulate supervisory regulations on state-owned commercial banks according to the international banking rules, especially the basic principles of the Basel Agreement. For example, the ratio of capital to risk weighted assets shall not exceed eight percent according to international standards. Commercial banks must design their credit policy and adjust their asset structure accordingly.

4. Development of overseas business—Chinese banks are developing their business overseas. By the end of 1993, BOC had 470 overseas branches, and PICC had sixty-seven overseas branches and offices.[43] Others have set up more than twenty offices abroad (PICC has three, ABC has two, PCBC has five, Bank of Communications has two, Pinan Insurance Company has three, Pacific Insurance Company has two, and Merchant Bank has one). Through the development of overseas business, the Chinese banks can obtain the latest information on international financial development, train the senior executives, and create commercial opportunities.

5. Competition—The large banks are facing new competition in banking business and credit cards. ICBC promotes its credit card business on television and markets the cards to companies and institutions. The Visa group is preparing to issue 100 million credit cards in China by 2000 and the state-owned banks are going to make every person in China hold one credit card in the next five years.

An increasing number of small and medium-sized banks and nonbank financial institutions have joined the financial market. They compete with larger banks for deposits, services, and interest rates. Foreign banks are also playing a more important role. Even though foreign banks cannot conduct businesses in Renminbi, the consultancy services they provide to local enterprises are becoming more attractive. All these new compeititive pressures on domestic banks definitely would lead the domestic banks to improve their business and management levels.

NOTES

1. *Annual Report*, People's Bank of China, 1992, Beijing, p. 38.

2. State Council Paper, No. 91, 1993.

3. *Annual Report*, People's Bank of China, Beijing, 1993, p. 16.

4. Liu, Hongru, 1991, *Financial Adjustment and Control*, Beijing: China Financial Publishing House, p. 306.

5. For a fuller discussion on the formula of China's money multiplier, see Liu (1991, pp. 284–307).

6. *China Financial Outlook 1994*, Beijing: China Financial Publishing House, p. 82

7. *PBC Statistics Monthly*, Beijing, 1993, various issues.

8. *China Financial Outlook 1994*, Beijing: China Financial Publishing House, pp. 87–88.

9. Jiang Wei-jun, 1994, "Interest Rate Adjustment: Background, Effect and Trend." in *Research Report on Market Economy*, Beijing: Beijing Market Economy Research Institute, p. 104.

10. *China City Finance and Banking Monthly*, Beijing: February-November, 1993, p. 64.

11. *Almanac of China's Finance and Banking*, 1992–1993, Beijing, pp. 505–516.

12. *China Financial Outlook 1994*, Beijing: China Financial Publishing House, 1994, pp. 78 and 88, and *Financial Times*, January 12, 1995, Beijing.

13. *China Securities Annual Report 1993*, Beijing: China's Financial Publishing House, 1993, pp. 5–13.

14. *Financial News*, March 17, 1994, Beijing.

15. *Almanac of China's Finance and Banking*, Beijing, 1988, p. 60.

16. Zhou, Zhenqiu, 1993, *A Research on China's Monetary Policies*, Beijing: China Financial Publishing House, p. 106.

17. *Annual Report 1992*, People's Bank of China, p. 13.

18. *Annual Report 1992*, People's Bank of China, p. 13.

19. *Annual Report 1992*, People's Bank of China, pp. 12–13.

20. *China Financial Outlook 1994*, Beijing: China Financial Publishing House, p. 18.

21. *China Financial Outlook 1994*, Beijing: China Financial Publishing House, p. 21.

22. *Chinese History on Finance and Banking from 1840*, Beijing: China Financial Publishing House, 1985, pp. 292–293.

23. For a detailed discussion on the development of banks in the postreform period, see Li (1994, pp. 32–33).

24. *Seminar Series on the Reform of the Chinese Financial System*, People's Bank of China, Beijing: China Financial Publishing House, 1994, p. 169.

25. *South China Morning Post*, March 11, 1995, Hong Kong.

26. *China News Digest*, March 21, 1995.

27. *China News Digest*, March 21, 1995.

28. *Almanac of China's Finance and Banking*, 1993, p. 3398.

29. *People's Construction Bank of China 40 Years Pictorial*, Beijing, 1994, p. 44.

30. *China Financial Outlook 1994*, Beijing: China Financial Publishing House, p. 90.

31. *Almanac of China's Finance and Banking*, Beijing: 1993, pp. 402–403.

32. *China Financial Outlook 1994*, Beijing: China Financial Publishing House, p. 76.

33. Calculations are based on *China Financial Outlook 1994*, Beijing: China Financial Publishing House, pp. 83–84.

34. *China News Digest*, March 16, 1995.

35. *China Financial Outlook 1994*, Beijing: China Financial Publishing House, 1994, pp. 91–93.

36. *China News Digest*, March 13, 1995.

37. Calculation is based on data from *China Financial Outlook 1994*, Beijing: China Financial Publishing House, pp. 83–84.

38. *China Financial Outlook 1994*, Beijing: China Financial Publishing House, p. 81.

39. *Almanac of China's Finance and Banking*, 1987, p. 60; 1988, pp. 58 and 437.

40. *China Financial Outlook 1994*, Beijing: China Financial Publishing House, p. 78.

41. *China Financial Outlook 1994*, Beijing: China Financial Publishing House, p. 85.

42. *China Financial Outlook 1994*, Beijing: China Financial Publishing House, p. 61.

43. Chen Yuan, 1994, *Seminar Series on the Reform of China's Financial System*, Beijing: China Financial Publishing House, p. 83.

REFERENCES

Chen, Yuan, 1994, *China Financial Outlook 1994*, Beijing: China Financial Publishing House.

Jiang, Weijun, 1994, "An Analysis on the Background, Efficiency and Trend of Interest Rate Adjustments," *Research Report on Market Economy*, Beijing: 93–108.

Li, Kui-Wai, 1994, *Financial Repression and Economic Reform in China*, Westport: Praeger Publishers.

Liu, Hongru, 1991, *Financial Control and Adjustment*, Beijing: China Financial Publishing House.

Zhou, Zhengqing, 1993, *Research on China Monetary Policy*, Beijing: China People's Publishing House.

2

Foreign Bank Lending to Chinese Industries: Criteria and Procedures

PANGSHUN CHAI and KUI-WAI LI

INTRODUCTION

The process of investment involves the transfer from the fund-surplus party to the fund-deficit party. Banks are intermediaries which act as the "invisible" hand in fund allocations. To a large extent, the productivity of investment depends on the way banks allocate their funds. Fund-surplus households usually do not have much information on the way fund-deficit organizations invest. Banks therefore play the role of ensuring that funds are allocated to the most productive investment projects so that the return could cover the principles as well as make a handsome profit for the banks. State banks in China are rather secretive in the way their funds are allocated. In this regard, foreign bank practices can be used as the reference point.

Large, well-established foreign banks apply a systematic approach in screening out investment projects with low returns. The entire process of loan application is divided into different areas through which investigations can be made impartially. There are basically three areas in which a foreign bank concentrates. First, the foreign bank will examine the status and background of the borrower, in particular, the borrower's ability to handle the loans and the repayment schedule. The project itself is another area of concern. The bank would seek a reasonable answer to questions concerning the industry, output marketability, project management, and its linkage effects. Various criteria are applied so that a scientific judgment is derived. The third area concerns the overall level of security in the recovery of the principal. In case the borrower cannot repay the principal, the bank would explore other channels to regain the principal.

Investigations have to be conducted with satisfaction before the foreign bank would agree to the loan. Studying the lending process of a foreign bank could give a good insight into the successful cases of bank loans. Indeed, the conservative nature of most established foreign banks ensures that loans are channeled to productive investments, while unproductive investments are screened out automatically. This ensures that output of the economy will rise. The linkage effects include a fall in inflation rate as supply is matched with demand, and a fall in government budget deficit as the number of loss-making state enterprises drops.[1]

THE BORROWER

The first movement in any investment project proposal must have the endorsement or approval from the economic committee (*jinwei*) of the department or ministry or commission concerned. These investment projects should fall in line with the overall development of the planning commission (*jiwei*). The borrower's type of enterprise can be seen from the project proposal. There are basically seven types of enterprises: government agent, state-owned, collectively owned, joint venture, solely foreign-owned, branch of a domestic enterprise, and branch of a foreign enterprise. In a case where foreign exchange (FX) loans are involved, the borrower has to obtain an authorized permit from the State Administration for Foreign Exchange Control (SAFEC) to borrow foreign exchange loans from abroad.

The proposal has to be supported by the enterprise's organization memorandum, registration certificate, business approval certificate, or foreign exchange business certificate if the borrower is a bank or financial institution. The borrower must identify the ultimate person who is empowered to execute documents. Most banks and financial institutions distribute their "FX loan quota" allocated from SAFEC to their main branches every year. Branches can borrow within their limit and report to SAFEC on a monthly basis their month-end outstanding debt balance.

State banks and financial institutions are authorized by SAFEC to borrow short-term (not over twelve months) and long-term (over twelve months) FX loans up to a certain amount every year. Foreign enterprises, including joint ventures and solely foreign-owned enterprises, do not need approval from SAFEC to borrow foreign loans, but the loan should be registered at SAFEC within fifteen days. Otherwise, interest payment and repayment of principal cannot be remitted to the lenders abroad. Banks and financial institutions have to report their outstanding FX loans periodically to SAFEC. Since the unification between the Renminbi (Rmb) and the Foreign Exchange Certificates (FEC) on January 1, 1994, all registered FX loans can use market rates quoted by their banks for payment of debt and interest.

THE LOAN ARRANGEMENT FLOW

The time involved in a loan arrangement differs from project to project (varies from two weeks to over four weeks), depending on the availability of approval documents and the extent of cooperation among the borrower, the lender, the guarantor, and other concerned parties. A loan arrangement has to go through several stages. We take a Swiss export buyer's credit for illustration.

Stage 1: Documents for application of loan—The borrower should possess the following documents when applying for a loan:

a. Loan application form;

b. Signed contract of purchase;

c. Project feasibility report and approval permits;

d. Foreign exchange loan quota;

e. Guarantor; and

f. Other documents that can support the application.

Stage 2: Swiss Export Risk Guarantee (ERG)—The supplier can assist the importer to apply ERG from the Swiss Government. The ERG is the basic document for banks to arrange a Swiss Export Credit, and the beneficiary of the ERG should be assigned to the lending bank.

Stage 3: Loan examination—The buyer's bank will examine the feasibility of loans, draft a Loan Assessment Report, and propose to the Head Office to utilize Swiss Export Credit under the Frame Loan Agreement with a Swiss bank. A set of loan application documents should be included.

Stage 4: Loan approval and confirmation of sales contract—The lending bank accepts the loan application, notifies the borrower's bank of the result of loan examination, and confirms with the borrower the contract agreement.

Stage 5: Payment—A five percent cash down payment is paid by the borrower to the supplier as advised by the lending bank. A ten percent down payment is made in the form of a Letter of Credit (L/C) issued by the buyer's bank, as advised through and by the lending bank. The rest of the eighty-five percent payment, as stated in the loan agreement, will be made to the supplier by the lending bank upon fulfillment of the L/C terms.

Stage 6: Repayment—The principal can be repaid in semiannual installments up to five years. Interest is paid every six months in arrears on outstanding loan balance. The loan flow is completed when the loan is repaid by the borrower via the buyer's bank.

THE LENDING CRITERIA

There are basically seven criteria a foreign bank uses, and weight is given to each of these criteria.

Advancement in Equipment and Technology

This criterion carries a weight of twenty percent. For a foreign bank, the first obvious criterion is the opportunity of exporting home-produced industrial plants and machinery to China. The bank acts as the intermediary not only between foreign savers and loan users in China, but also between home exporters and Chinese importers. Both the bank and the potential borrower can benefit from the application. The bank provides free information on various exportable industrial items. The borrower can then compare the technology from one overseas supplier with that of another, before deciding on the use of bank loans.

Guaranteed Repayment of Principal and Interest by the Partner Bank in China

This criterion also carries a weight of twenty percent. Securities that are available to the lender usually are guarantees and pledge of properties such as fixed assets (land use rights, buildings, machinery, and so on) and current assets (notes, bonds, shares, and so on). The Chinese civil law allows the pledge of "Land Use Rights" and other property, though land itself belongs to the state and cannot be pledged. There are, however, practical difficulties in recovering properties. First, it is difficult to urge people living in the property to move out. Furthermore, the lender cannot control the realization of the property because the lender has to entrust a state company to auction and to sell the property. Although land-use rights, equipment, shares, and bonds can be used as collateral, there is no standardized national law governing pledge and mortgage of properties. Some cities draw up their own rules, but there are differences between these rules. In short, bank guarantees and similar documents are still widely used instead of mortgages.

The concept of a company with limited liability is not widely used in China. Nearly all the state-owned and collective-owned enterprises are unlimited in nature. There are only a handful of newly formed conglomerates listed in the stock exchanges and some foreign-invested enterprises are limited companies. In general, secured loans get priority in repayment over nonsecured loans.

In the absence of a full debt guarantee, there are other potential financing structures. One is leasing and releasing. The lender can first lease the equipment to a reliable financial institution in China, which then re-leases the equipment to the end-user. Another possibility is refinancing. The borrower has to be a reliable financial institution in China and gives the loan to the end-user on its own risk. The third possibility is special-purpose deposits. In this case, the lender is acting as a depositor of the financial institution in China. Issuing shares and bonds is another potential channel. Some institutions in China are allowed to issue shares and bonds. Foreigners are not allowed to buy "A" shares and Renminbi bonds are issued domestically for local Chinese only. Shares and bonds open to foreigners include: "B" shares, which are traded in Security Exchanges in Shanghai and Shenzhen, and "H" shares, which are traded in the Hong Kong Stock Exchange. Other shares and bonds are issued in New York, London, Tokyo, and Singapore.

Profitability

The weight given to this criterion is twenty percent. For a medium-term loan, say five years, the general acceptable interest rate charged is 1.5 percent above LIBOR per annum net, though there is variation in the creditability of the borrower and guarantor. The arrangement fee should not be less than one percent flat of the loan amount. The participation fee, however, varies according to the amount of the loan.

A major element relating to profitability is risk. As far as country risk is concerned, most foreign banks apply the Moody credit ranking. China's country risk was upgraded to grade A in early 1994, recovering its pre-1989 position. An "A3" grade is given to long-term bonds, to the Bank of China, China International Trust and Investment Corporation, and People's Construction Bank of China. A "Baa1" grade is given to Guangdong International Trust and Investment Corporation. A "Prime 1" grade is given to Bank of China short-term foreign currency deposits. However, Moody downgraded the credit rating of the Bank of China, People's Construction Bank of China, Industrial and Commercial Bank of China, and Bank of Communications to Baa1 again in April 1995.

Industry risk is lower if the loan is invested in infrastructure industries, such as power generation, transportation, telecommunication, and export-oriented high-technology industries. This is because the development of these industries is encouraged by the state. After the implementation of the Austerity Plan in July 1993, which tightened credit expansion considerably, it was clear that only key infrastructure projects could obtain FX loan quota. In addition, borrowers should have sufficient cash flow for the payment of interest, principal, and other expenses. The grace period for light industry is not more than twelve months, or thirty months in the case of heavy industry.

Marketability of Output at Home and Abroad

A ten percent weight is given to the marketability of the output. The market identity of the product is important. Would it be a high-end or low-end product? Exportable product or domestically consumed product? A reliable independent market research report would be useful in supporting the proposal. In the case of large-scale industries such as energy and transportation, there is usually no problem with market potential. This is because demand for energy is generally large, and it is expected to grow as the economy prospers. Export-oriented industries should not have any problem, unless a major trade war between China and the outside world were to occur. China's domestic market has been ignored by investors for a long time. Such an attitude, however, is changing since China is still the largest market in the world. The domestic market should expand once income has reached a certain level.

Source of Raw Materials, Labor, and Overhead

This accounts for ten percent of the total weight. The lending bank is concerned generally with cost overrun, as that will impose pressure on cash flow and ability to repay the principal. Raw material supplies have to be specified clearly in the proposal. If the supply of raw materials comes from overseas, the risk involved will be larger. Training of workers is allowed if the project lasts for a number of years.

It is also the responsibility of the borrower to apply and get approval for tax exemption. There are two special tax issues. One is stamp duty. Since the beginning of 1994, a new set of value-added tax, business tax, and consumption tax have been implemented for all domestic and foreign enterprises alike. Stamp duty is levied at 0.005 percent of the loan amount on both parties. The other is a ten percent withholding tax in interest payment unless it is exempted by State Tax Bureau.

Feasibility Report, Approvals, and Availability of FX Loan Quota

This also accounts for ten percent in the total weight. Banks generally prefer to do business with clients they know. Borrowers and loan arrangers should choose lenders from the same bank as the one used by the supplier of equipment. This is important since some banks and exporters choose to support their prime clients, such as with export credit or buyer's credit that is covered by export insurance. Normally, foreign banks would request the borrower to supply a copy of the Business Registration Certificate, the borrower's Organization Memorandum, the annual financial report for recent years, and the Letter of Intent from the Guarantor. Borrowers also have to produce the following documents: incorporation and constitutional documents; joint venture contract and relevant MOFTEC approvals; government approval for borrowing; issue of guarantees, implementation of project; evidence of appointment of service agent by borrower and guarantor; legal opinion by a law firm in China; stamp duty and tax exemption certificates. Unless it is clearly stated in the loan document, the assignment of a loan needs the consent of the borrower and approval authorities.

Documentations usually follow European style. This includes: a) representations and warranties; b) positive and negative undertakings; c) default and waiver of default; d) choice of governing law and jurisdiction; and e) language used and assignment and transfer of lender's rights and obligations. However, loan documents can be amended to take account of local requirements and sensitivities of relevant parties.

Examples of positive undertakings include undertakings to fund cost-overrun and adequate capitalization, insurance, completion of all relevant government approvals and registrations. Examples of negative undertakings include: a) the restriction to create further charges; b) failure to fulfill contracts; c) failure to change the ownership structure; and d) failure to obtain loans or issue guarantees. Events of default include revocation or withholding of important government approvals or permits, misrepresentation and breach of warranties, termination of essential contracts, and cross-default.

Loan agreements must be registered at SAFEC within fifteen days of signing. The authorized person to sign on behalf of the Chinese side should be a legal representative named in the business license. The official seal should be affixed. As far as the law and language are concerned, a loan agreement between a foreigner and a Chinese legal person can choose either the Chinese law or the law of another country accepted by both sides as the governing law. Both parties can choose Chinese or any other language. However, Chinese is used for the purpose of registration of external debt at SAFEC. If legal proceeding is to be carried out in Chinese courts, Chinese language should be used.

Location of the Project

The last criterion forms the remaining ten percent of the weight. The coastal cities are more developed than inland areas in general. Investment projects situated in the Special Economic Zones and coastal cities are generally more preferred than projects situated in the interior regions.

LITIGATION AND ARBITRATION

In the event of a default, the lending bank will take the following steps to recover the loans:

a. A notification of default should be sent first to the borrower, then to the guarantor, then to SAFEC and other authorities concerned;
b. If there is no reply, a notification of legal proceeding to recover loans to all parties concerned will be issued;
c. If there is still no reply, the lender will call on the guarantor to repay the outstanding debt and interest;
d. If there is no further reply, action on arbitration and other informal means such as personal relationship and the mass media will be exercised;
e. The last resort will be to apply for a court order to take over the project and all assets of the borrower and guarantor.

The lending bank can consider arbitration as an alternative to formal legal proceedings. Beginning from 1991, China is a party of the New York Convention and has acceded to the Hague Convention. Application of reciprocal enforcement of arbitral awards must be made to the court before enforcement proceedings can be issued. The Hague Convention provides a formal channel for foreign judicial proceedings. Unless a convention for reciprocal enforcement is signed, a foreign judgment is unenforceable in China.

Arbitration is often used for settlement of disputes between the Chinese and foreign parties. Even before an application for arbitration is made, lenders should always be aware that other informal measures, such as personal discussions and negotiation, may be more effective. This usually can gain respect of both parties. However, if formal litigation proceedings have to be commenced, the lender has to produce documents and evidence that can support the claim. This includes payment default, breach of representation and warranties, breach of positive or negative undertakings, cross-defaults, termination of securities, and other major contracts. Usually, Hong Kong is chosen to proceed with the litigation. This is obviously because legal terms are clearly defined and there are more experienced lawyers in Hong Kong.

In China, there are different laws for terminating a company for failure to pay its debts. One is the Law of the People's Republic of China on Enterprise Bankruptcy promulgated on December 2, 1986, that applies to state-owned enterprises. There are also Municipal Regulations on the Liquidation of Foreign Investment Enterprises, which apply to foreign enterprises. These include: Guangdong Province Law on Enterprise Bankruptcy, Shanghai Municipality Liquidation of Foreign Investment Enterprise Regulations, and Beijing Procedure for Liquidation of Foreign Funded Enterprises.

There are broadly twelve procedures for terminating a company for failure to pay its debts:

1. To file an insolvency petition to the court in the locality of the enterprise;
2. Creditors are notified by court within ten days of the hearing of the insolvency petition;
3. Public announcement by the court of the hearing of the insolvency petition;
4. Creditors who are notified by court must prove their debts within one month;
5. Creditors who are not notified by court can prove their debts within three months;
6. Creditors who fail to prove their debts within the prescribed time will be deemed to have made a voluntary surrender of their claims irrespective of whether the debts are secured or not;
7. A creditors' meeting is formed to examine and admit proofs, to discuss and adopt proposals for conciliation, to discuss and adopt plans for realization of the assets of the debtor, and for distribution of the proceeds;
8. Within three months, debtors or the government department in charge of the debtor may apply for the reorganization of the debtor to be carried out in accordance with a draft conciliation agreement;

9. If a conciliation agreement is approved by two-thirds of the creditors present, it can be submitted to the court for approval, and it will become binding on all creditors once approved;

10. If there is no conciliation agreement, a liquidation committee will be appointed by the court to collect, realize, and distribute the assets of the debtor;

11. The secured creditor is entitled to enforce his/her security rights over the property; and

12. Proceeds of realization of the debtor are applied in the following order of priority: liquidation expenses; wages of employees and premium of labor insurance; tax and claims of unsecured creditors. If the assets of the debtor are insufficient to satisfy all the claims in the same class, such claims within the same class will be paid on a pro-rata basis.

CONCLUSION

Banks are intermediaries that match capital from fund-surplus households to fund-deficit investors. To a large extent, banks can determine the size and extent of investment through their lending activities. In the process, it is obvious that banks would make a profit. If capital is being allocated efficiently, however, a rise in output will lead to an increase in the supply of commodities, which can either be exported or be consumed locally.

Lending to Chinese industries has become one of the core businesses for many banks and financial institutions. In general, the risk of investing in China is relatively low and acceptable. Foreign banks tend to exercise a set of standard lending criteria for loan proposals. Altogether seven criteria are exercised to ensure the loans are secured. Security in loan repayment is the most important factor in all loans to Chinese industries. There are also channels through which the lender can recover the loans should the borrower fail to repay the interest or the principal.

The microeconomic activities of banks have wider macroeconomic implications. The interest rate acts not only as the cost of borrowing, but as a screening device banks use to promote productive investment. The criteria ensure that the project is economically viable and the ability to repay is maximized. If all banks behave similarly, capital resources will automatically be allocated to the most efficient investment projects.

NOTES

An earlier version of this chapter was presented in the 69th Western Economic Association Annual Conference, Vancouver, July 1994. The authors would like to thank the conference participants for their comments. The views expressed in this chapter belong entirely to the authors, and do not represent the views of the institutions with which they are affiliated.

1. For a fuller discussion on the economic linkages, see Li (1994, pp. 141–143).

REFERENCE

Li, Kui-Wai, 1994, *Financial Repression and Economic Reform in China*, Westport: Praeger Press.

3

The Development of Direct Foreign Investment in China

MEE-KAU NYAW

INTRODUCTION

During the Third Plenum of the Eleventh Central Committee of the Chinese Communist Party (CCP) held in December 1978, China adopted an "open door policy" that opened its economy to foreign investment. This was a major shift from its past self-reliance policy that resulted in a closed state of the Chinese economy. During the fourteen-year period, 1979–1992, China made great strides in its domestic economic development and foreign trade relations by establishing five Special Economic Zones (SEZs)— which include Shenzhen, Zhuhai, Shantou, Xiamen, and Hainan—fourteen open-trade coastal cities, coastal economic development zones, inland development areas, and, most recently, the New Pudong Area.[1] They are designated as target areas for attracting foreign direct investment.

In its quest for economic modernization, China has suffered from two severe bottlenecks: lack of savings for capital formation and foreign exchange constraints. Consequently, China has sought an inflow of foreign capital to increase its capital formation, and it has attracted export-oriented industries to the country to increase its foreign exchange earnings, thereby alleviating the two constraints. In addition, foreign investment has facilitated the transfer of technology and management techniques, both badly needed by China in its modernization drive. These have been the main objectives behind China's open door policy.

According to the classification used in China, utilization of foreign capital takes the following three forms: (a) foreign loans by foreign governments and international development agencies such as World Bank and Asian Development Bank (ADB); (b) direct foreign investment (DFI), which includes equity joint ventures (EJVs), contractual joint ventures (CJVs), wholly foreign-owned enterprises (WFOs), and joint development ventures (JDVs), which relate mainly to oil exploration; and (c) other foreign investment, which includes compensation trade, export processing, and international leasing.

An EJV, officially called a Sino-foreign joint venture, is a limited company jointly funded through equity by two or more investors. It has the status of a legal person, and the investing companies share profits or losses in proportion to their respective equity shares. A WFO is a branch founded by a foreign firm, or it can be an independent enterprise formed by a foreign company or a group of individuals outside China. It is wholly responsible for profits or losses. The third form, a CJV, is sometimes called a "cooperative venture," and it is probably unique to China. A CJV is a loose form of enterprise where Chinese and foreign partners cooperate in operations and management as prescribed in the contract. The Chinese side often provides land, natural resources, labor, local equipment, or facilities, but does not contribute equity funds. The foreign partners often provide funds, technology, major new equipment, and materials. Under a CJV, profits or losses are split according to a ratio agreed upon beforehand. Finally, a JDV is a joint investment by Chinese and foreign interests that is limited primarily to exploration of off-shore oil resources. The purpose of the venture is not to share profits but to share oil resources. Output, once produced, is divided between both sides according to contract terms.

TRENDS AND STRUCTURAL FEATURES, 1979–1993

Table 3.1 shows the utilization of foreign capital from 1979 to 1993. During this period, total contractual or pledged DFI and other foreign investment totaled 228.4 billion U.S. dollars, while total realized value of DFI was sixty-six billion U.S. dollars. In addition, eighty-six billion U.S. dollars in foreign loans (realized value of 71.8 billion U.S. dollars) was pledged for the period 1979–1993. During the early years, foreign investment followed a zigzag path. It grew slowly in the initial years but suffered a drastic decline in 1986 due to deterioration of the investment climate. When the Chinese government started to take serious action to rectify the

Table 3.1
Utilization of Foreign Capital, 1979–1993

(100 million U.S. dollars)

	Foreign Loans[1]		Direct Foreign Investment[2]		Other Foreign Investment[3]		Total	
	Projects	Value	Projects	Value	Projects	Value	Projects	Value
Contractual								
1979-1989	510	517.34	21.776	337.56	-	44.93	22.286	899.92
1990	98	50.99	7.273	65.96	-	3.90	7.371	120.85
1991	108	71.61	12.978	119.77	-	4.45	[4]13.086	195.83
1992	94	107.03	48.764	581.24	-	6.12	[4]48.858	694.39
1993	158	113.06	83.437	1,114.36	-	5.31	[4]83.595	1,232.73
1994	97	106.68	47.549	826.80	-	4.08	47.646	937.56
Realized								
1979-1989	-	393.21	-	154.95	-	29.69	-	577.85
1990	-	65.35	-	34.87	-	2.68	-	102.90
1991	-	68.88	-	43.66	-	3.00	-	115.54
1992	-	79.11	-	110.07	-	2.84	-	192.02
1993	-	111.89	-	275.15	-	2.56	-	389.60
1994	-	92.67	-	337.67	-	1.79	-	432.13

Notes: (1) Includes loans by foreign governments and international development agencies, (2) Direct foreign investment includes the following forms: equity joint ventures, contractual joint ventures (cooperative ventures), wholly foreign-owned enterprises, and joint development ventures (petroleum), (3) Includes compensation trade, export processing, and international leasing, (4) Excluding projects in "other foreign investment" category.

Source: Zhongguo Tongji Nianjian (China Statistical Yearbook) (various years); *Zhongguo Tongji Zhaiyao 1992* (A Statistical Survey of China 1992), *Zhongguo Jingji Nianjian* (China Economic Yearbook) (various years); *1994 China Foreign Economic Statistical Yearbook.*

situation, foreign investment began to gradually recover until the outbreak of the prodemocracy movement in Beijing in the summer of 1989. After the Tiananmen Incident in June 1989, China was sanctioned by a number of Western countries. In addition, an economic retrenchment program initiated in 1988 to curb high inflation rates had an adverse effect on FDI in 1989. According to the data published by the Ministry of Foreign Economic Relations and Trade (MOFERT), renamed the Ministry of Foreign Trade and Economic Cooperation (MOFTEC) at the 8th National People's Congress held in early 1993, the pledged DFI projects had declined from 5,945 in 1988 to 5,779 in 1989, representing a negative growth rate of -2.8 percent. Total commitments in 1989 recorded only a moderate growth of 6.1 percent as compared to 1988, and the number of EJVs and CJVs declined by 6.4 percent and 27.3 percent, respectively.[2]

In the second half of 1990, direct foreign investment in China began to recover as Western countries gradually normalized their relations with China, in particular after the lifting of economic sanctions by France, which had initially adopted a tough stance against China's crackdown on the prodemocracy movement. Foreign investors flocked back to China after a cooling-off period, and DFI continued to increase in 1991. The high growth rates in 1992 and 1993 were partially due to the huge investments in real estate from overseas. Certainly the optimism of DFI in China was spurred by Deng Xiaoping's visit to Southern China in January 1992, when he argued for more rapid development of the open door policy. It was also helped by the adoption of the "socialist market economy" doctrine at the 14th CCP Congress held in October 1992. According to a report by Reuter News Agency, total commitments of foreign investment to China during the first nine months of 1992 had far surpassed those of Indonesia, Malaysia, and Thailand, three of the booming Southeast Asian countries which compete with China for foreign direct investment.[3]

The relative shares of various forms/types of foreign investment have changed over the years in China. As presented in Table 3.2, in the first few years of opening to the outside world, China's utilization of foreign funds was realized mainly through contractual joint ventures, joint oil development ventures, and "compensation trade and export processing ventures." Together, these accounted for eighty-two percent of foreign investment during 1979–1984. EJVs and WFOs were relatively unimportant during that period. CJVs and "compensation trade and export processing ventures" in particular were generally smaller in scale and of low-skill labor-intensive industries which were located mainly in four SEZs and the Guangdong Province. A majority of the foreign investors took advantage of low wages and cheap land prices in China. In addition, the forms of CJVs and export

Table 3.2
Percentage Shares of Various Forms of Foreign-Invested Enterprises to Total Foreign Investment, 1979–1993 (contractual values)

Year	EJVs	CJVs	WFOs	Joint Development	Other Investment*	Total Foreign Investment (in 100 million U.S. dollars)
1979-1984	13.4	45.6	4.6	23.5	12.9	103.3 (100%)
1985	32.1	55.2	0.7	5.7	6.3	63.3 (100%)
1986	41.3	40.8	0.6	2.4	14.9	33.3 (100%)
1987	45.2	29.7	10.9	0.01	14.1	43.2 (100%)
1988	50.6	26.2	7.8	1.0	14.4	61.9 (100%)
1989	42.3	17.2	26.3	3.2	11.0	62.9 (100%)
1990	38.7	17.9	35.0	2.8	5.6	69.9 (100%)
1991	49.0	17.2	29.5	0.7	3.6	124.2 (100%)
1992	49.6	22.6	26.7	0.07	1.1	587.3 (100%)
1993	49.3	22.8	27.2	0.3	0.4	1,119.7 (100%)

Note: * Includes compensation trade, export processing, and international leasing.
Source: Computed from *Almanac of China's Foreign Economic Relations and Trade* (various years).

processing ventures were quite flexible and usually required no cash outlay by Chinese partners.

As shown in Table 3.2, EJV have become increasingly important since 1985. The number of WFOs also surged after 1987 whereas CJVs and "other investment ventures" declined. The increase of WFOs was due mainly to three factors. First, there was a huge surge of DFI from Taiwan in the late 1980s (see pattern of investment flows below). Taiwan investors usually are inclined to control their own companies rather than to cooperate with partners. Second, considerable costs and time involved in the coordination of technology and management deemed essential in EJVs and CJVs was avoided by establishing WFOs.[4] And third, there was greater acceptance by the Chinese Government of WFOs which are export-oriented and bring into China much needed foreign-exchange earnings. It is worth noting that many EJVs and WFOs have been established by well-known multinationals and conglomerates from all over the world. China has been quite successful in attracting large-scale, high-tech foreign enterprises to invest in the country in recent years.

By 1993, investors from over fifty countries or areas had invested in China (see Table 3.3). Hong Kong/Macau has been the largest investor area taking up 62.2 percent of total direct investment during 1979–1991. Before 1990, the State Statistical Bureau of China did not separate Hong Kong from Macau in its published foreign investment figures. Despite this, it is known that most of the flows of foreign investment are from Hong Kong whereas Macau accounts for only a minute share.

It should be stressed that published DFI figures for Hong Kong are overstated. Part of the investment flow from Hong Kong was in fact originated in Southeast Asia. Some overseas Chinese and Taiwan business-men invested in the mainland through subsidiaries registered in Hong Kong to avoid scrutiny from their home countries. Investing in China by wealthy overseas Chinese businessmen is politically sensitive in some Southeast Asian countries such as Indonesia, which broke diplomatic relationship with China after the Indonesia Communist Party was linked to the *coup d'état* in 1965. The two countries reestablished diplomatic ties only in 1992. Since then, the Indonesian government has adopted a more positive attitude toward its ethnic-Chinese citizens regarding investments in China. In Taiwan, investors were legally prohibited from investing in China prior to 1990, although Taiwanese businessmen found ways to circumvent govern-ment restraints by registering ventures through Hong Kong. The rule was relaxed in 1990 to allow Taiwanese firms to invest in the mainland through proper registration with the Taiwan Government. Consequently, future accounting for DFI through Hong Kong/Macau will be more accurate, but

Table 3.3

Shares of Direct Foreign Investment by Leading Countries/Areas, 1979–1993

(100 million U.S. dollars)

Countries/Areas	Projects					
	1979-1991		1992		1992	
	(No.)	(%)	(No.)	(%)	(No.)	(%)
Hong Kong /Macau	31,453	75.1	31,892	65.4	50,868	60.9
USA	2,000	4.8	3,265	6.7	6,750	8.1
Japan	1,891	4.3	1,805	3.7	3,488	4.2
Germany	111	0.3	130	0.3	320	0.4
Singapore	558	1.3	742	1.5	1,751	2.1
United Kingdom	132	0.3	126	0.3	348	0.4
Australia	181	0.4	358	0.7	769	0.9
Canada	187	0.5	394	0.8	759	1.1
Taiwan	*3,851	-	6,430	13.2	10,948	13.1
All countries /Areas	-	-	48,764	100	83,437	100
	Contractual Values					
	(Amt.)	(%)	(Amt.)	(%)	(Amt.)	(%)
Hong Kong /Macau	325.7	62.2	415.3	71.5	767.5	68.9
USA	50.1	9.6	31.2	5.4	68.1	6.1
Japan	39.1	7.5	21.7	3.7	29.6	2.6
Germany	10.9	2.1	1.3	0.2	2.5	0.2
Singapore	9.1	1.7	10.0	1.7	29.5	2.6
United Kingdom	7.3	1.4	2.9	0.5	19.9	1.8
Australia	3.4	0.6	2.8	0.5	6.4	0.6
Canada	3.2	0.6	3.2	0.5	11.8	1.1
Tawian	*34.3	-	55.4	9.5	99.5	8.9
All countries /Areas	-	-	581.2	100	1,114.4	100

Note: * 1983-1991.

Source: Zhongguo Jingji Nianjian (various years); *Almanac of China's Foreign Economic Relations and Trade* (various years); Taiwan's data for 1983-1991 are from *China Daily* (Beijing), December 30, 1992.

data on investment flow for previous years coming from Hong Kong and Macau include Taiwan and other Southeast Asian interests.

Moreover, there are some China-funded firms in Hong Kong and Macau that have established joint ventures with other domestic Chinese firms. The so-called "bogus blue-eyed" joint ventures were established to take advantage of the preferential treatment given to joint ventures. Clearly, the existence of the "reverse investment," as it is often called by the Chinese, overstates the flow of foreign investment funds from Hong Kong. However, its magnitude is unknown as no official data have been published by China.

After Hong Kong, the second largest foreign investor in terms of DFI value for the period 1979–1991 was the United States, followed by Japan and then Germany. Taiwan's DFI should be noted here. China began to publish investment figures from Taiwan only in 1990. According to the figures released by *China Daily*, there were 3,815 foreign-invested projects with contractual or pledged value of 34 billion U.S. dollars for 1983–1991. Pledged investments increased significantly in 1992 and 1993, which were equivalent to 1.6 and 2.9 times of that pledged during the period of 1983–1991 respectively (Table 3.3). The relative position of Taiwan increased from fourth in 1991 to second in 1992 and 1993, only after Hong Kong.[5] According to a report published by the Chung-Hua Institution for Economic Research, a semigovernment think-tank based in Taipei, there were over 10,000 cumulative Taiwanese-invested projects in the mainland with a total contractual value exceeding sixty-eight billion U.S. dollars in 1992.[6] This surpassed the U.S. investments. Investment flow from South Korea also has become increasingly important. In 1991–1992, South Korea's investment position climbed from obscurity to fifth place after Hong Kong, Taiwan, the United States and Japan.[7] China established full diplomatic relations with South Korea in 1992, which marked the end of hostility between the two countries following the Korean War. This breakthrough will certainly have a positive effect on the flow of Korea's direct investment into China due to geographical proximity of the two countries. Historically South Korea has had close ties with Shandong Province, which, today, is the key recipient of DFI from South Korea, and it is expected to remain so in the future.

As illustrated in Table 3.4, investment projects made by Taiwan and Hong Kong are small in scale, with an average value of 0.9 million U.S. dollars (1983–1991) and 1.03 million U.S. dollars (1979–1991), respectively. The average project size for Hong Kong investors had increased in 1992 and 1993. The average size of DFI from Germany is the largest with 9.81 million U.S. dollars, followed by the United Kingdom (5.53 million U.S. dollars) and the United States (1.51 million U.S. dollars) during 1979–1991. The

Table 3.4
Direct Foreign Investment Based on Contractual Values, 1979–1993

Countries/Areas	Average Value per Project (Million U.S. dollars)		
	1979-1991	1992	1993
Hong Kong/Macau	1.03	1.30	1.51
Taiwan	*0.90	0.86	0.91
USA	2.51	0.96	1.01
Japan	2.07	1.20	0.85
Germany	9.81	1.00	0.78
Singapore	1.63	1.34	1.69
United Kingdom	5.53	2.27	5.71
Australia	1.88	0.77	0.83
Canada	1.71	0.80	1.23

Note: * = 1983-1991.
Source: Computed from Table 3.3.

average Japanese DFI project is quite small (Table 3.4), but the Japanese DFI in China accounts for only 1.1 percent of Japan's total overseas investment and 6.3 percent of its total Asia investment for the period 1982–1984.[8] In view of Japan's huge economic power, its proximity to China, and its traditional cultural ties with China, the relatively small total DFI has been disappointing. This can be explained partially by the relative difficulty in transferring Japanese technological know-how to China, and partially by the huge bilateral trade surplus in Japan's favor. China has been critical of Japan's reluctance to invest more, particularly when good performance of Japanese DFI is taken into consideration.[9] Given the improved investment climate in China in recent years, Japan needs to respond more positively to China's demand.

China's direct foreign investments by geographical distribution in terms of both amounts and percentage shares are presented in Tables 3.5 and 3.6, respectively. Four SEZs accounted for 20.2 percent of total DFI during 1979–1989. Shenzhen, the first SEZ established in China, topped the list and absorbed 13.2 percent of DFI. This was partly due to its proximity to Hong Kong. Apart from the SEZs, DFI was concentrated in the nine "open coastal provinces," which accounted for over seventy percent of FDI during 1990–1993. Guangdong Province attracted the largest amount of total investment, whilst Jiangsu, Fujian, and Shandong provinces had increased their relative shares during 1990–1993 (Tables 3.5 and 3.6).

Table 3.5

Direct Foreign Investment in China by Geographical Distribution (realized values)

(Million U.S. dollars)

	1979-1989	1990	1991	1992	1993
SEZs	3,152.05	654.63	969.18	1,216.33	2,550.48
Shenzhen	2,045.76	388.94	398.75	321.66	672.21
Zhuhai	497.37	69.10	134.33	172.53	399.93
Shantou	175.25	123.86	303.10	158.61	440.94
Xiamen	433.67	72.73	310.76	563.53	1,037.40
Open Coastal Cities					
Dalian	250.16	201.29	261.11	-	-
Tianjin	313.89	83.15	93.88	116.05	232.57
Qingdao	97.37	45.88	46.47	-	-
Shanghai	1,258.74	177.19	164.20	789.96	2,317.62
Guangzhou	913.37	180.87	231.61	554.20	1,278.28
Open Coastal Provinces					
Liaoning	435.40	248.31	313.60	439.16	1,227.31
Hebei	97.63	39.35	44.37	173.82	357.35
Shandong	455.39	150.84	179.50	973.35	1,843.19
Jiangsu	406.22	141.10	233.24	1,402.93	3,001.85
Zhejiang	219.07	48.44	91.62	293.98	1,032.71
Fujian	799.78	290.92	402.68	1,416.33	2,867.45
Guangdong	6,541.68	1,459.84	1,822.86	3,551.50	7,498.05
Hainan	302.22	100.55	176.06	451.60	734.49
Guangxi	279.76	30.25	38.71	180.26	872.03
Beijing	1,517.66	276.95	284.88	349.84	666.94
Total	15,495.00	3,242.51	4,056.38	11,231.53	26,130.56

Source: Figures for 1979-1989 are derived from Y. Y. Kueh, "Foreign Investment and Economic Change in China," *The China Quarterly*, No. 131 (September 1992), Table 3, p. 649; 1991-1993 figures are from *Almanac of China's Foreign Economic Relations and Trade* (various years).

Table 3.6
Shares of Foreign Direct Investment in China by Geographical Distribution
(realized values)

	1979-1989	1990	1991	1992	1993
SEZs	20.5	20.2	23.9	10.8	9.8
Shenzhen	13.2	12.0	9.8	2.9	2.6
Zhuhai	3.2	2.1	3.3	1.5	1.5
Shantou	1.3	3.8	7.5	1.4	1.7
Xiamen	2.8	2.2	7.7	5.0	4.0
Open Coastal Cities					
Dalian	1.6	6.2	6.4	-	-
Tianjin	2.0	2.6	2.3	1.0	0.9
Qingdao	0.	1.4	1.2	-	-
Shanghai	8.1	5.5	4.1	7.0	8.9
Guangzhou	5.9	5.6	5.7	4.9	4.9
Open Coastal Provinces					
Liaoning	2.8	7.7	7.7	3.9	4.7
Hebei	0.6	1.2	1.1	1.5	1.4
Shandong	2.9	4.6	4.4	8.7	7.1
Jiangsu	2.6	4.4	5.8	12.5	11.5
Zhejiang	1.4	1.5	2.3	2.6	4.0
Fujian	5.2	9.0	9.9	12.6	11.0
Guangdong	42.2	45.0	44.9	31.6	28.7
Hainan	2.0	3.1	4.3	4.0	2.8
Guangxi	1.8	1.2	1.0	1.6	3.3
Beijing	9.8	8.5	7.0	3.1	2.6

Source: Computed from Table 3.4.

As DFI surged during the period 1990–1993, there were some shifts of geographical distribution. The four SEZs remained important, but their shares of DFI had declined relative to coastal provinces in 1992 and 1993. In the "open coastal cities," Dalian and Shanghai recorded the largest increase in terms of percentage share. Although Guangzhou's DFI increased in absolute terms throughout the period, its relative share remained rather stable at about 5.5 percent. Open coastal provinces continued to absorb the lion's share of DFI with larger percentage shares during 1990–1993 as compared to the period 1979–1989. After being promulgated as a separate province in 1987, Hainan was able to attract an increasing share of DFI, and Guangdong continued to remain vibrant. On the other hand, Beijing's DFI declined in relative terms over the period 1990–1993. Another notable recent development is that inland areas have attracted more DFI, although their relative values are not very significant. Traditionally, businessmen from Hong Kong and Taiwan have concentrated their investments in the Pearl River Delta and Fujian Province; there is a notable trend that more investors from Hong Kong and Taiwan are seeking investments in the Yantze River Delta and some inland areas.

The sectoral distribution of DFIs for 1979–1993 is shown in Table 3.7, but a brief explanation of the classification for economic sectors is necessary. According to the United Nations' standard classification of economic sectors, "mining and quarrying" is considered a primary sector whereas in China it is included in the "manufacturing" group as a secondary sector. Also, in China only primary sectors (e.g., agriculture, forestry, husbandry, and fishing) and secondary sectors (e.g., industry, transportation, postal service, and building) are considered "productive" sectors while categories under the service sector (e.g., commerce and catering) are classified as "nonproductive." Before 1984, economic sectors were broken down into twenty-one subgroups. These were later consolidated into eleven subgroups. As illustrated in Table 3.7, there were fluctuations in the relative share of economic subsectors throughout the period 1979–1993. When China first opened its economy to foreign investors, one of its primary objectives was to attract import-substituting industries to the country. Thus, it attracted a significant amount of DFI in the industrial sector during the initial years (Table 3.7). On the other hand, China also absorbed a substantial amount of direct investment in the hotel industry. During 1983–1984, the "tourism and hotel industry" accounted for 21.6 percent of total DFI with a value of 103,440 million U.S. dollars.[10] With respect to EJV investment, 36.8 percent came from the tourism and hotel industry with a value of 50,857 million U.S. dollars.[11] Foreign investors concentrated on the service sector during those early years because the investment climate in

Table 3.7
Direct Foreign Investment by Economic Sectors (contractual basis)

Economic Sectors	Percentage Share				
	1979-1989	1990	1991	1992	1993
A.F.H.F.	3.1	1.8	1.8	1.2	1.1
I.	52.9	84.4	80.3	56.9	45.9
B.	1.6	2.7	1.1	3.2	3.5
C.P.T.	1.3	0.6	0.8	2.7	1.3
C.C.	4.7	1.7	1.4	2.5	4.1
R.P.S.	25.2	6.8	12.6	31.1	39.3
H.S.S.	0.4	0.6	0.5	0.7	0.4
E.C.A.	0.4	0.1	0.5	0.2	0.4
S.R.G.	-	0.5	0.2	0.1	0.5
F.I.	-	-	-	0.0	0.1
Others	10.5	0.8	0.8	2.2	3.4
Total Value (100 Million U.S. dollars)	337.6	66.0	119.8	581.2	1,114.4
	Average Size Per Project (Million U.S. dollars)				
A.F.H.F.	0.99	0.54	0.68	0.67	0.70
I.	1.14	0.85	0.83	0.85	0.91
B.	1.03	4.19	1.69	1.63	1.23
C.P.T.	0.85	0.78	1.45	3.28	1.63
C.C.	1.51	1.16	0.12	0.96	0.95
R.P.S.	5.44	2.85	3.77	3.99	3.87
H.S.S.	2.07	2.67	2.14	4.34	2.32
E.C.A.	1.75	0.40	1.20	0.76	0.99
S.R.G.	0.33	1.12	0.30	0.28	0.67
F.I.	-	-	-	3.77	5.24
Others	2.89	0.88	0.96	1.23	1.08
Total Value (100 Million U.S. dollars)	1.55	0.91	0.92	1.19	1.34

Note: A.F.H.F. = Agriculture, forestry, husbandry, and fishing; I. = Industry; B. = Building; C.P.T. = Communications, post, and telecommunications; C.C. = Commerce, and catering; R.P.S. = Real estate, public utilities, and servicing; H.S.S. = Hygiene, sports, and social welfare services; E.C.A. = Education, culture, and arts; S.G.C. = Science, research, and general technical services; and F.I. = Financial investment.
Source: Computed from *Zhongguo Jingji Nianjian* (various years); *Almanac of China's Foreign Economic Relations and Trade* (various years).

industry was less than satisfactory (see following sections on investment policies and regulating framework). At the same time, the payback period for investment in hotels was shorter than in industry, which was attractive to many investors.

With the promulgation in 1986 of the Provisions of the State Council for the Encouragement of Foreign Investment (the so-called twenty-two-article provisions), the industrial investment climate has improved. Also, the Regulations on Guiding Foreign Investment Operations, approved by the State Planning Commission in 1987, played a role in attracting investors to ventures in the industrial sector. Consequently, there has been a larger share of DFI in the industrial sector (47.9 percent in 1987), but direct investment in the tourism and hotel sector was still substantial (28 percent for 1987). Because of the glut of hotel rooms piled up from earlier investments, China temporarily "halted" further investments in hotels in 1988. Thus, foreign direct investment in industry continued to increase significantly in terms of both relative shares (over eighty percent after 1989) and absolute values. The Tiananmen Incident in 1989 dealt a serious blow to tourism, and DFI in hotels shrunk even further, but as people's memory faded, tourism fully returned to normal by 1992. DFI in manufacturing was concentrated in low-end, labor-intensive industries rather than capital or skill-intensive enterprises. This was generally demonstrated by the small size of projects. In 1993, the average size of an industrial project was 0.91 million U.S. dollars. Larger-scale projects were normally found in the "real estate, public utilities, and services" subgroup, which includes hotel development (see Table 3.7). There are indications that China has been able to attract more capital-intensive projects in recent years. According to a high-ranking Chinese official, "productive" (i.e., non-service-related) projects accounted for ninety percent of total projects approved; "most of them are either technically advanced or export-oriented."[12] Reports in the press showed that an increasing number of projects of this kind are being signed with foreign investors. For example, a joint-venture automobile plant in Chung-chun and a large-scale petrochemical plant were signed with Volkswagen and Royal-Shell Dutch, respectively, in 1991. The former was designated as a "state project" by the Chinese government.[13]

PERFORMANCE OF FOREIGN-INVESTED ENTERPRISES

In a questionnaire survey of thirty-four EJVs located in Shenzhen SEZ in 1986, Henley and Nyaw found that the performance of the EJVs was rather mixed. Empirical findings of firms with regard to planned profit targets were as follows: surpassed target (9.4 percent), achieved target as planned (40.6 percent), failed to achieve target (31.3 percent), some losses (15.6 percent), and heavy losses (3.1 percent). With regard to "foreign exchange earnings," 23.5 percent of firms indicated that there were net gains, 44.1 percent achieved a balance, and 32.4 percent had deficits. As far as overall performance of EJVs was concerned, the following findings were given: "very successful" 3.0 percent, "basically successful" 24.2 percent, "cannot tell yet" 24.2 percent, "not very successful" 9.1 percent, and "basically a failure" 9.1 percent.[14]

If EJVs in the Shenzhen Special Economic Zone are indicative of the nation as a whole, it seems that one-third of China's EJVs have not performed well. This was substantiated by a remark made by Yu Xiaochung, Assistant Minister of MOFERT, in late 1991. According to Yu, China's *san-zi* enterprises (i.e., three forms of foreign-invested enterprises, or EJV, CJV, and WFO) had reversed from their earlier trend of low-performance to one characterized by "normality" in 1987. By the first half of 1991, however, about seventy percent of the nation's 16,000 *san-zi* enterprises under actual operation were profitable, remitting 4.35 billion yuan of taxes to the State's treasury.[15] The number of enterprises running at a loss was decreasing.

Based on a 1991 survey conducted by the Foreign Investment Management Bureau of MOFERT, economic efficiency of *san-zi* enterprises did not differ much among the various open coastal areas and inland provinces. Differences in economic efficiency were related to different lines of industry, forms of investment, orientation of marketing, or managerial capabilities. The survey showed that ventureship between foreign investors and large state-owned enterprises had generally performed better. Based on another survey of 1,000 foreign-invested enterprises conducted by Fujian Province Statistical Bureau, performance by technologically advanced/large-scale capital-intensive enterprises was significantly superior to that of smaller enterprises in the same industry.[16]

The poor performance of foreign enterprises could be attributable to several factors. First, new enterprises in the surveys had only been in operation less than a year, and their profit picture was not yet known. Second, in order to avoid taxes, enterprises could resort to "transferring" profit elsewhere (often in dubious ways), thus showing net losses in their income statements. Some enterprises evaded tax payments by outright fraud and deception. Third, enterprises had genuine difficulties. The second reason, that of hiding profits through transfers, seemed to be predominant in China. Given the widespread corruption among Chinese officials, and the unreliably low standard of accounting systems in China, it was extremely difficult to unearth malpractices.

Performance of foreign-invested enterprises at the national level for the year 1992 was not yet reported for verification here; however, based on scattered data released so far, performance in 1992 was probably among the best since the open door policy was launched in 1979. For example, in Guangdong Province foreign enterprises accounted for a large share of the total national value of DFI in China (Table 3.6), and in mid-1990, 46.6 percent of the province's 2,569 foreign-funded enterprises were losing money. Lack of raw materials, energy shortages, stagnant domestic demand, inconsistent policies, and other reasons were cited for such poor performance.[17] By the end of 1992, however, this trend was reversed. In a survey conducted by the Guangdong Foreign Economic Relations and Trade Commission in 1992, it was shown that about ninety percent of the 6,505 *san-zi* enterprises were making profits. Net profit for the first half of 1992 was 1.28 billion yuan, an increase of over twenty percent compared to the same period in 1991.[18] This may demonstrate the experience gained by both foreign and Chinese partners in operating *san-zi* enterprises, ultimately resulting in an increase of economic efficiency. In particular, Chinese managers had learned many of the intricacies of a market economy, such as market pricing of products and operations management of enterprises.

Compared to the outstanding performance of Guangdong and other coastal provinces, the inland Sichuan Province did not perform well. Sichuan had only 1,600 foreign-invested enterprises in 1992, which is only 6.4 percent of the number in Guangdong. According to a survey of 118 *san-zi* enterprises in Sichuan, only forty-six percent were profitable while more than fifty percent were losing money. A poor investment climate and an inadequate infrastructure were certainly important factors contributing to less-than-satisfactory performance; however, many foreign partners did not remit their investment funds to their enterprises as pledged.[19] This has become more serious in other areas as well in recent years.

DEVELOPMENT STRATEGIES AND FOREIGN INVESTMENT POLICIES

Before the adoption of the open-door policy in 1979, China's socialist modernization program strictly adhered to the principle of "self-reliance" to the exclusion of "assistance from outsiders." This principle was based on an important speech made by Mao Zedong in 1952 on China's economic development. However, assistance from outsiders did occur and had various connotations in different periods. In the 1950s, China received low interest loans from the Soviet Union and, with Soviet technical assistance, built 149 large industrial projects. Soviet assistance came to an abrupt stop in 1960 when relations between the two countries deteriorated over ideological conflicts. Subsequently, China began actively soliciting assistance from several Western countries. During 1963–1968 it imported over 80 technological items and industrial projects (fifty-two percent of which were "turnkey" or complete projects) from Japan, the United Kingdom, France, West Germany, Sweden, Italy, and Austria. These were valued at over 100 million U.S. dollars, and were financed mainly by export credits and deferred-payment systems of the exporting countries.[20] Importation of foreign technology was seriously hindered during the Cultural Revolution which commenced in 1966.

With the downfall of the Gang of Four in 1976, Hua Guofeng, a Maoist who succeeded Mao Zedong as Chairman of Chinese Communist Party (CCP), launched the so called "Leap Forward with a Foreign Character" (*yang-yue-jin*). Within a short span of one year in 1977, China signed contracts with Western countries worth more than 780 million U.S. dollars, seventy percent of which were "turnkey" industrial projects.[21] However, such drastic change, and at such a fast pace, strained China's foreign reserves, and project importation was scaled down. Then in 1978, Hua was out-maneuvered by Deng Xiaoping and his associates at the 3rd Plenary Session of the 11th CCP Congress. Dengist Reform and the open door policy were established as guidelines for long-term, systematic economic development.

Much has been written on the motives behind Deng's reversal of China's foreign economic policy.[22] However, the great success of China's neighboring "Four Little Dragons" (South Korea, Hong Kong, Taiwan, and Singapore) certainly had a great impact on Deng and his associates. One common feature of the phenomenal economic growth of the Four Little Dragons during the last two decades was the openness of their economies. In the Dengist view, China would have to follow suit or lag behind and remain poor. The latter could be detrimental to the future stability of the nation.

The open door policy called for utilization of foreign capital and a speeding up of the process of economic development in China. However, policy-makers were careful not to inhibit the development of local industries by driving them out of domestic markets in the initial process. Four Special Economic Zones were first set up to attract foreign investment. Later, other economic and technological development areas, open coastal cities, development zones, and open coastal provinces were established.

The Chinese government also formulated a set of strategic targets for guiding foreign investment in light of state industrial plans and specific situations of recipient areas or regions. State industrial plans have changed over the years. Prior to 1978, the Stalinist or Maoist strategy emphasized development of heavy industry. During the early 1980s, and in spite of the new reform program, the state investment allocation was still "strongly skewed towards the preferential growth sector of heavy industry."[23] The current state industrial plan is aimed at achieving a more diversified industrial base with transfer of new technology and managerial capability from abroad. Because of capital shortage, foreign investors are expected to bring in machinery, equipment, and raw materials while their Chinese counterparts are expected to provide cheap labor and land for production destined for export. In addition, foreign-invested firms are expected to balance their own foreign exchanges.

In order to generate hard currency needed to finance various state industrial plans, Zhao Ziyang launched a new initiative in 1987 by arguing that Chinese coastal areas should participate in the international division of labor, or what he called the "international great cycle" or "placing two heads outside, pursuing big imports and big exports" (*liantou zaiwai, dajin dachu*).[24] Essentially this meant that development in the coastal areas would rely entirely on the outside world for both inputs and manufactured exports. This approach is different from the import substituting strategy pursued by some developing countries. They solicit foreign investment to invest in their countries destined predominantly for a domestic market by resorting to protectionist measures such as high tariffs or nontariff trade barriers. In contrast, the "international great cycle" approach linked China more closely to the international economy. Zhao was replaced by Jiang Zemin after the June 4 Incident in 1989, and his "international great cycle" approach has rarely been mentioned since then. This does not imply that the approach has been abandoned, however, but rather that the strategy has been amended by discarding the big-push overtone. It should be pointed out that unlike the export-led strategy of the Four Little Dragons, China did not open up its vast domestic market for foreign competition during the period 1979–1990. Since 1990, however, China has begun to liberalize its policies and open domestic markets in response to international pressure and China's strong desire to join the General Agreement on Trade and Tariff (GATT). The World Trade Organization (WTO) was formed on January 1, 1995, replacing the GATT. China's development strategy, nevertheless, is inherently inward-looking, although it is bound to evolve gradually toward a more open economy.

China's foreign investment policy is comprised of various laws, regulations, and provisions that were formulated to change the industrial mix of the country, to effect investment flows to certain designated geographical areas, to target particular forms of investment, and to protect the interests of foreign investors. Since 1979 more than 200 laws and regulations have been introduced which, today, constitute a complex web of regulating mechanisms.

The first piece of legislation on foreign investment in China was the law of the PRC on Chinese-Foreign Joint Ventures (hereafter referred to as the "Joint Ventures Law") promulgated by the State Council in July 1979. It is very brief with only fifteen articles, and it lacks substance. Subsequent laws and regulations were passed on income taxes, company registration, labor management, trademarks, contracts, advertising, and various other matters relating to foreign-invested firms. Then, in September 1983, the Chinese government adopted the Regulations for the Implementation of the Law of PRC on Chinese-Foreign Joint Ventures. This occurred more than four years after the promulgation of the Joint Venture Law, but it contained 118 articles that codified and elaborated the 1979 Joint Venture Law and other laws and regulations that had been issued since 1979. Essentially, the Joint Venture Law spelled out the following preferential treatments or salient features of an EJV:[25]

a. An EJV in SEZs, economic and technological development zones, and Hainan pays an income tax of only fifteen percent; a *new* joint venture may be exempted from income tax in the first two years and allowed a fifty percent reduction in taxes for the third to fifth years.

b. It is exempted from import duties on imported advanced equipment.

c. It can repatriate abroad all its profits as well as funds it receives upon expiration or early termination of the venture.

d. Its foreign employees can remit all after-tax income abroad.

e. There is no fixed export ratio for the products it produces (but normally an EJV is expected to balance its foreign exchange budget by its own resources).

f. It has the right to hire its own staff and workers based on individual merits.

g. It can seek arbitration by judicial means in China or in a third country if dispute of the concerned parties cannot be resolved.

These apparently attractive investment incentives were not without problems. For example, foreign investors found that they ran into a host of problems with the Chinese bureaucracy. It was widely reported in the Hong Kong and overseas media that overseas investors were dismayed by the practice of Chinese officials of levying fees indiscriminately or making up arbitrary rules. The influential *Time Magazine* reported that Chinese cadres "often made up taxes, rules and regulations as they went along, rather than following any written policy."[26] As a result, foreign-invested firms in China found that their profits were eroded by hundreds of unforeseen expenses. The incident of Beijing Jeep, a joint venture of American Motors in the United States and a Chinese state-run auto maker, is a case in point. Because of a serious foreign-exchange crisis caused by a consumer-product buying spree in 1985, China launched an across-the-board clampdown on import purchases, which affected AMC's imports of parts from its Canadian factory. The financial problem was finally resolved only after Zhao Ziyang personally stepped in to allocate financial resources to Beijing Jeep.[27] Consequently, confidence by foreign investors was seriously damaged, and total DFI in China dropped significantly in 1986 (see Table 3.7).

In view of the very negative response from overseas investors, China acted swiftly to enact the "Provisions of the State Council for the Encouragement of Foreign Investment" (twenty-two-article provisions) in October 1986. This was intended to rectify the inadequacies or limitations of past laws and regulations on foreign investment. Furthermore, it provided additional incentives to foreign-invested firms. The twenty-two-article provisions are definitely one of the most important documents on foreign investment in China. Essentially, the provisions grant strong incentives to both "export enterprises" and "technology enterprises," which have priority in allocations for water supply, electricity, transportation, and communication equipment. This infrastructural support has been critical to the success of foreign-invested enterprises because of a prevailing unreliable and underdeveloped infrastructure of the nation. If a "technology enterprise" is an EJV, the preexisting tax holiday is extended by three additional years at half the tax rate. In addition, lower land-use fees are granted to the two forms of enterprises if they are not in busy urban sectors of large cities. They also have priority in obtaining short-term loans in foreign exchange or *Renminbi* from the Bank of China and other Chinese financial institutions. In addition, foreign-invested enterprises have gained protection against unreasonable charges as local governments are required to comply with the "Notice of the State Council on Resolutely Curbing the Indiscriminate Levy of Charges on Enterprises," which is applicable to both state-owned and foreign-invested enterprises. This was, of course, a welcome move by the State Council as far as foreign investors were concerned.

As indicated earlier, foreign investment policies have been formulated to achieve an optimal industrial mix in China. In a speech to senior MOFERT officials on December 24, 1991, Vice-Premier Tian Jiyun stated that "the important work at present is to strive for improving the quality of foreign investment projects (including economic efficiency and technical standards) to make them develop to a higher level." He reiterated that preferential policies should be used to lure foreign investment from export-oriented and technologically advanced foreign enterprises, particularly transnational corporations and large conglomerates with advanced management experience and worldwide networks.[28] This could be characterized in economic development terms as an unbalanced growth strategy. It is a strategy of selecting key industries for development to spark a reaction in other industries that are affected by, or part of, the key industry's value chain.

In the twenty-two-article provisions, "advanced technology" is broadly defined to include technology that China lacks in all economic sectors except the service industry. This is extended to technology that can help China develop new export products, or technology needed by an import substitution industry. These are broad guidelines, but they have been useful in granting favorable incentives to enterprises through credit, taxation, tariffs, and supply of raw materials.

In 1987, the State Planning Commission adopted "Regulations on Guiding Foreign Investment Operations," which outlined the general principles and administrative procedures in dealing with foreign investments. Investment in so-called "productive industry" is generally welcomed. The 1987 Regulations also provided a detailed list of industries as guidelines in directing the flow of foreign investment into China. The list may change to reflect needs and specific situations of various provinces, cities, or areas, but generally, industries fall under the following three subgroups: preferred group, restricted group, and prohibited group. A preferred group includes primary industries such as textiles, chemicals, petroleum, machinery, automobile, scientific equipment, nuclear plant or equipment, and building equipment. A restricted group includes industries such as fisheries, beverages, shipbuilding, real estate, finance, and insurance. A prohibited group includes projects in arts and crafts, mail communication, airlines and airport management, foreign trade, storage, broadcasting, and military equipment. In recent years, China has emphasized that foreign investment policy should direct the flow of the capital to sectors of agriculture, energy, transportation, and urgently needed raw materials. Vice-Premier Tian Jiyun made this policy statement clear in December 1991.[29] Based on the broad definition of "advanced technology," it would include any technology related to energy and transportation and thus incentives would be awarded accordingly.

Protection of investment is a major concern of foreigners investing in China and this is due to two obvious reasons. First, the PRC is a socialist country, and when the CCP took power in 1949, it confiscated properties of both the so-called Chinese bureaucratic capitalists and Western companies. Nationalization of foreign investors' properties also has occurred in Third

World, socialist countries, resulting in tremendous losses. These recollec-tions are very much in the minds of foreign capitalists or multinational managers when they consider investments in China. Second, foreign inves-tors are fearful of drastic political changes that could affect the existing open door policy. This is understandable, as in the past PRC policies have oscillated between radicalism and pragmaticism. In order to allay these fears, Article 2 of the PRC Joint Venture Law in 1979 asserted that "the Chinese Government protects, in accordance with the law, the investment of foreign joint ventures, the profits due them and their other lawful rights and interests in a joint venture." Unfortunately, no clear provisions or mechanisms were stipulated. In enforcing the law, other Asian countries have more specific laws and provisions for protecting the interests of foreign investors. To strengthen the confidence of foreign investors, China moved one step forward to legitimize foreign investment in the country by including a new article in the revised Constitution of the People's Republic of China, adopted at the 5th Session of the Fifth National People's Congress in December 1982. Article 18 of the revised Constitution stipulates that "the PRC permits foreign enterprises, other foreign economic organizations and individual foreigners to invest in China and to enter into various forms of economic cooperation with Chinese economic organizations in accordance with the law of PRC." The article further stresses that the "lawful rights and interests of all foreign-invested enterprises are protected by the law of PRC." Obviously, such recognition of the legitimate rights of foreign investors has great symbolic value to them.

Since 1982, China has taken concrete actions to sign bilateral agreements on investment protection with a number of countries. First, two bilateral investment protection pacts were signed in 1982. More pacts were signed in subsequent years. In 1992, China signed a record number of seventeen protection pacts with other countries. During 1982–1992, it signed a total of forty-seven pacts with forty-eight countries (Belgium and Luxembourg shared one pact with China), including the United States, Canada, Japan, Australia, European Economic Community (EEC) members, and countries in Latin America, the Middle East, Eastern Europe, Africa, Southeast Asia, and the Commonwealth of Independent States. Another thirteen agreements are now under negotiation or in the planning stage.[30] Signing bilateral agreements on investment insurance and protection with other countries would imply that China is willing to adopt the practice of international rules for dealing with flows of DFI between two countries. Admittedly, this would boost the confidence of foreign investors.

On the organizational level, the Joint Venture Law stipulates that disputes between the signing parties should be resolved, if possible, internally by the board of directors. This is the preferred procedure, but should it fail, disputes could be referred to a Chinese arbitration organization. The Joint Venture Law also permits foreign partners to choose arbitration outside China. In the early years of China's open door policy, foreign investors were very hesitant to submit disputes to arbitration because it was felt that this might jeopardize their business relations with China. This attitude has changed, and more and more disputes have gone to arbitration in the last few years.

Inside China, arbitration cases are handled by the China International Economic and Trade Arbitration Commission (CIETAC). This organization is based in Beijing under the auspices of the China Council for the Promotion of International Trade. China is a signatory to the New York Convention on the Recognition and Enforcement of Foreign Arbitral Awards, and, consequently, arbitration results are currently recognized by over eighty countries or areas. Arbitration by CIETAC has increased significantly in the last few years. It has become the second busiest arbitration center in the world, handling about 900 cases in 1992.[31] This was second only to the tribunals handled by the famous Institute of Arbitration of the Stockholm Chamber of Commerce. Although CIETAC is widely credited as an relatively inexpensive, fair, and expeditious forum for resolving disputes, many foreign investors found that it is very difficult to enforce arbitration awards in China. Many cases have been reported in which regional courts in China refused to enforce awards against local economic interests. For example, a British company won a case against a Ningxia company. Yet the Ningxia local court refused to enforce awards even after the Beijing court's repeated requests for immediate settlement.[32] This makes a mockery of the entire legal system in China, which badly needs changing. Unless the arbitration awards are enforceable, foreign investors may become less willing to go to CIETAC for arbitration.

MAJOR RECENT DEVELOPMENTS

There were several major developments of DFI in China since 1991. First, China relaxed its restrictive policy by permitting greater foreign participation in its service industry. This created a euphoria for foreign investment opportunity, and many firms turned to China in large numbers to invest in the lucrative service sector, including retailing, accounting, consulting, advertising, and finance/insurance industries. In the retail sector, China now allows foreign companies to establish department stores in selected cities on a case-by-case basis. There is a stipulation that foreign products cannot exceed fifty percent of the store's sales volume, and the firms must balance their foreign exchange accounts.[33] Some famous department store companies in Hong Kong, such as Sincere, Wing On, and Giordano, and Japan's Yaohan and Seibu, established joint-venture stores in China in 1992. Sun Hung Kai Property Ltd., a giant property development company, signed an agreement with a Beijing company valued at 255 million U.S. dollars to redevelop Dong An Market, a famous department store in the busy Wang Fu Jing area in Beijing.[34] In addition, chain restaurants and stores such as Café-de-coral, Fairwood, McDonald's, Park-N-Shop, Welcome, 7–Eleven, and Watsons, among others, entered China's domestic market in 1992 or earlier. International accounting and consulting firms such as Arthur Anderson and Price Waterhouse also established footholds in China.[35] In 1994 China began to allow foreign insurance companies to operate in China; American International Assurance (AIA) was the first multinational insurance company to open a branch inside PRC. During the past few years several commercial banks from Hong Kong and elsewhere have also been permitted to open branches in China, although they are prohibited from taking Renminbi deposits, which are restricted to state Chinese banks. Restrictions on Renminbi deposits may also be liberalized in due course, and if this occurs, it will be a significant shift in policy away from state-controlled currency transactions.

Second, there has been a great surge of property investment by foreigners since 1992, subsequent to China's adaptation of a land-leasing experiment modeled after Hong Kong's land system. This system began in 1987, and under the experiment, the state retains ownership of land but can lease to developers. Since the experiment has been introduced, it has generated billion of dollars in official revenue.[36] Hong Kong's land developers are the active players, with Tian An China Investment Co. leading the group by focusing its property business solely in China. Hong Kong's giant real estate developers, such as New World Development Co., Hopewell, Wharf Holdings, and Cheung Kong Holdings, have accelerated their interests in China. The latter two companies entered the China market with major investments in 1992.

One-fourth of China's total contractual foreign investment was destined for property development in residential, commercial, and industrial projects alone in 1992.[37] Hong Kong firms had gained an estimated 200 million square feet of lease-rights on land in China by late 1992, and total projects were valued between 1.5 and 2.5 billion U.S. dollars.[38] Without question, a large percentage of these leases are being held for speculative purposes. Yet there are active development projects in the Pearl River Delta, Hainan, Shanghai, Beijing, Fujian, and Yangtze River Delta areas.

Third, since 1992 China has signed many huge projects with foreign investors for infrastructure projects such as highways, power plants, harbors, and ports. One of the top priorities of China's modernization program is to inject funds into infrastructure development, and due to shortage of domestic funds, China has been actively soliciting funds from abroad to bridge the gap. So far, most private investment in infrastructure projects has come from Hong Kong. Gordon Wu of Hopewell Holdings led the way by investing in the Guangzhou-Shanzhen-Zhuhai Highway as well as power plants in Shajiao of Guangdong Province. China Light and Power also made a significant investment in a nuclear power plant in Daya Bay. New World Development Co., Hutchison-Whampoa, Wharf Holdings, and China Light and Power have signed major contracts with China for investment in highways, power plants, electrified railways, liquefied gas, and various other infrastructure projects.

In April 1993, Vice-Premier Zou Jiahua announced that China would adopt the international "BOT" form (build, operate, and transfer) as a means to channel investment into the infrastructure projects. The BOT scheme allows foreign investors to have contractual rights in managing and operating projects while the Chinese government only collects taxes. When a contract expires (usually in fifteen years), the entire project would be turned over to China. According to Zou, China has plans to liberalize the existing monopolistic market structures in the energy, telecommunications, and transportation industries.[39] Demand for infrastructural facilities is immense if China continues its existing market reform. This will provide additional opportunities for foreign investors to tap this expanding sector.

Fourth, there was an attempt by the Chinese government to "privatize" some of its state-owned enterprises. This was accomplished by converting enterprises to Sino-foreign joint ventures, establishing new share-holding companies with foreign participation, or simply leasing them to foreign investors. Poor performance by state-owned enterprises, whether large or small in size, is no secret. Currently, there are about 100,000 state enterprises, one third of them operating at a loss, and another third only breaking even. These figures were probably understated as a result of a low depreciation policy and poor accounting standards that fail to capture many hidden costs. Due to this dismal record, the Chinese government had to allot nearly twenty percent of its expenditure budget and eighty percent of its bank loans to prop up state-owned enterprises. In 1991, the state industrial sector incurred a loss of 5.30 billion U.S. dollars and losses continued to increase.[40] This has been a very heavy burden for the central government to bear. A reform policy meant to invigorate the inefficient state enterprises by various means, including expansion of enterprise autonomy, has been less than satisfactory.

In 1992, the Chinese government launched a variety of "marketization" schemes for participation by foreign investors in state-owned enterprises on an experimental basis. The most notable case occurred in the city of Quanzhou, in Fujian, which signed a joint venture agreement with Hong Kong–based China Strategic Investment Ltd. by selling forty-one of its forty-two state-run industrial firms in December 1992. If the 42nd enterprise had not been engaged in a joint venture with another foreign company, it would have been a total "sale." It was reported that China Strategic Investment Ltd. is injecting Rmb 240 million for a sixty percent controlling share in the newly created company called Quanzhou C.S.I. (Holdings) Ltd.[41] The latter is currently restructuring the forty-one enterprises by closing down some of the inefficient firms and expanding the more profitable ones. In another example, a Hong Kong firm took a fifty-one percent controlling share in Wuhan No. 2 Dyeing and Printing Factory in July 1992. This was the first time in PRC history that a foreign enterprise took a controlling share of a state-owned factory.[42]

Apart from Quanzhou, Wuhan city in Hubei was negotiating with Taiwan and Hong Kong investors in late 1992 to sell thirty of its state enterprises. Earlier a bankrupt textile-dyeing firm was sold by Wuhan to a Hong Kong entrepreneur.[43] In Qingdao, the city has recently selected several state enterprises for possible joint ventureship with foreign investors.[44] Since 1993 the trend to "sell" state enterprises has accelerated.

Another form of foreign participation in existing state-owned enterprises is by leasing them to foreign investors. In Sichuan Province, one of its fourteen prime enterprises in passenger-car manufacturing was leased to a Hong Kong–based firm for a rental of Rmb 63 million to be paid annually for a contract period of fifteen years. The contract stipulates that the Hong Kong firm would have to inject funds and to transfer modern technology to the leased firm while the former is solely responsible for its profit and loss. The firm was the first of its kind in China, and the lease took effect in July 1992.[45]

Another form of foreign participation in state-run enterprises is through establishment of new share-holding companies. One of the large-scale ball-bearing industrial enterprises in Harbin, with about 20,000 staff and workers, signed a share-holding contract with a Hong Kong–based firm in April 1993. The foreign investor injected Rmb 108 million into the newly established company for a share of forty-five percent.[46] This is the first case where a large-scale state industrial firm established a partnership with a foreign firm.

China also welcomes foreign investors interested in buying state enterprises that are declared bankrupt. Recently, a state printing equipment firm in Shenzhen was in receivership through a court order. Later it was announced that the firm would be sold through auction and foreign investors were welcome to bid.[47]

Various forms of foreign participation in Chinese state-owned enterprises, as illustrated above, seem to indicate that China is endorsing a process of "privatization," particularly for less efficient firms. However, it would be unrealistic to expect that a great number of state-run enterprises will follow suit. Some sensitive problems such as job arrangements for employees who are used to the security of the "iron rice bowl" policy need to be resolved, and privatization procedures must be resolved to avoid social instability.

Last, but not least, since 1991, the State Council has approved the establishment of twelve "bonded zones" (or free trade areas) to further encourage trade and investment. These run from the northeast to the south along the coast, including Dalian, Tianjin, Waigaoqiao (Shanghai), Zhangjiagang, Fujian, Shatoujiao, Guangzhou, Haikou, Qingdao, Ningbo, Xiamen, and Fuzhou. Shantou, Yantai, and Beihai have also joined other coastal cities to establish bonded zones lately.[48] Among the bonded zones, Shatoujiao was the first, and the smallest one, which began operation in 1991. The bonded zones, modeled after other successful free trade zones in Asia, are established mainly in the Economic and Technological Development Areas, or SEZs.

A bonded zone allows free mobility of capital, goods, and executives. This mobility has a significant impact on luring foreign investments. Industries related to foreign trade and exports, such as processing, storage, reexport, trading, finance, and property development, are targeted for development in the bonded zones. Each of the twelve bonded zones has developed its own preferential policies for investments, but a national policy for all bonded zones has yet to be formulated.[49] Generally speaking, foreign-invested enterprises established in the bonded zones enjoy all privileges available to other economic and technological development zones. In addition, they are exempted from import and export duties, production taxes, and industrial consolidated taxes if their products are exported. In Guangzhou's bonded zone, there is free convertibility of foreign currency, and companies enjoy a fifty percent reduction of taxes in tobacco and liquor. The bonded zone in Guangzhou has attracted 130 million U.S. dollars in foreign investment, including construction of an eighty million U.S. dollars exhibition center in 1992.[50] Given additional preferential treatment, the bonded zones should appeal to many export-oriented foreign firms. Xiamen's free trade zone, for example, would have great appeal to Taiwanese investors in light of its geographical proximity and close economic ties between two sides of the Taiwan Straits.

PROBLEMS AND OBSTACLES

Problems have received increasing attention by Chinese officials in charge of DFI policies. There are five aspects: "fake" joint ventures, evasion of taxes, appraisal of properties, preferential policies in different areas, and the status of "high-tech zones."

Chinese officials have become increasingly concerned about the rising number of "fake joint ventures." These become apparent when, after signing a contract, foreign investors' pledged capital fails to materialize. During 1991–1992, Guangdong Province canceled several hundred fake foreign-invested enterprises.[51] The problem in Sichuan province is more serious with approximately fifty percent of pledged capital by foreign investors unaccounted for during 1992; in 1991 the figure was thirty percent.[52] Some of the "fake" ventures are due to poor feasibility studies, poor management, conflicts of partners, or, in some instances, fraud. There were also some investors who actually had no capital of their own but rather sought to utilize the newly established foreign firm as a vehicle to borrow funds from domestic financial institutions, thus passing the risks entirely to Chinese partners. In addition, some foreign-invested firms that were losing money decided to no longer inject additional funds, thus making their ventures inoperative.

Tax evasion by some foreign-invested enterprises has also been quite serious, particularly in smaller companies. These companies incur "losses" by taking advantage of loopholes in tax laws, such as artificially raising prices of imported raw materials or lowering prices of exported products. Another tactic has been to "wind up" the original company, replacing it with a newly registered company, thereby continuing to enjoy tax benefits after the initial tax-exemption period has expired. Some companies also resort to moving their enterprises to new areas, allowing them to apply for new tax exemptions with local authorities.[53]

Whether value of land and other state assets have been properly appraised is another major concern. Many state assets have been appraised at artificially low prices by local authorities in order to attract joint ventures. Some local authorities even set ceilings on state assets to attract foreign investment. According to an official of the Bureau of State Owned Property, less than ten percent of the state properties are properly appraised.[54] On the other hand, some foreign investors imported old or unwanted equipment and then priced the equipment as new to artificially increase the book value of the joint ventures. These investors have come mainly from Japan, Hong Kong, and Taiwan.[55] How much revenue has been lost due to these unethical tactics may never be known. According to a crude estimate by a state official, revenue loss to the state treasury resulting from overpricing of equipment amounted to several hundred million Renminbi alone in 1992.[56]

Another problem encountered by China in attracting foreign investment is related to the discrepancy of preferential treatment in different areas. In order to attract foreign investors, local authorities compete with each other by offering a variety of favorable terms. Many of these are in violation of state provisions and tax laws. In August 1993, the State Council issued a stern warning to local authorities to abide by the state laws.[57] Earlier this issue was specifically highlighted in the Outline of the Ten-Year Programme (1991–2000) and the Eighth Five Year Plan (1991–1995) for National Economic and Social Development which was adopted at the 4th Session of the Seventh National People's Congress in March 1991.[58] Although competition among local authorities may work to the advantage of some foreign investors, confusion may arise due to ambiguity of national and local regulations. Foreign investors are generally more concerned with factors other than tax incentives in assessing the investment climate.

Development zones are designed by either the state, province, or county. State-level development zones are approved by the Science and Technological Commission. Forty-seven development zones had been established by 1992, mainly located in the coastal open cities.[59] There are, however, many development zones designated by local authorities. According to the New China News Agency, there are close to 2,000 development zones throughout the country, taking up 15,000 square kilometers of land.[60] Many of these zones, however, are not approved by either state or provincial authorities. Local authorities are generally overzealous to jump into the fray to attract foreign investment without careful prior planning. Therefore, many have been found to underperform or to simply stay idle after establishment. For example, one county in Sichuan appropriated 2,000 acres of farm land, offering it to Taiwan investors, hoping that the latter would invest two billion N.T. dollars in development capital. But the investment funds were never remitted, and consequently the land remained idle for many years.[61] This case was certainly not an isolated one. Steps are now being taken by the State Council to assess all development zones in accordance with stipulated criteria, such as projects and work completed, amount of pledged and realized capital, management capabilities and other factors, and so forth. Under this new assessment system, development zones that fail to meet the criteria can be closed, and "lifetime" status of the zone will no longer be guaranteed. Zones in local counties without proper approval from provincial authorities will be closed.[62]

The problems outlined above are presented from the perspective of Chinese authorities. A different set of problems emerge when viewed from the perspective of foreign investors. They are concerned more with obstacles that inhibit foreign investment in China. For example, the existing regulatory framework remains unsatisfactory, and unpublished rules and regulations continue to influence company operations. Some rules and regulations, published or otherwise, are inconsistent, thus leading to ambiguity. In addition, the scope of authority and responsibility in various government departments is often vague, thus inhibiting foreign investment. Apart from the regulatory environment, other obstacles to investment include inadequate protection of property rights; existence of arbitrary fees imposed by some local authorities; excess barriers to local markets; lack of a national liquidation law; and bureaucratic interference in the wage-setting process which hampers the ability of foreign-invested enterprises to practice market-oriented policies, i.e., its prerogative to recruit, retain, and motivate employees.[63] All these issues need to be carefully evaluated and the problems resolved.

CONCLUSION AND PROSPECTS

Without question, China has made great strides in attracting foreign direct investment since 1979. The impressive growth of DFI has impacted on structural changes of many segments of the Chinese economy, especially the industrial and service sectors. Many of the economic changes that occurred were probably inconceivable before 1979. In the initial years of the open door program, however, China was fraught with problems of building a framework conducive to attracting foreign investment. Broadly speaking, these problems could be viewed as "hard" and "soft" sides of the investment environment. On the hard side, the infrastructure bottleneck has been a disincentive to foreign investment. Some improvements have been made over the years, but it is not expected that the problems will be solved quickly. A high priority is attached by both central and provincial governments to improve China's physical infrastructure. Coupled with an enthusiastic participation by private-sector interests in recent years, China could alleviate the development bottlenecks significantly. In the final analysis, a long-term commitment is required by the government to build up a modern infrastructure over the next several decades.

Strengthening the soft side of the investment environment seems to be crucial for China in the short run, and it may influence infrastructure development. Improving the soft side of the investment climate can be accomplished mainly through policy adjustments that address the problems and obstacles in attracting foreign direct investment. Investment laws also need to be uniform among constituent areas and consistent in their application. Although laws governing foreign investment are important, attitudes toward the rule of law are even more crucial. A case in point is the nonenforcement of arbitral awards in China.

China is moving increasingly toward economic liberalization after Deng Xiaoping's southern tour in early 1991. The most important change since adoption of the open door policy is perhaps the "market mentality" which now deeply imbues Chinese cadres. Ideological conflicts between Chinese officials and foreign investors seem to be fading as dogma is replaced by a sense of pragmatic "economism." These will facilitate "marketization" to take root in China. Clearly this is the trend that is currently taking place, and China seems prepared to further open its domestic economy to foreign investment. For example, in a joint venture contract, the standard ratio between exports and domestic sales has been seventy percent, but now it is possible to negotiate the ratio downward to as low as fifty percent.[64] In addition, Shenzhen and Hainan are adopting the international practice of company registration, i.e., to register a company directly without going through various levels of bureaucratic red tape.[65] The liberalization trend is likely to spread to other coastal open cities. Furthermore, China's impending membership in WTO will provide further impetus in liberalizing the domestic economy. This will appeal to more and more foreign investors given the sheer size of the country and improved income level of the Chinese people.

NOTES

1. Shenzhen, Zhuhai, Shantou, and Xiamen were proclaimed SEZs in 1980. Hainan Island, formerly part of Guangdong Province, gained provincial status in 1987 and has since been designated a SEZ, the largest among the five. In 1984, the following fourteen coastal port cities were opened to the outside world: Dalian, Qinhuangdao, Tianjin, Yantai, Qingdao, Lianyungang, Nantong, Shanghai, Ninbo, Wenzhou, Fuzhou, Guangzhou, Zhanjiang, and Beihai. Economic and development areas were set up within them. In 1985, China further opened the Yangtze River Delta, the Pearl River Delta, and the Minnan Delta to foreign investors.

2. Calculated from MOFERT, *Almanac of China's Foreign Economic Relations and Trade*, 1989/90 and 1990/91.

3. *Sing Tao Daily*, October 4, 1992, Hong Kong.

4. K. Hiraiwa, "Foreign Investment in PRC, 1990–1991," *China Newsletter*, JETRO No. 96, January-February, 1992, p. 11.

5. *China Newsletter*, No. 96, 1992, p. 12.

6. Reported by *Wen Wei Po*, April 18, 1993, Hong Kong.

7. See *Wen Wei Po*, January 6, 1993, Hong Kong.

8. *The World and Japan's Foreign Direct Investment* (various years), Japan, quoted in Fan Yungmin, *Industrialization and Foreign Direct Investment in China*, Shanghai: Shanghai Institute of Social Sciences, 1992, p. 179.

9. *Ibid*, pp. 173–178.

10. MOFERT, *Almanac of Foreign Trade and Economic Relations*, 1984 and 1985.

11. *Zhonghuo Tongji Nianjian* (China Statistical Yearbook), 1985.

12. Wu Sufen, "China's Absorption of Foreign Investment Achieves Remarkable Results," in *Almanac of China's Foreign Economic Relations and Trade*, 1992/93, p. 51.

13. K. Hiraiwa, *op. cit.*, p. 12.

14. J. S. Henley and M. K. Nyaw, "The System of Management and Performance of Joint Ventures in China: Some Evidence from Shenzhen Special Economic Zone," *Advances in Chinese Industrial Studies*, Vol. 1, Part B, pp. 277–295.

15. Quoted by Xinhua News Agency, November 20, 1992, reported in *Ta Kung Pao*, November 21, 1991, Hong Kong.

16. *Ta Kung Pao*, November 21, 1991, Hong Kong.

17. *South China Morning Post*, June 12, 1994, Hong Kong.

18. *Ta Kung Pao*, December 30, 1992, Hong Kong.

19. *Sing Tao Daily*, April 22, 1993, Hong Kong.

20. Fan Yungmin, *op. cit.*, pp. 1–4.

21. Ibid, p. 5.

22. See, for example, studies by Samuel P. S. Ho and R. Huanemann, *China's Open Door Policy: The Quest for Foreign Technology and Capital*, Vancouver: The University of British Columbia Press, 1984; and Y. C. Jao and K. C. Leung, eds., *China's Special Economic Zones: Policies, Problems, and Prospects*, Hong Kong: Oxford University Press, 1986.

23. Y. Y. Kueh, "Foreign Investment and Economic Change in China," *China Quarterly*, Vol. 131, September 1992, p. 638.

24. This coastal development strategy was first proposed by Wang Jian, a research fellow associated with the Institute of Economic Planning at the State Planning Commission.

25. See *Regulations for the Implementation of the Law of PRC on Chinese-Foreign Joint Ventures*, September 30, 1983; and Chu Baotai, *Foreign Investment in China: Questions and Answers*, Beijing: Foreign Language Press, 1986.

26. See *Time Magazine*, June 2, 1986.

27. See the story by Jim Mann in *Beijing Jeep: How West Business Stalled in China*, New York: Simon and Schuster, 1989.

28. Tian Jiyun's speech was delivered at the National Working Conference on Foreign Economic Relations and Trade on December 24, 1991. His speech was reprinted in *Almanac of China's Foreign Economic Relations and Trade*, 1992–93, pp. 13–17.

29. *Ibid*, p. 15.

30. *China Daily*, Business Weekly, January 10–16, 1993, Beijing.

31. *Ta Kung Pao*, April 7, 1993, Hong Kong.

32. This case was mentioned in a speech by Lee Kuan Yew, former Prime Minister of Singapore, at a World Economic Forum held in September 1992 in Beijing. See *Sing Tao Daily*, October 1–3, 1992, Hong Kong. The case was more fully discussed in a paper by Bersani. See Mathew D. Bersani, "Enforcement of Arbitration Awards in China," *The China Economic Review*, May-June, 1992, pp. 6–10.

33. So far, Ministry of Commerce has allowed fourteen cities including Beijing, Shanghai, and Guangzhou to discuss joint-venture retail deals. See "Trend and Issue," *China Business Review*, September-October, 1992, p. 4.

34. Liang Bosong, "An Analysis of the Current Status of Foreign Enterprises," *Hong Kong and Macao Economic Digest*, January 15, 1993, pp. 32–33.

35. *Express News*, December 9, 1992.

36. M. C. Ross ad K. T. Rosen, "China's Real Estate Revolution," *China Business Review*, November-December, 1992, p. 44.

37. *Ming Pao*, January 4, 1993, Hong Kong.

38. M. C. Ross and Kenneth T. Rosen, "The Great China Land Rush," *China Business Review*, November-December, 1992, p. 51.

39. *Wen Wei Po*, April 24, 1993, Hong Kong.

40. See Kathy Chan, "Hong Kong-China Venture Overhauls State-Run Firms," *Asian Wall Street Journal*, December 22, 1992; and James McGregor, "China's State Enterprises Think Private," *Asian Wall Street Journal*, January 8–9, 1993.

41. *Asian Wall Street Journal*, December 22, 1993.

42. *United Daily News*, July 31, 1993, Hong Kong.

43. *Asian Wall Street Journal*, January 8–9, 1993.

44. *Ta Kung Pao*, January 1993, Hong Kong.

45. *Ta Kung Pao*, July 27, 1993, Hong Kong.

46. *Ta Kung Pao*, May 1993, Hong Kong.

47. *Hong Kong Times*, July 1992.

48. *Ming Pao*, December 24, 1993, Hong Kong; and *China Daily*, Business Weekly, January 10–16, 1993, Beijing.

49. *Wen Wei Po*, November 24, 1992, Hong Kong.

50. *Ming Pao*, December 24, 1992, Hong Kong.

51. *Ta Kung Pao*, February 10, 1993, Hong Kong.

52. *Sing Tao Daily*, April 22, 1993, Hong Kong.

53. *Ming Pao*, December 7, 1992; and February 10, 1993, Hong Kong.

54. *Ming Pao*, December 21, 1993, Hong Kong.

55. *Ming Pao*, May 3, 1993, Hong Kong.

56. *Ta Kung Pao*, March 10, 1993, Hong Kong.

57. *Ta Kung Pao*, August 23, 1993, Hong Kong.

58. Li Peng, *Report on the Outline of the Ten-Year Program and the Eighth Five Year Plan for National Economic and Social Development*, Beijing: People's Press, 1991, p. 134.

59. *Ming Pao*, December 23, 1992, Hong Kong.

60. This high figure probably includes those under planning by the local authorities, but it was not stated in the news item. See *New China News Agency*, March 9, 1993.

61. *Sing Tao Daily*, April 22, 1993, Hong Kong.

62. *Ming Pao*, February 17, 1993, Hong Kong.

63. Some of the obstacles are discussed in a U.S.-China Business Council's Report presented to China. The Report was published in *China Economic Review*, September-October, 1992, pp. 6–10.

64. *South China Morning Post*, December 28, 1992, and *Hong Kong Economic Times*, December 7, 1992. According to a well-known Hong Kong business leader heavily investing in China, it is possible to see all products of a joint venture in the domestic market if there is a demand. See *Hong Kong Economic Times, ibid.*

65. *Ta Kung Pao*, December 8, 1992, Hong Kong.

4

Foreign Direct Investment, Trade, and Development in China

RAYMOND H. F. KWOK

FOREIGN DIRECT INVESTMENT IN CHINA

Over the past fifteen years, China has made a significant effort in building and stabilizing her domestic economy. To accomplish the various goals, China had focused on the development of FDI and foreign trade. During the period 1989–1991, the Chinese government eschewed a set of policy reforms geared to improve foreign access to China's domestic markets. The reforms call for new foreign investment in business enterprises which either are export-oriented, or earn foreign-exchange, or those embodied with advanced technology.

At present, China is second only to the United States as the largest recipient of foreign capital in the world. According to World Bank figures, foreign capital inflows into China in 1991, 1992, and 1993 were, respectively, eleven billion, twenty-four billion and twenty-seven billion U.S. dollars. As foreign capital inflows into all developing countries grew by 12.5 percent in 1993, China's share was fifteen percent, which was no higher than her 1992 share. The influx of foreign investment has filled some gaps in China's shortfall in capital and has therefore contributed to the country's economic development. In the future, foreign investment would become more diversified in terms of industries and regions and a more balanced pattern would emerge.

FDIs in China have been concentrated mainly in labor-intensive manufacturing industries, and labor-intensive manufacturing products recorded the highest growth. In other words, the growth of FDI in the early 1980s promoted the export growth, and subsequently economic growth. This can be examined by using a simple correlation coefficient analysis:

$$\rho_{ij} = \sum_{t=1}^{k} (e_{it} - \bar{e}_i)(e_{jt} \; \bar{e}_j)/(n-1) \, S_i \, S_j \tag{1}$$

where ρ_{ij} is the correlation coefficient of e_i and e_j, $\bar{e}_i$ and S_i are the means and the standard deviations of e_{it}, respectively.

Table 4.1 indicates that the correlation coefficients between these three variables are positive and significant in the period 1979–1993. The square of correlation coefficient indicates the percentage of common variance between these variables. The percentage of common variance between FDI and exports is about seventy-four percent, while the percentage of common variance between FDI and GDP is about eighty percent. This implies that seventy-four percent of export performance and 80 percent of economic performance are the result of the influence of FDI.

As the economy continued to growth at an annual average rate of 9.3 percent over the period 1979–1994, the prospects of selling to a market of 1.2 billion people began to take on more weight in luring foreign investors. Moreover, the country's breakneck economic growth underscores the pressing need to upgrade her infrastructure with foreign capital and expertise. The government thus began to allow foreign investors who utilize large

Table 4.1
Correlation Matrix Between FDI, Exports, and Economic Growth, 1979–1993

	FDI	Exports	GDP
FDI	1.00	0.86	0.88
Exports	0.86	1.00	0.89
GDP	0.88	0.89	1.00

amounts of capital and advanced technology to sell primarily in the home market.

According to the Chinese statistics, contracted FDI in 1993 were 111 billion U.S. dollars, and grew by ninety-one percent over 1992, while the utilized amount was twenty-six billion U.S. dollars, which grew by 134 percent over 1992. The amounts of FDI in 1993, both contracted and utilized, were roughly equal to the cumulative total of FDI in the first fourteen years of the open door era (1979–1992). By the end of 1993, the cumulative contracted and utilized FDI in China were 217 billion and sixty billion U.S. dollars, respectively. In addition, the number of contracts also surged significantly in 1993 as compared to the past fourteen years.

More than 100 countries and territories have now invested in China. Overseas Chinese from Hong Kong, Macau, and Taiwan continued to account for more than two-thirds of total foreign investment in China, in terms of both the number of investors and the amount invested. Also at the top of the list are investors from the United States, Japan, Singapore, Britain, Thailand, Canada, and Germany. The implementation of market-oriented reforms encouraged more foreign capital inflows to the Chinese economy, stimulating economic and industrial development, especially the bottleneck industries. However, the 1993 investment boom has led to economic over-heating, followed by harsh downturns. Alarmed by this situation, Vice-Premier Zhu Rongji, who took the reins of the People's Bank of China for more than two years between July 1993 and 1995, unveiled a sixteen-point austerity plan aimed at enforcing financial discipline, achieving monetary order, and laying down precise directions for economic growth. The move led to increased efforts on the part of the central authorities to tackle the problems.

China allocates most foreign resources into export-oriented manufacturing industries. During the period 1979–1993, the percentage shares of manufacturing industry on the number of projects and contract value were the largest at 74.1 percent and 52.8 percent, respectively. However, with the structural changes in the Chinese economy, the pattern of investment began to change also. In 1989, for example, 83.3 percent of FDI was in the manufacturing sector, and mainly concentrated on the exports sectors. However, by 1993, its share had dropped to 45.9 percent while the relative share of real estate and public utilities had shot up to 39.3 percent from 9.4 percent in the same period. Although the manufacturing industry continues to capture a large amount of FDI, it is increasingly being targeted at the domestic market. FDIs have begun to concentrate more on the infrastructural developments so as to maintain a longer economic life. This can also be confirmed by looking at the share of investment in different sectors in the last fourteen years. The gap in the share between these two sectors has been narrowed, suggesting that the development of infrastructure has become the major task.

Owing to their convenient location and better infrastructural development, the southern and coastal provinces have always been the favorite spots for foreign investors. As a consequence, income levels in these provinces have been improving more rapidly than in other regions, resulting in greater disparity in income and employment opportunities. Comparing the overall average over the last fourteen years, coastal areas occupy the largest share in terms of project totals and contract value. Guangdong ranks the first among the fifteen provinces, taking up one-third of overall foreign investment. In addition, foreign capital continues to concentrate in the seven major provinces, which together took up almost seventy percent of contract value.

In order to achieve a more balanced development pattern, the authorities are encouraging investments moving into the inland provinces. In response to the government's policy and to the rising costs in the coastal areas, FDI is spreading to other regions. One interesting observation which may be linked to the regional diversification of FDI is the declining share of Guangdong in total FDI and the rising share of Shanghai in recent years. In 1991, for example, Guangdong accounted for forty-two percent of total FDI, while Shanghai accounted for only a mere three percent. By 1993, the picture had changed dramatically with Guangdong's share falling to twenty-seven percent while Shanghai's share rose to eleven percent, reflecting the development priorities accorded to Shanghai and its growing importance as an economic and financial center. By contrast, in spite of its political and cultural importance, Beijing has remained an insignificant destination of foreign investment. The share dropped from 5.2 percent to 2.4 percent in the same period.

Despite its steady long-term uptrend, FDI in China has experienced short-term fluctuations that tie in closely with the stop-go economic policy cycle of the Chinese economy. For instance, in terms of the contracted value, FDI registered a substantial increase of 124 percent and forty-three percent, respectively, in 1985 and 1988 when the Chinese economy was growing rapidly. However, it dropped to fifty-two percent in 1986 and recorded a marginal growth in 1990 as a result of economic retrenchment. Moreover, the utilized ratio (utilized amount/contracted amount) dropped steadily from sixty percent in 1989 to twenty-three percent in 1993, implying that the economic projects generated from the FDI have slowed down. In other words, although the Chinese economy has maintained a double-digit growth over the last three years, the anti-inflationary measures have slowed down the process of economic projects, leading to an uneven distribution of resources and uneven economic development across the country.

RELATIONSHIP BETWEEN FDI AND EXPORT PERFORMANCES

The Chinese government's goal of maximizing foreign exchange earnings is to finance its priority import program. Accordingly, the most important criterion for judging·the performance of FDI projects in China is the ability of the foreign-funded enterprises to balance their foreign exchange requirements. In other words, it is interesting to evaluate how FDI can promote China's exports and, thus, generate exchange earnings.

Table 4.2 indicates that external trade grew very fast over the last fourteen years. Exports grew at an average annual rate of thirteen percent and imports at an annual average rate of fourteen percent. Moreover, the share of exports and imports in the world market also increased dramatically. The share of exports increased from 0.88 percent in 1979 to 2.5 percent in 1993, while the share of imports grew from 0.98 percent to 2.7 percent in the same period. Although exports increased rapidly in the last decade, China suffered trade deficit in most years. In 1993, China ran a trade deficit of twelve billion U.S. dollars, the highest in the last fourteen years. However, this was not a cause for concern as China had huge net capital inflows, and a surplus in the capital account implied a corresponding deficit in the current account. In other words, foreign investment can also be used as an important tool to balance the external account.

Since most foreign investments are concentrated in the export-oriented, manufacturing industry, foreign direct investments play a significant role in promoting China's exports. Table 4.3 shows the breakdown by forms of trade (see Sung, 1994). General trade refers to trade conducted by China's foreign-funded operations, including compensation trade, which has become relatively insignificant, foreign-invested ventures (joint ventures, cooperative ventures, and wholly owned foreign enterprises), and processing/assembling operations.

It should be noted that foreign funds in foreign-invested ventures are regarded as foreign direct investment because of foreign ownership and control in each of the three kinds of foreign-invested ventures. Foreign funds in compensation trade and processing/assembling operations are classified under commercial credit instead of foreign direct investment because the Chinese partners fully own the enterprises involved, and they pay for foreign machinery and technical assistance with output or with labor services.

Table 4.2
External Trade (billion U.S. dollars)

Year	Exports	Imports	Total Trade	Trade Balance
1979	13.66 (0.88)	15.67 (0.98)	29.33 (0.93)	-2.01
1980	18.12 (0.96)	20.02 (1.02)	38.14 (0.98)	-1.90
1981	22.01 (1.20)	22.02 (1.13)	44.03 (1.15)	-0.01
1982	22.32 (1.28)	19.29 (1.06)	41.61 (1.17)	3.03
1983	22.23 (1.31)	21.39 (1.21)	43.62 (1.26)	0.84
1984	26.14 (1.45)	27.41 (1.45)	53.55 (1.45)	-1.27
1985	27.35 (1.50)	42.25 (2.23)	69.60 (1.87)	-14.90
1986	30.94 (1.55)	42.90 (2.07)	73.84 (1.81)	-11.96
1987	39.44 (1.68)	43.22 (1.78)	82.66 (1.73)	-3.78
1988	47.52 (1.77)	55.28 (1.99)	102.80 (1.88)	-7.76
1989	52.54 (1.80)	59.14 (1.96)	111.68 (1.88)	-6.60
1990	62.09 (1.86)	53.35 (1.55)	115.44 (1.70)	8.74
1991	71.84 (2.10)	63.79 (1.79)	135.63 (1.94)	8.05
1992	85.00 (2.30)	80.61 (2.12)	165.61 (2.21)	4.39
1993	91.80 (2.50)	104.00 (2.70)	195.80 (2.60)	-12.20

Note: Figures in parentheses are percentage shares in world trade.
Source: International Financial Statistics Yearbook, International Monetary Fund.

In 1993, foreign-invested ventures accounted for 27.5 percent of China's exports, while processing/assembling operations accounted for another seventeen percent. Combining these two, foreign-funded operations accounted for a total of forty-five percent of China's exports. As this represents almost half of China's exports, it clearly indicates that the role of foreign investment is very important in China's export drive.

In addition, the exports of foreign-invested ventures soared by forty-five percent while the exports of processing/assembling operations grew by only four percent. In recent years, foreign-invested ventures have been allowed to sell a substantial portion of their output in the internal market, and many

Table 4.3
China's Trade by Forms of Trade, 1993

	Exports		Imports		Trade Balance (Billion U.S. dollars)
	US$ Bil.	Growth rate (%)	US$ Bil.	Growth rate (%)	
General trade	43.2	-1.0	38.1	13.1	5.10
Foreign-funded operations	41.5 (45.2)	17.2	55.1 (53.0)	40.4	-13.60
Compensated trade	0.3 (0.3)	5.1	330.0 (0.3)	32.1	-0.02
Foreign-invested ventures	25.2 (27.5)	45.4	41.8 (40.2)	58.6	-16.60
Processing/ assembling operations	16.0 (17.4)	4.3	13.0 (12.5)	2.5	3.00
Total	91.8	8	104	29	-12.20

Note: Figures in parentheses represent percentage share of the total.
Source: China's Customs Statistics, Beijing.

processing/assembling operations have thus been converted to foreign-invested enterprises. Thus, the rate of growth of exports by foreign-invested enterprises overstates the growth of foreign investment. In other words, foreign-funded operations have clearly performed well in exporting as compared to the general trade. Exports from China's foreign trade corporations (general trade) had decreased by one percent in 1993. It was estimated that if this situation continued, foreign-funded operations would account for well over half of China's exports in 1994.

A REGRESSION MODEL

The impact of FDI on exports and growth can be examined by looking at the impact of FDI on foreign trade, and then the impact of foreign trade on economic development.

Impact of Foreign Trade on Economic Growth

The effect of foreign trade on economic growth can be explored by a simple one parameter model:

$$GNP = \alpha + \beta EXP \qquad (2)$$

The parameter β explains how exports (EXP) affect economic growth (GNP). In general, most developing economies will apply the export-led strategies in their early stage of economic development. That is, more resources will be allocated to industries with comparative advantage in exports. Through the expansion of the export sector, this stimulates economic growth. Therefore, a large and positive β implies that the effect of foreign trade on economic development is significant.

Impact of Foreign Investment on Foreign Trade

The expansion with respect to FDI and its effect on foreign trade is explicitly taken into consideration. Expanding Equation (2) as follows:

$$\beta = \eta + \lambda FDI \qquad (3)$$

Equation (3) states that the effect of foreign trade on economic growth is a function of foreign direct investment. Thus, the sign of the parameter, λ, indicates the importance of FDI to foreign trade opportunities. A large λ indicates that the effect of foreign trade on economic development is positive, and the economy is successful in attracting FDI. In other words, if the export sector is profitable and competitive in the world market, and if the government allows foreign investors to participate in these sectors, it will attract foreign capital inflow. Under these circumstances, foreign investment will play a significant role in driving the growth of exports and the economy. A negative coefficient suggests that FDI could actually reduce the positive contribution of foreign trade to economic development. It may imply that the growth of output from FDI is channeled back to the internal market.

Full Model

Finally, by substituting Equation (3) into Equation (2), we obtain:

$$GNP = \alpha + \eta EXP + \lambda FDI * EXP \qquad (4)$$

Equation (4) specifies the effect of foreign trade and FDI on economic development. We can analyze not only the simple relationship between economic growth and foreign trade, and between foreign trade and FDI, but also consider the combined effect of foreign trade and FDI on economic growth. If λ is positive and significant, it implies that the growth of FDI can stimulate the export volume. High export volume will in turn prompt the economy to grow further.

EMPIRICAL RESULTS

By using the data from 1983 to 1993, the empirical results in Table 4.4(a) indicate that the foreign trade is positively and significantly associated with economic growth. A one percent growth in foreign trade causes economic growth in China to increase by 0.5 percent. Moreover, the explanatory power is quite high, at eighty-six percent, indicating that export growth is one of the important factors determining the economic growth in China during the period. As the Chinese economy has started to transform into a market economy and is being more integrated into the world market, the growth of external trade will continue to play a significant part in stimulating the Chinese economy.

As mentioned before, the correlation between FDI and export is significant. The simple regression result indicates a similar finding. Table 4.4(b) shows the estimated regressions of exports on FDI. Although the coefficient is small, the t-statistic is still marginally significant at a ten percent level. This result is consistent with the finding of Sung (1994), who showed that foreign-funded operations occupied almost half of China's exports, and that FDI is one of the major forces driving export growth. A one percent growth in FDI can stimulate exports to grow by 0.07 percent. In the early stage of economic development, owing to abundant labor supply and cheap cost, most foreign investors would concentrate on the manufacturing industries. Since most of these industries are export-oriented, a surge in FDI can increase the manufacturing output, and hence, the export growth. Moreover, government policies also encourage manufacturers to produce export goods, so as to gain more export earnings. Moreover, the growth of FDI has a significant impact on export performance. Kueh (1992) states that regions with a higher export share generally enjoy a higher output share.

Recently, the Chinese government began to channel foreign investment into bottleneck industries, especially infrastructure projects, so as to maintain long-term economic growth. With these changes, economic reforms can be extended to the inland provinces rather than just concentrate on the

Table 4.4a
Estimate of Regression of Economic Growth on Exports

α	EXP	R^2	$s(\eta)$	D-W
3.90 $(8.12)^*$	0.50 $(4.09)^*$	0.86	0.05	2.52

Table 4.4b
Estimate of Regression of Exports on FDI

α	FDI	R^2	$s(\eta)$	D-W
3.96 $(4.61)^*$	0.07 $(1.80)^\#$	0.99	0.004	2.30

Table 4.4c
Estimate of Regression of Economic Growth on Exports and FDI

α	EXP	COM	R^2	$s(\eta)$	D-W
4.84 $(11.20)^*$	0.08 (0.42)	0.02 $(1.80)^\#$	0.85	0.08	1.71

Note: * = Significant at five percent level. # = Significant at ten percent level.
EXP = growth rate of exports; FDI = growth rate of Foreign Direct Investment; COM = combined factor of exports and FDI. *t*-statistics are in parentheses. R^2 is the adjusted coefficient of determination, $s(\eta)$ is the residual error. D-W is the Durbin-Watson statistic.

coastal areas, promoting more balance of growth among different regions. However, this is not an easy task, as infrastructural investment may not be very profitable and return on investment is often slow as compared with export-oriented manufacturing industries. Another problem of diverting foreign investment out of the traditional manufacturing industries is the guaranteed return on bottleneck industries. The debate over the approved rate of return on the infrastructure projects illustrated the conflicting interests between the Chinese authority and foreign investors. However, if the problems can be solved, FDI will no longer concentrate only in the manufacturing industries and the export sector, but will also diversify to long-term investment and benefit the interior regions.

CONCLUSION

Foreign direct investment has become a well-established and important part of economic activity in China. The strategy of seeking to maximize foreign exchange earnings through export-oriented foreign investment has meant that Sino-foreign joint ventures have been largely excluded from the domestic economy.

However, the Chinese government is aware that there are limits to the expansion of foreign investment. For example, the accumulation of a substantial trade surplus, which China presently enjoys with Western countries, would invite political pressures from trade-deficit countries for a reciprocal opening of the domestic market. In other words, the Chinese government is likely to use foreign capital to enhance the capacity of import-substitution industries. This is regarded as the "third wave" of foreign investments characterized by attention to China's retail market, capital, and technology-intensive projects in the infrastructure sector, and to industries in the service sector (banking, real estate, retail sales, consulting services, accounting firms, and information service).

The Chinese government has started to implement policies to divert foreign investments into inland provinces and to the infrastructure and service sectors, and away from the traditional export-oriented industries. However, any significant shift in policy towards a genuine import-substitution foreign investment regime will necessarily require a further deregulation in the large and medium scale state-owned industrial enterprises. This would encourage a further integration of the Chinese economy with the rest of the world. If these policies are successful, the Chinese economy can grow even faster than previously and can maintain its influence in the international markets.

REFERENCES

Kueh, Y.Y., 1992, "Foreign Investment and Economic Change in China," *China Quarterly*, No. 131, pp.637–690.

Sung, Yun W., 1994, "Foreign Investment and Trade," in Joeseph Cheng, ed., *China Review*, Hong Kong: OUP, Chapter 12.

5

Japan's Direct Investment in China: Current Situation, Prospects, and Problems

TOSHIHIKO KINOSHITA

INTRODUCTION

Japan's direct investment in the People's Republic of China (China) in FY1994 reached 2.6 billion U.S. dollars at an all-time high, up fifty-two percent on foreign direct investment (FDI) on a registration basis. It was the second highest figure, next to its FDI in the United States at 17.3 billion U.S. dollars, which has been the largest receiver of Japan's FDI for many years.

Meanwhile, the aggregate number of contact-based projects and the amount of FDI to China approved by the Chinese government marked a sharp decrease in 1994, after a continuous growth in the preceding five years as shown in Table 5.1. FDI from Hong Kong, which had been by far the largest investor in China, also fell by a large percentage. Investment from Taiwan, the second largest investor for the past several years, and that from the United States also fell noticeably. The Chinese government reported that despite a decrease in the inflow of contract-based FDI, there was a sizable increase of twenty-three percent on the basis of actualization. One observation is that China has entered a new phase from merely quantity to quality in receiving FDI. The decrease of FDI on the contractual basis in 1994 was apparently related to the tight monetary policy and other restrictive policies (e.g., on real estate business, etc.) adopted by the government of China.

Table 5.1
FDI in China, 1994

	No. of Projects	Amount (Billion U.S. dollars)
On Contractual Basis:		
Hong Kong/Macau	21,389 (-56.5)	40.5 (-45.2)
Taiwan	4,429 (-59.5)	3.4 (-65.4)
U.S.A.	3,035 (-55.1)	3.6 (-47.5)
Japan	2,228 (-36.1)	3.5 (+118.8)
World Total	47,490 (-43.0)	81.4 (-26.6)
On Actualization Basis:		
Hong Kong		15.9 (-8.1)
Taiwan		2.3 (-27.7)
Japan		1.7 (+30.7)
U.S.A.		1.5 (-29.4)
World Total		33.8 (+22.8)

Note: ( ) = Percentage change over 1993.
Source: Ministry of Foreign Trade and Economic Cooperation, China, *China Directory*, Radiopress Inc., Beijing, 1995.

DETERMINATION OF FDI AND THE INVESTMENT CLIMATE

Japanese investors, long awaited as one of the most active investors in China because of Japan's proximity to China and their strong corporate power as a whole, were generally inactive in investing in China until 1991. Japanese firms increased their FDI in China sharply beginning in 1992 (see Table 5.2). The trend continued into the middle of 1995. Other major investors, such as those from Hong Kong and Taiwan, which invested heavily in China for a decade until 1993, sharply curbed their investments in 1994. This shows that corporate advantages (and disadvantages) and/or perceptions of China between Japanese and the latter two economies are different.

Before making a close comparison, one has to look at the determinants of FDI and the "investment climate" in general. Basically, there are push factors from the investor's (or source country's) side and pull factors in the host country (in this case, China). Both of these factors constitute the

Table 5.2
Japan's FDI in China

	By Japanese Statistics (FY, Registration Basis)		By Chinese Statistics (CY, Contract Basis)		
	No. of Cases	Amount (Million U.S. dollars)	No. of Cases	Amounts (Million U.S. dollars)	No. of Projects in All of China
1979-1983			52	95	186
1979	3	14			
1980	6	11			
1981	9	26			
1982	4	18			
1983	5	3			
1984	66	114	138	203	1,856
1985	118	100	127	471	3,096
1986	85	226	94	210	1,492
1987	101	*1,226	110	301	2,230
1988	171	296	237	276	5,940
1989	126	438	294	440	5,769
1990	165	349	341	460	7,271
1991	246	579	599	812	12,932
1992	490	1,070	1,805	2,172	48,757
1993	700	1,691	3,488	2,960	83,251
1994	636	2,565	2,228	3,516	47,475
1979-1994	2,931	8,727	9,410	12,450	221,403

Note: * = Included a special type of oil development loan of one billion U.S. dollars.
Source: Ministry of Finance, Japan; Ministry of External Trade and Economic Cooperation, People's Republic of China.

conditions for making FDI in a host country, subject to its investment climate as evaluated by potential investors in Japan (see Kinoshita, 1982).

There are various push factors. First is "managerial resources of a firm," the most important concept in FDI. It is a package of management knowhow, production/sales expertise, financial capability including credit in the capital/money market, and various property rights of a potential investor. It brings about a firm-specific advantage which enables overseas investment. The more firms nurture managerial resources, the more likely they will want to, and are able to, invest overseas. The existence and transfer of managerial resources distinguish FDI from portfolio equity investment, which pursues interest, dividends, and capital gain, without holding ownership of overseas ventures. When host countries wish to receive managerial resources from overseas as a vital source of technology transfer, job opportunities, domestic or export demand, and so on, they will give priority to FDI.

Another factor for a firm is the existence (or expanding trend) of factors in the home country that cause a reduction in international competitiveness of its product. This factor is crucially important—especially for export-oriented FDIs. Currency appreciation and a higher level of wages and salaries in the home country, for example, tend to cause a loss of international competitiveness, other things being equal. The third factor is a corporate strategy that responds to those of rival firms at home and overseas. One move by a rival firm to invest in a certain country will influence the firm's decision.

As far as the pull factors are concerned, foreign investors will never invest in a foreign country without the existence of such factors. For import-substitution-type FDI or FDI in the service sector, the existence of a sizable domestic (or regional) market and its growth potential is crucial. However, if foreign firms think they can continue to engage in business through trade (export) with their counterparts without any problems, they will seldom set up local subsidiaries to meet local demand by spending additional funds. In most developing countries, however, there are barriers such as higher tariffs, import quotas, or a lack of comprehensive industrial policies to nurture local firms.

For investors aiming at establishing export facilities beyond just having a service function, the existence of, and easier access to, reasonable factor costs is crucial, though this is not the only condition necessary for high value-added industries. For most foreign investors, how to maintain the good quality of a product in the international market is the biggest interest. Naturally, the quality of human resources who can provide good R&D or high value-added activities becomes a key factor.

The distance from the home country is, in many but not all cases, one of the most important factors. This is particularly true for small enterprises where the time factor for owners or other decision makers is severely constrained.

Finally, regarding regulations on capital (FDI) inflow, the more open the capital market of a host country, the easier it is for foreign investors to invest. Deregulation of capital inflow has proceeded steadily in developing countries, which has boosted worldwide FDI dramatically these days.

Three other necessary conditions are interrelated with the pull factors. One is facilitation of transport and reasonable transportation costs. This is more or less related to distance. With the advancement in technology, however, perceived distances tend to shorten. The second condition is the availability of an international information network. No competitive firm in the world can operate currently without facsimile, for example. The third factor is the development and/or existence of related industries. For certain industries, main parts and materials may be shipped by an investor's own airplane. But some others cannot operate efficiently without related industries nearby. Chemical, steel, and automotive industries are typical examples.

The investment climate is no less important when compared with the pull and push factors. This is because foreign investors will select the best place for their overseas operation. Firms will not select a place where hyperinflation is taking place or where they cannot send their staff because of security or sanitary reasons. Host countries with the best investment climate, such as Singapore, Malaysia, and Hong Kong, have been reciprocated by favorable FDI inflows for years and those without good climates have failed to attract and absorb FDI. A favorable investment climate in host countries includes: a) a stable political and social situation; b) good macroeconomic management; c) a good public infrastructure, including good primary/vocational educational system; d) a consistent, fair treatment toward foreign investors/their subsidiaries (preferably, no discrimination between domestic capital and foreign capital); and e) others such as a good legal system, sound financial system, convenience of everyday life for foreigners, good security, and cooperation of trade unions, if they were to be set up.

CURRENT SITUATION OF JAPAN'S FDI IN CHINA

Unlike most East Asian developing market economies, China did not wish to attract FDI until the end of the 1970s because of ideological reasons. China was a highly planned economy for three decades since its independence in 1949 and viewed FDI as a weapon of "imperialism." However, in 1979, the Chinese authorities led by Mr. Deng Xiaoping completely altered their basic policy and adopted a "socialistic market economy" and a "reform and open" policy. A law encouraging inducement of FDI in the form of joint venture was promulgated in July of that year. This was a revolutionary change in China's history. Related laws and regulations and policies to set up special economic zones for foreign firms, to provide incentives for FDI, including a permit to set up even 100 percent foreign-owned subsidiaries, have been promulgated ever since. Responding to worldwide requests, Chinese authorities have also made related laws and regulations.

The Sino-Japanese joint ventures began in 1980. Hitachi set up a color-TV factory in Fujian. Otsuka began to produce a medical product in Tianjin. Japan's equity share in both cases was fifty percent. The invested amount of each project was relatively small—three to seven million U.S. dollars. Another project was a hotel venture in Fujian. The following year saw two small joint ventures, one of which was in Beijing. There were none in 1983, however. Thus Japanese firms were not generally active in making FDI in China during this period. The Chinese government, pursing a "reform and open" policy, did not conceal its frustration, saying that Japanese were too timid in investing in China compared with its very active external trade with China. The situation generally improved over time. A tax treaty to avoid double taxation between the governments of Japan and China was concluded in 1983. Then laws on brands and patents were enacted. Various missions were sent reciprocally, and study meetings were often convened to examine problems among the parties concerned. In the latter part of 1983 Japanese FDI in China began to increase gradually. An oil development joint venture supported by both governments began around this time with big expectations. Implementation guidelines and additional tax incentive measures were announced in September 1993.

By the end of 1985, sixty-three Japanese subsidiaries were set up in China, as Table 5.3 illustrates. This figure does not include a large number of tiny contractual investment projects without any equity participation (under unincorporated joint venture agreements or compensation trade agreements, etc.). Since then, the number of newly established Japanese subsidiaries has continued to grow from thirty in 1986 to sixty-one in 1989. This increase partly reflected the yen's sharp appreciation vis-à-vis the U.S. dollar as a result of the Plaza Accord in the fall of 1985. However, the economic adjustment policy in China in 1989, which contained inflation, as well as the Tiananmen Square incident in June 1989, provided a negative impact on inward FDI, including that from Japan. Hence, the number of new Japanese entrants decreased to forty-three in the following year.

Table 5.3
Number of Japanese Subsidiaries in China (by questionnaire survey)

Year	Number of Firms
1981-1985	63
1986	30
1987	34
1988	56
1989	61
1990	43
1991	74
1992	110
1993-July 1994	433
Total	904

Note : The figures excluded the large number of relatively small projects without incorporation. Chinese statistics show that 292 cases were approved by the authority between 1979 and 1985, for instance.
Source: Toyo Keizai, *Chugoku Shinshutsu Kigyo Sooran*, 1995, p.53.

The Japanese economy, which had been overheated, suffered a collapse of the "bubble economy" in 1991, and that caused an overall shrinkage of its outward FDI. However, FDI to China was not negatively affected. Japanese firms began to be strongly interested in investing in China. Actually Japan's FDI in China increased drastically since 1992. Japan's FDI to China was 1.1 billion U.S. dollars in FY1992 (increased from 579 million U.S. dollars in FY1991), 1.7 billion U.S. dollars in FY1993, and 2.6 billion U.S. dollars in FY1994 on a Japanese government registration basis (small investments whose individual amount is less than 100 million yen are currently omitted owing to a lack of need to register).

Incidentally, 1992 was the remarkable year when Mr. Deng Xiaoping visited southern regions of China in winter and called strongly for an acceleration of the "reform and open" policy. Tycoons in Hong Kong boosted their investment in China then. Taiwanese followed. The increase in Japan's FDI in China since 1992 was so fast and so large in amount, though far smaller than those made by Hong Kong and Taiwan, that it caused great concern in other Asian developing countries, which feared that inward FDI in their respective countries might dry up.[1]

In fact, a large number of Japanese subsidiaries, as many as 543, were set up in China between 1992 and July 1994 (see Table 5.3). The number is equivalent to two-thirds of the entire number of subsidiaries set up since 1980. By area, Japanese firms invested nationwide except in Tibet, but the major portion was placed in coastal areas (including Beijing and Shanghai). Shanghai is the biggest recipient, holding 199 Japanese subsidiaries, followed by big provinces and municipalities/cities such as Guangdong (142), Beijing (129), and Liaoning (120). This was in sharp contrast to FDI from Hong Kong, whose investments have been concentrated in Guangdong, including Shenzhen, and those from Taiwan in the nearest Fujian province and its neighbors.

Up to 1994, the aggregate number of Japanese investments in electric/electronic machinery and textile occupied some sixty percent of the total up to 1994.[2] In the case of the electric/electronic machinery industry, investments have been widely made in relatively well-developed regions such as Dalian, Beijing, Shanghai, Guangdong, Jiangsu, Zhejiang, and Xi'an. This reflects the diversified requirements or wishes of Japanese firms: a) some badly need related industries to meet high localization ratio to lessen the financial requirements for foreign exchange and to strengthen price competitiveness of their products, b) some seek reasonable factor costs such as wage, land price, transportation cost for export and/or inland distribution, and c) some are attracted by fast-growing local/regional markets. The main areas of electrical devices invested by major Japanese multinational enterprises are shown in Tables 5.4 and 5.5.

Investments in the textile industry have been heavily focused on regions such as Jiangsu, Zhejiang, Shandong, and Shanghai, which have easy access to cheap labor of good quality, and abundant industrial water in some cases. For example, Nantong in Jiangsu can provide a good factory site for an integrated synthetic fiber production. Toray had decided to deploy a sizable investment there for several years. Japan's FDI in auto-related industries has been limited mainly due to a relatively small market in China in the past and its somewhat unclear industrial policy on auto industries. However, its domestic demand is now growing quickly. Domestic production of cars in China in 1995 was estimated to be 1.6 million and that in the year 2000, 2.6 million. And a new policy guideline on auto manufacturing was made public recently. Thus, the situation has changed and it is expected that big investments will be made by some large Japanese auto manufacturers in the coming years. Those investments will be concentrated in rather well-developed industrial areas. The other major investments included cement factories (joint ventures of Onoda, Mitsubishi Material, Nihon Cement, etc.), beer production by Suntory, Kirin, and Asahi, manufacturing of motor bikes or their engines by Honda, Yamaha, and Suzuki, a glass factory (Asahi Glass), and food-processing investments (Ajinomoto, Nisshin Oil, etc.).

Recently, Japanese firms also began to make large amounts of investments in the service sector, such as department stores and supermarkets in

Table 5.4
China's Position in Japan's FDI in Asia (million U.S. dollars)

	FY1991			FY1992			FY1993		
	Case	Amount	%	Case	Amount	%	Case	Amount	%
China	246	579	9.8	490	1,070	16.7	700	1,691	23.5
Hong Kong	178	925	15.5	154	735	11.4	184	1,238	18.7
Korea	48	260	4.4	28	225	3.5	33	245	3.7
Indonesia	148	1,193	20.1	122	1,676	26.1	97	644	9.7
Singapore	103	613	10.3	100	670	10.4	100	670	10.1
Taiwan	87	405	6.8	48	292	4.5	41	292	4.4
Malaysia	136	880	14.8	111	704	11.0	92	800	12.1
Thailand	258	807	13.6	130	657	10.2	127	578	8.7
Philippines	42	203	3.4	45	160	2.5	56	207	3.1
Others	29	71	1.2	41	236	3.7	48	272	4.1
Total	1,277	5,936	100.0	1,269	6,425	100.0	1,478	6,637	100.0

Note: These figures do not include reinvestment.
Source: Ministry of Finance, Japan.

Table 5.5
FDI in China by Japanese Firms

Name of Firm	Location	Form of FDI	Annual Production Capacity
For the Production of Television Sets			
Sanyo	Guangdong	Joint Venture	650,000
Victor	Shanghai	Joint Venture	50,000
Hitachi	Fujian	Joint Venture	800,000 Brown tubes 1.6 million
Matsushita	Beijing	Joint Venture	Brown tubes 2.6 million
For the Production of Air Conditioners			
Matsushita	Guangdong	Joint Venture	300,000 Compressors
Mitsubishi Electric	Guangdong Shanghai Beijing	Technical Assistance	
Hitachi	Shanghai	Joint Venture	250,000 Compressors
	Shanghai	Technical Assistance	
Sanyo	Shenyang	Joint Venture	400,000 Compressors
	Shenyang	Technical Assistance	
	Guangdong	Joint Venture	150,000
Sharp	Shanghai	Joint Venture	400,000

Source: Mitsubishi Research Institute, *Handbook on China-related Information*, Soosoosha, Japan, 1995, pp.140-142.

addition to hotels, which started in the 1980s (see Table 5.6). This is mainly due to the deregulation policies on retail business since 1992 and the fast-growing purchasing power of the people, particularly in large cities. Many Japanese banks also set up branches in accordance with China's recent financial deregulation policies and the active trading and FDI activities of Japanese firms.

As for the push factors, most Japanese firms have ample competitive managerial resources. This is shown by the fact that Japan is now one of the biggest investors overseas. There is a salient feature in the case of Japan that not only large firms with worldwide brand names, but millions of small firms, make FDI. In the case of the United Stares, major investors are world-famous "multinationals" and only a limited number of small firms invest overseas.

Japanese firms have nurtured their competitive edge by a growing technological backlog. It began with borrowed technology in the pre– and post–World War II period and has improved through "Kaizen" efforts every day, and eventually by their own R&D activities. They tend to set up subsidiaries overseas rather than selling patents or knowhow, as many

Table 5.6
FDI in China by Japanese Supermarkets and Department Stores (includes ongoing plans)

Name of Firm	Location	Date
Yaohan	Shenzhen	September 1991
	Shenzhen	April 1993
	Shanghai	December 1995
Isetan	Shanghai	July 1993
	Tianjin	December 1993
Daiei	N.A.	N.A.
Seiyu	Beijing	September 1993
Ito-Yokadoo	Shenzhen	1992
Jusco	Qingdao	1996
	Shanghai	1996

Source: Same as Table 5.5, p. 129.

Western firms prefer to do. The abrupt and continuous yen appreciation vis-à-vis the U.S. dollar has accelerated the "globalization strategies" of Japanese firms. Over time, many overseas factor costs denominated in U.S. dollars, including wages, land prices, materials, and energy costs, have become cheaper than domestic costs. In general terms, knowledge- and capital-intensive industries can still maintain international competitiveness, but those producing labor-intensive, energy-related and low-tech (or completely standardized) products are losing their price competitiveness. Hence, the firms must choose a survival strategy: release workers, increase the importation of cheaper materials, alter the product mix to a higher value-added content, or invest overseas to reduce production cost for export to Japan/Third World countries or to meet local demand.

Corporate strategies to cope with rival firms both at home and overseas constitute an additional driving force for outward FDI. For instance, when a rival firm relocates its production site to China, where it can reduce production costs sharply, other firms producing the same product may have to consider how to respond. This can lead to a "bandwagon" effect on the part of other firms. This is particularly true for products whose product differentiation is difficult. This may be the major reason why a number of small Japanese firms have invested in "special economic zones" to produce cheaper apparel, optical goods, electrical devices, food processing, and miscellaneous goods with little product differentiation. They are doing so in order to keep an equal footing, at the minimum, with their rivals. Many other Asian firms based in Hong Kong, Taiwan, and Korea are adopting similar strategies. However, many Japanese firms which are equipped with better managerial resources are aiming at relocating facilities to produce firm-specific but standardized products. They need better quality of labor, related industries, better materials, and so forth.

As already stated, the location factor is no less important. Coastal areas of China are very convenient in terms of access from overseas, especially for small Japanese firms. This is why firms located in the Kyushu and Kansai districts in Japan are generally more active in dealing with China than those in the Kanto area. However, specific places that Japanese firms have selected are somewhat different from those of Hong Kong, Taiwan, and Korea.

At first, many Japanese subsidiaries were export-oriented because of China's industrial policy that their domestic markets were not open to foreign subsidiaries and, more important, that foreign subsidiaries had to bring in or earn foreign currency to meet foreign exchange requirements in order to purchase foreign parts and materials and to repatriate dividends, if any. Over time, however, many Japanese firms began to notice China's fast-growing domestic market. The sale volume of durable goods and its import of these goods have expanded at a pace higher than expected. The emerging middle class of China has shown a strong desire to purchase luxury items such as electric home appliances, motor bikes, personal computers, and even small cars. To make the situation better for foreign firms, the Chinese government began to gradually open its domestic market to foreign capital because of: a) the strong purchasing power of the people, and their diversified need for good products; b) the extension of the "reform and open policy" to urge competition to improve the quality of domestic products; c) the strong wish or pressure from overseas including the reentry to GATT (WTO since 1995); and d) the need to nurture internationally competitive local/localized industrial groups. China's new national goal to aid state-owned enterprises in difficult situations, financially as well as technically, also influences the policy to induce foreign capital to provide them with new chances to absorb better managerial resources. Many Japanese firms actually set up joint ventures with Chinese state-owned enterprises.

PROSPECTS AND PROBLEMS OF JAPAN'S FDI

Prospects

Japan's FDI, which began to grow rapidly in FY1992, is still rising. In the meantime, those from Hong Kong, Taiwan, and the United States fell drastically in 1994 and in the first quarter of 1995. These countries increased their FDI in Southeast Asian countries instead. What made the difference? Are the Japanese firms more optimistic about China's future than investors in Hong Kong and Taiwan?

The difference partly stems from the fact that firm-specific advantages between Japanese firms and those of Hong Kong, Taiwan, and ethnic Chinese in Southeast Asia are somewhat different. The latter have advantages in their investments in real estate, construction, and infrastructure building in addition to light industries. When the Chinese government adopted economic (monetary and industrial) policies to contain inflation, they led to a slowdown of foreign money entering into such areas as real estate and construction, Hong Kong and Taiwanese firms were badly affected but Japanese firms were not. Some Japanese subsidiaries were, however, negatively affected in such a way that their Chinese counterparts could not provide money to undertake or expand joint ventures.

There may be other reasons why foreign capital inflows have slowed down, for instance, the uncertainty of China's sociopolitical situation and growing labor disputes. Some have optimistic views, some do not. Many large Japanese firms tend to recognize at present that China has good potential for the future and that the current "reform and open" policy of the goverment is generally well accepted by Chinese people and that there would be no alternative even in the future. These firms usually include China in their globalization strategies. They send missions to China from time to time to update their information on policies of the Chinese government. Some smaller firms in the same industrial group will follow their affiliated large firms. But others, mostly independent small firms, will behave differently. Being pressured by further yen appreciation and domestic recession, many of these firms are actively investing mainly in China's coastal area. There will be, however, a new wave of large investments in China in the area of auto manufacturing.

In the meantime, the Export-Import Bank of Japan had undertaken a questionnaire survey mainly of leading Japanese firms, on Japan's outward FDI every year. The last one was undertaken in the summer of 1994 (see Tejima and Nakashima, 1995). This survey covered only manufacturing but is widely known for its accuracy. A total of 382 firms, with 5,400 overseas subsidiaries, responded to the survey. The survey illustrates, for instance, how many major Japanese firms are planning to invest in China.

The survey finds that within (approximately) the next three years, out of a total number of newly projected overseas investment, some thirty percent are expected to be made in China, which is followed by four Association of Southeast Asian Nations (ASEAN) countries, except Singapore (twenty-five percent), and Asian Newly Industrializing Economies (ANIES) (ten percent). By industry, twenty-two percent of their total planned projects in the world will be in the area of electric/electronic machinery/devices (fifteen percent in parts manufacturing) and seventeen percent in auto manufacturing (fourteen percent auto parts manufacturing), followed by the chemical industries. Major areas of Japan's FDI in China will also be in the manufacture of electric/electronic machinery/devices, automobiles, and precision machinery. Nonmanufacturing FDI will include those in the distribution system and some infrastructure projects on a build-operate-transfer (B.O.T) scheme. China has been selected as the most promising host country for FDI in the long-term (around ten years) perspective. Hence, the generally optimistic view of Japanese firms on China is clearly revealed.

There are no statistics on how much of China's exports to Japan is derived from Japanese subsidiaries in China. However, they are no doubt the major exporters to Japan. Evidently, Japanese trading houses are also playing a large role in this area. Japan's imports from China amounted to 27.6 billion U.S. dollars in 1994, up thirty-four percent over the previous year, which was bigger than its exports to China by 8.9 billion U.S. dollars. Japan's imports of manufactured goods from China expanded at an annual rate of thirty percent up until 1994, from 1985 when the Plaza Accord was made. Thus, trade and FDI seem to be strongly interrelated.

Currently the attention is focused on China's auto industry, which requires a huge amount of investment. Technology transfer to attain higher localization ratios is not easy. This explains why big motor company groups of Japan, such as Toyota and Nissan, generally are not enthusiastic about investing heavily despite invitations by Chinese authorities to do so. This contrasts with some German, French, and American car manufacturers, which have been more active in investing in China.

However, the situation has changed dramatically, as mentioned earlier, since the Chinese government formally made public a new industrial policy in 1995 to nurture strong auto manufacturers as a main pillar of China's industry. It clarifies the comprehensive industrial policy of Chinese authorities for the first time. Whole industries are classified into three categories: (A) those to be encouraged; (B) those to be limited; and (C) those to be prohibited. Category A comprises FDI in the areas of (i) new types of agriculture and fertilizer; (ii) newly developed materials; (iii) advanced electronic parts; (iv) precision machinery; (v) private airplanes; (vi) mobile telecommunications; (vii) infrastructure; (viii) biotechnology; (ix) agriculture in desert-like areas; and (x) auto parts.

Despite the fact that FDI in auto-parts manufacturing is classified as Category A, auto assembly is not included in this preferential category. A recent Chinese report states that it is in Category B which is still under examination. The number of foreign car-assembly firms to be allowed to newly enter in 1996 or afterward will be severely controlled through the following conditions:[3]

a. Form of venture: joint venture; wholly owned by foreign firm(s) is not permitted.

b. Limit of equity share of foreign firm(s): less than forty-nine percent.

c. Location: designated place by Chinese authorities.

d. Limit regarding partners: designated partner(s) by Chinese authorities.

e. Limit on enterprising: obligation of localization is required.

Until this new policy was announced, there was a guideline of 3–3–2 for auto production under the 8th Five-Year Plan: three groups for big cars, three for small cars, and two for smaller cars. Three European and U.S. auto manufacturers, namely, Volkswagen, Peugeot-Citroen, and Chrysler, set up five joint ventures with Chinese state-owned enterprises and have produced big and small cars. Japan's involvement by now is generally weak. Daihatsu, one of the Toyota group companies, joined the second category group to produce small cars on a contractual technical assistance basis (not in the form of joint venture). Also, Fuji Heavy Industry and Suzuki Motor have provided Chinese partners with technical assistance to produce smaller cars. Isuzu established a joint venture to produce engines with an annual capacity of 70,000 units. Though the door is to be reopened, it is assumed that only a very few assemblers could enter in 1996 or afterward. Japanese auto manufacturers, such as Toyota, Nissan, and Mitsubishi (with a Malaysian counterpart producing the national car—Proton Saga), have expressed their wish to the Chinese authorities to join the program.[4] There is a precondition, however, that parts producers of each group shall invest in China first, while no indication is given on what firm(s) will eventually be selected as designated assembler(s). That is the biggest obstacle for potential investor groups (Iwahara, 1995, p. 156). Under the current situation, Toyota decided to raise its equity ratio of Daihatsu from 16.6 percent to 33.3 percent. This is apparently related to Toyota's strategy to enter Chinese auto manufacturing (*Nihon Keizai Shimbun*, September 20, 1995).

Problems

A number of problems exist in China as compared with other Asian countries. Laws and regulations regarding FDI are too vague and not fair to foreign investors. Some investors are concerned about the social infrastructure, e.g., the shortage of electricity and the transportation problem. Others worry about how to attain "foreign exchange balance" in making domestic-market-oriented projects. Some cannot find appropriate partners. Good materials are usually in short supply. There are also many bureaucratic problems, and a lack of discipline in many areas of the country.

China has all the problems that any developing country has. However, the fact that China still retains a basically planned economy, though aiming at a market economy, increases the complexity of the problems encountered by foreign investors. Trade is easier than FDI should foreign investors try to produce an internationally competitive product in China. It is also a fact that the situation has improved year after year through serious discussions among the concerned parties. New laws and regulations and their guidelines have been promulgated. Bureaucrats have became accustomed to dealing with foreigners. Heads of many municipalities attempt to solve problems. Many existing Japanese subsidiaries are reportedly recording profits with some exceptions. Japanese trading houses which have accumulated good human resources as well as the knowhow to conduct business in China have played an important role in helping Japanese manufacturers and firms in the service sector to set up subsidiaries.

Recently, however, Japanese firms or their subsidiaries are faced with new problems, such as high inflation and its impact on workers' wages and social welfare, tax (rebate) issues regarding the introduction of value-added taxes, shortage of local money derived from the recent tight monetary policy, abrupt changes of the guideline on working hours, and the new selective industrial policy.[5]

Potential Japanese investors are strongly requesting Chinese authorities to help them solve these problems. Some problems will be solved soon. Some will not, for many of them are structurally rooted. Chinese authorities are also faced with serious problems—high inflation and the people's frustration with it, growing shortage of domestic supply of food and oil, decrease of arable land, a widening income gap between the rich and the poor and that between the coastal areas and inner provinces, and how to attain conditions to be a member of WTO at the earliest date. How these problems are tackled by the Chinese authorities will influence, more or less, the management of existing foreign subsidiaries and forthcoming FDI in China. How to implement the new industrial policy may also affect foreign investors. The new policy is clearly a carrot-and-stick policy. The Chinese side wishes to grow indigenous and expand the number of localized firms, to attain a higher localization ratio, and to increase other "national interests." Hence, conflicts may take place in the area of relatively low-tech industrial fields in the foreseeable future.

CONCLUSION

Issues concerning Japanese FDI in China are multifaceted. Japanese firms will continue to make sizable investments in China in the future. China's political or socioeconomic turbulence or business fluctuations from time to time will, of course, influence Japan's FDI in China. However, the economic relationship of the two countries could be largely complementary in many respects and thereby could take advantage of growing trade and FDI. Many Japanese firms will engage in more FDI for their restructuring or reengineering. China also needs much FDI of good quality for various reasons. Japanese firms and their subsidiaries have generally been good corporate citizens there and wish to remain so. The Japanese broadly believe that China's "reform and open" policy has been strongly supported by the people and that there can be no alternative. The international community also wants China to become a part of the global economy and to coexist in the new world order, toward which Japan and other countries should make the utmost effort.

It is understandable that Chinese authorities have newly decided on a selective industrial policy. True, quality is more important than just quantity or the amount or number of projects. Chinese authorities well know that the country cannot necessarily receive qualitative investments only through an industrial policy. Indeed, what counts more for foreign firms is improvement of the investment climate; the push and pull factors are equally important. At the same time, we can foresee the possible results of converging interests of the two countries by increasing trade and FDI. The day will come when Japan and China will find it necessary to coordinate their respective industrial policies to attain their mutual benefit.

It has been said that it is through human relations rather than laws and regulations that things are decided upon and solved in China. However, decision making mainly through human relations tends to bring about unfairness or sometimes even corruption. Contracts work efficiently under good laws. It is important that new laws are being made public. But to make a law is one thing and to implement it properly is another. To educate people that everyone stands equal before the law and to nurture good judges and lawyers are the first steps toward observing it. Such efforts in China are eagerly awaited by the international community. China's government is expected to take initiatives on this issue. At the same time Japanese and other foreign investors are urged to study and prepare for the newly published laws, such as the Labor Law and Product Liability Law, as well as Chinese judicial system so as to reduce possible legal conflicts (Takahashi, 1994).

It is crucially important that Chinese authorities and people pay due attention to natural environment issues related to industrialization and urbanization, and to the significance of hard/soft infrastructure. There will be no need to detail the importance of the natural environment. As for social infrastructure, some are rather optimistic, thinking that many of those projects could be privatized and would be easily funded. This may be true particularly in the area of power generation and superhighways. Big corporations in Hong Kong have been and will continue to be active in this field. Japanese firms are also showing much interest in doing so. However, many of them could not be privatized for one reason or another. How to fund them will constitute one of the important issues for the future economic growth of China. China can count on the economic cooperation of Japan to a certain degree, but self-help efforts must also be made.

NOTES

1. These concerns of non-Chinese Asian developing economies and their competition to invite FDI represent one of the strong driving forces for them to further deregulate capital inflow. In fact, however, Japan's FDI in other Asian developing countries also increased and was not entirely concentrated in China (in FY1994, China's share in Japan's entire FDI in Asia rose slightly to 26.4 percent compared with 23.5 percent in FY1993).

2. Out of the total sales amount of Japanese subsidiaries in China, those in electric/electronic machinery shared some fifty-four percent in FY1993, followed by those in general machinery (twenty-one percent) and transport machinery (fifty-one percent) (MITI, 1995).

3. The new auto manufacturing policy passed in 1994–1995 by the Chinese government was as follows:

a. Local production in 2000 shall cover over seventy percent of domestic demand.

b. Number of passenger cars produced shall be over fifty percent of all cars. They shall be largely for family use.

c. Production of motor bikes shall be mainly for domestic demand; some can be exported.

d. Auto manufacturers shall be reorganized as follows by 2000. The biggest group of firms shall be limited to two or three. The medium-sized ones ("mini-midget giants") shall be limited to six or seven. For those producing motorbikes, the total is eight to ten.

e. The next step of reorganization by 2010 shall be to make three to four big auto manufacturing groups through mergers of the biggest and medium-sized firms. Likewise for motorbikes, to three to four biggest corporate groups.

4. *Nihon Keizai Shimbun* reported on July 14, 1995, that Nissan has materialized a plan to set up joint venture in China with Nanjing Auto Works, a large Chinese state enterprise, to produce engines with an annual capacity of 150 thousand units and, independently, basic auto parts for commercial cars.

5. It should be noted that while these problems are widely reported in Japan and other countries by the press, few Chinese citizens are informed of the existence of these problems.

REFERENCES

Iwahara, Taku, 1995, *A Guidebook on China's Auto-Industry*, Tokyo, May.

Kinoshita, Toshihiko, 1982, "Japan's Financial and Technology Cooperation to China—with special reference to its foreign direct investment," in Sekiguchi, S. (ed.), *Japan's Foreign Direct Investment to Pan-Pacific Region*, Nihon Keizai Shimbunsha, Tokyo, August: 119–145.

Takahashi, Masatake, 1994, "New Revisions of Laws: What Are Their Impacts?", *Chuuookooron Special Issue: All Perspectives on Business with China*, No. 2, December: 272–281.

Tejima, Shigeki, and Hiroyuki Nakashima, 1995, *Results of Questionnaire Survey on Japan's Outward Foreign Direct Investment—an FY1994 Issue*, Research Institute for International Investment and Development, Export-Import Bank of Japan, 21, No. 1, January.

Toyo, Keizai Shimposha (ed.), 1995, *Data Book on Japanese Foreign Direct Investment in China* (a special issue), Tokyo.

6

Taiwan's Trade and Investment in China

POCHIH CHEN and CHAK-YUEN KAN

INTRODUCTION

Significant economic differences in the per capita income and wages between the Taiwan Province and Mainland China have produced a good potential for economic complementarity. Moreover, a considerable number of Taiwan citizens who migrated from China after World War II still have close relatives and friends in China. This creates many opportunities for economic cooperation between Taiwan and China. However, due to political and military conflicts between Taiwan and Mainland China since 1949, there was virtually no economic relationship nor cooperation between them until the 1980s. In addition, China's self-sufficiency policy in the 1950s and 1960s also hindered her economic developments with other noncommunist countries. The indirect relationship between Taiwan and Mainland China through a third economy was negligible before the 1980s. The importation of herbs through Hong Kong was probably the only significant item in Taiwan's trade with China at that time.

When Mainland China decided to adopt economic reform and open door policies in 1978, China also changed its policy against Taiwan from one of a hardline military liberation policy to a peaceful unification policy. Although the new policy is still not free from military risk, China tries to use economic means to lure Taiwan, or at least Taiwanese businessmen, away from the pursuance of an independent Taiwan. Chinese leaders thought that increasing economic dependence of Taiwan on the Mainland and reducing the income gap would increase the possibility of unification. A number of privileges have also been given to Taiwanese businessmen (see Kao, 1995).

Changes also took place in Taiwan. Democratization and the removal of Martial Law have given rise to a great potential to do business with the Mainland. The Taiwan authority officially permitted Taiwanese to visit China in 1987, after a long period during which many Taiwanese visited China informally. Indirect import from China has also officially been allowed since 1989, while indirect export and investment to China were officially allowed in 1990. All these permissions actually came long after the actual trade and investment had occurred. Even though these permissions do not cover all kinds of industries, they give the Taiwanese a direct means to meet people from the Mainland. Many Taiwanese now believe that the economic relation with China can be separated from the political conflict.

With the change in policy between Taiwan and the Mainland, their economic relations started to grow quickly in the 1980s. However, it is argued that the growth in economic activities is mainly the result of the underlying economic factors rather than the policies adopted.

THE DEVELOPMENT OF TRADE

With a different stage in economic development between Taiwan and the Mainland, there are many opportunities for trade to occur. The differences in wage rate, in natural resource endowment, and in technology are the sources of potential benefits of trade or economic cooperation. Moreover, similar customs and language of the people involved and the personal relationships and kinship ties will certainly reduce the transaction cost and enhance the potential trade flow. Therefore, the trade between Taiwan and China grew rapidly when indirect trade was allowed.

The trade between Taiwan and the Mainland through Hong Kong is of two main kinds: transshipment and reexports (see Kan, 1994).

Transshipment Trade

According to the Hong Kong Census and Statistics Department, transshipment refers to "cargo that is consigned on a through bill of lading from a place outside Hong Kong to another place outside Hong Kong but is or is to be removed from one vessel (ship, vehicle, train or aircraft) and either returned to the same vessel or transferred to another vessel within Hong Kong waters." Hence, the transshipment trade shows the weight and volume of cargoes without corresponding monetary values.

Since 1983, transshipment trade statistics have been collected by the Hong Kong Census and Statistics Department (see Table 6.1). Except in 1984 and 1985, the weight of Taiwan's exports to China was always bigger than Taiwan's import from China during the years 1983–1994. The transshipment trade has been expanding rapidly as a result of favorable policies exercised by the Taiwan authority.

Reexport Trade

The value of Taiwan's exports to China is less than Taiwan's import from China in general (see Table 6.2). Taiwan exports to China rose rapidly in 1980, with a growth rate of 994.4 percent. By 1994, the exports of Taiwan

Table 6.1
Transshipment Trade Between Taiwan and the Mainland Through Hong Kong, 1983–1995

	Taiwan's Export to China		Taiwan's Import from China	
	Weight (tonns)	Volume (CBM)	Weight (tonns)	Volume (CBM)
1983	4,267	11,777	1,573	5,370
1984	318	1,066	3,269	7,070
1985	226	711	1,666	4,286
1986	1,392	5,101	828	1,741
1987	1,912	5,027	934	1,235
1988	8,096	14,360	2,595	5,556
1989	53,450	125,220	6,662	19,496
1990	81,195	219,610	12,447	25,921
1991	345,700	840,550	87,610	155,728
1992	872,292	2,310,981	211,026	388,275
1993	1,152,363	3,132,763	221,410	428,625
1994	1,227,000	3,200,000	442,000	876,000
1995	1,718,000	4,371,000	557,000	1,100,000

Source: Census and Statistics Department, Hong Kong.

Table 6.2
**Reexport Trade Between Taiwan and the Mainland Through Hong Kong,
1970–1995**

	Taiwan's Export to China		Taiwan's Import from China	
	Value (Million U.S. dollars)	% Share in Taiwan's Export	Value (Million U.S. dollars)	% Share in Taiwan's Import
1970			1.80	0.11
1971			2.52	0.13
1972			7.94	0.31
1973			16.77	0.44
1974	0.01	a	21.40	0.30
1975	0.01	a	25.67	0.43
1976	0.00	a	41.07	0.54
1977	0.03	a	30.62	0.35
1978	0.05	a	46.72	0.42
1979	21.5	0.13	56.30	0.38
1980	235.0	1.19	76.20	0.39
1981	384.2	1.70	75.20	0.35
1982	194.5	0.88	84.00	0.44
1983	157.9	0.63	89.90	0.44
1984	425.5	1.40	127.80	0.58
1985	986.9	2.21	115.90	0.58
1986	811.2	2.04	114.20	0.60
1987	1,226.5	2.30	288.90	0.83
1988	2,242.2	3.70	478.70	0.96
1989	2,896.5	4.38	586.90	1.12
1990	3,278.3	4.88	765.40	1.40
1991	4,667.2	6.12	1,126.00	1.79
1992	6,287.9	7.72	1,119.00	1.55
1993	7,585.4	8.93	1,103.60	1.43
1994	8,517.2	9.15	1,292.30	1.51
1995	9,882.8	8.84	1,574.20	1.51
1995*	14,783.9	13.23	3,098.10	2.99

Note: * = Figures from the Custom Statistics of the People's Republic of China. a = Less than 0.01 percent.
Source: Census and Statistics Department, Hong Kong; Mainland Affair Committee, Taiwan; China Custom Statistics, People's Republic of China.

to China via Hong Kong were 8,517.2 million U.S. dollars, accounting for 9.15 percent of the total exports of Taiwan.

Since the trade between Taiwan and China is indirect through a third party, the actual amount is not easy to trace. For instance, the amount of exports from Taiwan to Hong Kong in recent years has been much greater in Taiwan's statistics than in Hong Kong's statistics. It is believed that a major reason for this gap is that some exporters declared their exports to China as exports to Hong Kong through Taiwan's customs, and usually this gap is captured by the transshipment trade. If this gap is regarded as exports to China, Taiwan's exports to China constituted 17.21 percent of Taiwan's total exports in 1994, sixteen percent higher than they were ten years ago. China is already Taiwan's second biggest export market.

Hong Kong and China together accounted for twenty-three percent of Taiwan's exports in 1994, which was close to Taiwan's exports to the United States It is expected that Hong Kong and China together will soon exceed the United States to become Taiwan's biggest export market. Moreover, the share of Hong Kong and China in Taiwan's exports has also become much greater than their shares in other Asian countries. For instance, their shares in the exports of South Korea, Singapore, and Japan in 1993 were only 14.08 percent, 11.25 percent, and 11.08 percent, respectively, but their share in Taiwan's export was 21.7 percent, and their shares in other East Asian countries and other advanced countries were less than ten percent. One can conclude that trade development between Taiwan and China has been quite astonishing.

In contrast and according to official statistics, Taiwan's imports from China did not grow at a comparable rate. The share of Taiwan's indirect imports from China through Hong Kong grew by merely 1.51 percent in 1994. However, the shares of China in the imports of Japan and the United States in 1993 were 8.58 percent and 5.38 percent, respectively. This phenomenon is partly due to Taiwan's import restrictions on Chinese products and partly due to smuggling activities. China's share in Taiwan's imports seems to be too low and there is much room for further expansion. However, differences in the international comparative advantages could be another important reason, as, for example, the shares of China in the imports of South Korea and Singapore in 1993 were only 3.71 percent and 2.82 percent, respectively.

Taiwan's investment in China is probably the most important reason for the relatively high exports from Taiwan to China and the low imports from China. Taiwan has more than twenty thousand firms investing in China. A major reason for these Taiwanese firms to invest in China is to produce the traditional exports of Taiwan.

TAIWAN'S INVESTMENT IN CHINA

Taiwan's investment in China has become important since 1987 when the New Taiwan (N.T.) dollar started to appreciate against the U.S. dollar. The amount of Taiwanese investment in China approved by the People's Republic of China was merely twenty million U.S. dollars before 1987, but the investment approved in 1987 alone was 100 million U.S. dollars, and the investment approved in 1988 reached 420 million U.S. dollars (see Lee, 1994). The amount approved in 1993 reached 9,965 million U.S. dollars, equivalent to 4.6% of Taiwan's GDP. The total Taiwanese investment approved by the People's Republic of China up to 1993 was 18.9 billion U.S. dollars, equivalent to about nine percent of the total approved foreign investment of China. Taiwan has become the second biggest source of foreign investment for China (Lee, 1994).

Table 6.3 shows the cases and amount of Taiwan investment in China by region from 1991 to February 1995. Guangzhou, Jiangsu, and Fujian were the main areas in China for Taiwan investment. Electronic and electric appliances, precision instruments, plastic products, and foods and beverages are the target industries for Taiwan's investment in China.

COMPLEMENTARITY IN DEVELOPMENT AND IN PRODUCTION

A major reason for the Taiwanese to invest heavily in China is the economic structural adjustment in Taiwan. In conventional theories, the major motivations for direct foreign investment include the expansion of markets, avoidance of trade barriers, utilization of the host country's resources, taking advantage of the differences in government regulations and tax systems, enhancement or realization of monopoly power, obtaining higher rates of return on capital, and so forth. In the case of Taiwan, an additional important benefit is the vertical complementarity in production, namely the division of labor in production and specialization in production processes. Another form of vertical complementarity is the continuous shift of the international comparative advantage of some products or production processes from one region to another. The first type of complementarity is called "complementarity in production," and the second type of complementarity is known as "complementarity in development."

If there are no transportation costs, transaction costs, and other kinds of trade barriers, the cheapest way to produce a commodity is to transfer each production process to the location where the cost of production is the lowest. However, a perfect division of labor is usually impossible. If regions having

Table 6.3
Taiwan's Investment in China by Region

Region	1995		1991-1995	
	Case	US$1,000	Case	US$1,000
Mainland China	490	1,092,713	11,254	5,644,483
Guangdong	114	222,748	3,640	1,686,849
Guangzhou	14	49,571	470	253,436
Shenzhen	26	20,910	917	369,894
Zhuhai	2	9,500	102	52,879
Fujian	52	121,656	1,794	777,625
Fuzhou	7	34,568	372	165,527
Xiamen	25	31,433	603	306,558
Hainan	1	649	164	73,665
Jiangsu	163	394,772	2,514	1,678,680
Shanghai	89	224,160	1,313	829,263
Zhejiang	27	57,425	587	262,019
Sichuan	3	6,500	182	101,281
Hebei	48	83,194	780	364,053
Henan	4	2,902	142	26,879
Shandong	8	24,043	356	147,694
Northeast region	15	43,539	320	139,666
Others	19	79,286	405	231,643

Note: Taiwan's investment in China was officially permitted in October 1990.
Source: Investment Commission, Ministry of Economic Affairs, Taiwan, 1995.

different comparative advantages are close to one another in geography and culture, these regions may have a high possibility of cooperation in production. The structure of industry in a country changes with the stage of economic development. When a country becomes more and more capital-abundant, the share in capital-intensive production will probably increase, while the share of labor-intensive production will decline. Owing to the changes in international comparative advantage over time, some industries will decline or even fade out when the country becomes more developed, and some less developed countries will take over the market. Therefore, production will shift from the more developed region to the less developed region, as argued in the "flying geese" hypothesis.

Industries usually have some industry-specific factors of production or inputs. These include industry-specific machines, technology and know-how, market information and channels, trademarks and goodwill, and specialists in designing or production. Domestic demand for and the domestic value of these specific factors or inputs will decline when the industries using these inputs decline or phase out in the process of restructuring. However, if these specific factors or inputs can be exported to other countries where these industries can grow, they probably can obtain much higher prices. Consequently, the reutilization of these specific factors of production or inputs is an important reason for international investment. International investment can make the returns of these factors or inputs higher than the returns they would have when they continue to be used in the mother country. On the other hand, this kind of international investment can also allow the host country to obtain these specific factors or inputs at lower cost than if the host country has to develop these specific factors and inputs itself. As a result, the mother country will find it easier to get rid of the old industries and move into new industries, while the host countries can also develop their new industries much more easily. Therefore, the international investment that transfers these specific factors and inputs from one region to another can promote industrial development and growth in both regions easily. If there is a different degree of economic development between two regions, then the transfer of declining industries from one region to the less developed region is beneficial to both. This is "complementarity in development."

Since many of the specific factors such as designing, management, and marketing are related to human capital, the efficient transfer of these factors often requires mobility of skilled workers. Therefore, the transfer of production and human factors would be easier if the host region had a similar background in culture, custom, and language. Moreover, if two regions are close enough geographically, industries in the home region can still support or cooperate with the transferred industry to yield a higher export level of the host region. This forms a complementarity in production.

The concept of complementarity in development can be used to explain the investment from Taiwan to China in the past few years. The results of sampling surveys indicate that the lower wage rates and the sufficient supply of labor in China represent the most important reason to attract investors from Taiwan. The similarity in language and custom is the second important reason, while lower rents or land cost in China are the third important reason. The second reason is obvious, but both the first and the third reasons have become more important in recent years when economic conditions in Taiwan have changed drastically.

There was a huge trade surplus in Taiwan in the 1980s, with a ratio of trade surplus to GDP reaching nearly twenty percent in 1986. Since 1985, international pressure to reduce the trade surplus has become so intense that the N.T. dollar has appreciated against the U.S. dollar rapidly. The exchange rate appreciated from about forty N.T. dollars per U.S. dollar to twenty-six N.T. dollars per U.S. dollar between 1985 and 1989. As a result, the appreciation of the N.T. dollar in the second half of the 1980s was higher than most other currency appreciations in the world.

In addition, the wage rate in Taiwan rose rapidly in the 1980s. This was partly the direct result of the Labor Law passed in 1983, which raised concern for labor welfare, and partly due to the booming economy, particularly growth in the service sector in the second half of the 1980s. Consequently, the unit labor cost in the manufacturing sector increased much faster than that of all major competitors in the Asian region, with Japan probably the only exception, and the international competitiveness of Taiwan's traditional labor-intensive exported products worsened drastically. In order to maintain the same degree of market competitiveness, Taiwan has to switch from the traditional labor-intensive exports to other exports which can widen Taiwan's comparative advantage (Chen, Schive, and Chu, 1994).

The pressure for structural change in exports after 1985 was further reinforced by two factors, namely the decline of domestic investment since 1980 and the falling share of the manufacturing sector in GDP. Although the appreciation of the N.T. dollar was caused mainly by the huge trade surplus, insufficient domestic investment also had a role to play in Taiwan's trade surplus before 1985. Therefore, the policy of reducing trade surplus almost solely by exchange rate appreciation puts a very high pressure on Taiwan's export sector.

The manufacturing sector, which is the major tradable goods sector in Taiwan, also faced another adjustment pressure. The share of the manufacturing sector in Taiwan compared to most developed countries was quite high in the early 1980s. The experiences of many developed countries indicate that the share of the manufacturing sector in GDP increases in the early development stage and decreases in the later stage. The highest level of this share in the major Western countries was about forty percent of GDP. Taiwan reached a record share for manufacturing in GDP of 39.70 percent in 1987, but fell to only thirty percent in 1994. This declining ratio means that the manufacturing sector has grown slower than the rest of the economy. Certain industries in the manufacturing sector have encountered mounting pressures and difficulties. Investing in China has become the only choice for many labor-intensive industries.

Besides changes in labor cost, inflation in land prices, which rose more than three times in the latter half of 1980s, had not only forced new investors to go abroad, but also enabled old firms and other landlords to acquire more funds for foreign investment by selling their land at high prices. The rising demand for environmental protection at home, increasing global competition, and government incentives offered by the host economy have been mentioned by investors as reasons for investing abroad.

Owing to changes in the economic conditions, outward investment from Taiwan has increased drastically since 1986. Because of geographical proximity and the similarity in language and custom, China probably has the strongest attraction to investors from Taiwan. Since the stages of economic development in Taiwan and China are different, the potential for utilizing complementarity in production and development is very high. For instance, the share of highly labor-intensive products in Taiwan's exports to the United States was 46.27 percent in 1991, while the share was 57.70 percent for China. In addition, 68.18 percent of China's exports to the United States belonged to low human-capital-intensive products, while the ratio was only 37.60 percent for Taiwan. In general, Taiwan has a comparative advantage in products with low labor intensities and high capital intensities or higher human-capital intensities. Taiwan's comparative advantages are in the production of intermediate products, machinery, heavy chemical products, and high-tech products (Chen, 1994; Chen, Schive, and Wu, 1991).

This suggests that Taiwan would invest in the labor-intensive industries in China. Investment was made when there were structural and policy changes in Taiwan in the late 1980s. Between 1990 and 1992, seventy-three percent of Taiwanese investment approved in China was in the manufacturing sector, while the national total of foreign investment in the manufacturing sector approved in China was only fifty-eight percent. In contrast, only fourteen percent of Taiwanese investment was in finance, insurance, and real estate industries, but China's national total of foreign investment in these sectors was twenty-six percent. Taiwanese investments are more concentrated in the manufacturing sector. Within the manufacturing sector itself, the majority of Taiwanese investments are concentrated in the traditional export industries of Taiwan such as electrical and electronic machinery and appliances, miscellaneous products, food, metal products, plastic products, textiles, and wearing apparel.

THE INFLUENCE OF TAIWAN'S INVESTMENT ON CHINA'S EXPORTS

In the past few years Taiwan's investment in China has concentrated mainly on producing Taiwan's traditional manufactured goods (see Lin and Chung, 1992). Lee (1994) estimated that the exports of China created by Taiwanese firms amounted to fifteen billion U.S. dollars, equivalent to twenty percent of the total exports of China in 1992. The actual exports of Taiwanese firms in China may be lower than this estimate because the export ratio of some industries such as the food-processing industry may be much lower than eighty-eight percent. According to Lee (1994), miscellaneous products are the biggest item of Taiwanese firms' exports from China, followed by wearing apparel, and electrical and electronic machinery and appliances. The export created by Taiwanese firms in each of these three industries exceeded two billion U.S. dollars.

Although part of the exports by Taiwanese firms in China may create their own markets or replace the exports of other countries, their original target was to replace the traditional exports of Taiwan. The huge amount of Taiwanese investment in China and the huge amount of exports it created imply that a significant portion of Taiwan's traditional exports might have been replaced by the exports of Taiwanese firms in China. It is not easy to identify the exact amount of Taiwanese exports replaced by China, not to say the amount replaced by Taiwanese firms in China. This is because the market shares of many countries are changing at the same time.

In order to provide some reasonable estimates, we classify Taiwan, Hong Kong, South Korea, China, and the ASEAN countries into a share-increasing group and a share-decreasing group for each product in a specific market. One can assume that the share of Taiwanese products lost was replaced by other economies in the first group in proportion to the share they gained if the total share gained by the first group is higher than the total share lost by the second group. When the total share lost by the second group is higher, we divide the share gained by each economy in the first group into the share that replaced the products of the second group in proportion to the share lost by the economies in the second group.

On the basis of these assumptions and using the most detailed commodity classification available, we find that China has to a considerable extent replaced Taiwanese products. Table 6.4 shows the estimated amount of the market share of different categories of Taiwanese products replaced by China as a proportion of the current market share of Taiwan. It is evident that the replacement is quite serious in the categories of middle-labor-intensive, low-capital-intensive, low-human-capital-intensive, and consumer nondurable goods.

The estimated amount of Taiwanese products replaced by Chinese products formed an important source of the export growth of China. Table 6.5 shows that twenty-one percent of China's export of consumer durable goods to Japan was originally in the market share of Taiwan. This replacement of Taiwanese products in the Japanese market might have increased China's export to Japan by as much as fourteen percent in 1993. In the U.S. market,

Table 6.4
Taiwan's Export Replaced by China as a Percentage of Taiwan's Export to Each Market in Each Category

Classified by Input Factor Intensities

Country/Year	Degree of Labor Intensity			Degree of Capital Intensity			Degree of Humam Capital Intensity			Degree of Energy Intensity		
	High	Mid.	Low	High	Mid.	Low	High	Mid.	Low	High	Mid.	Low
Japan 1988-1993	32.5	62.4	6.0	10.7	49.7	57.7	12.4	22.3	49.5	5.0	53.0	22.4
E.C. 1989-1992	21.0	10.6	11.7	10.7	9.6	38.7	5.3	10.2	36.7	6.2	21.2	12.7
U.S.A. 1989-1993	26.1	27.8	16.5	12.5	13.0	93.9	6.2	17.1	61.0	13.0	32.3	22.9

Classified by Industry

	(1)	(2)	(3)	(4)	(5)	(6)	(7)	(8)	(9)	(10)	(11)	(12)	(13)	(14)	(15)
Japan	6.6	14.2	38.0	86.6	32.3	7.8	20.8	114.9	25.4	34.1	3.2	22.2	41.0	26.6	36.9
E.C.	3.1	14.0	1.5	14.0	28.0	5.3	3.6	37.3	21.4	6.7	3.7	7.12	25.4	7.4	22.2
U.S.A.	25.4	6.6	0.6	58.6	6.8	8.5	7.0	66.0	29.0	10.8	0.9	10.5	42.7	10.1	38.2

Note: (1) = Agriculture, forestry, livestock, and hunting products; (2) = Processed food; (3) = Beverage, and tobacco preparation;
(4) = Energy and materials; (5) = Construction materials; (6) = Intermediate products A; (7) = Intermediate products B;
(8) = Consumer non-durable products; (9) = Consumer durable products; (10) = Machinery; (11) = Transportation equipment;
(12) Heavy chemical enterprises products; (13) = Non-heavy chemical enterprises products; (14) = High technology products;
(15) = Non-high technology products.
Source: a) Taiwan Institute of Economic Research; b) Chen, Schive, and Wu (1991).

Table 6.5
Taiwan's Export Replaced by China as a Percentage of China's Export to Each Market in Each Category

Classified by Input Factor Intensities

Country/Year	Degree of Labor Intensity			Degree of Capital Intensity			Degree of Human Capital Intensity			Degree of Energy Intensity		
	High	Mid.	Low	High	Mid.	Low	High	Mid.	Low	High	Mid.	Low
Japan 1988-1993	13.0	19.5	2.0	6.9	14.7	13.9	3.0	18.4	13.7	2.5	17.5	7.8
E.C. 1989-1992	5.9	7.9	4.4	4.2	6.1	7.3	6.6	7.4	5.9	2.6	6.0	7.0
U.S.A. 1989-1993	10.0	17.9	13.6	13.1	12.1	14.1	7.1	21.5	12.7	9.5	19.5	10.0

Classified by Industry

(1)	(2)	(3)	(4)	(5)	(6)	(7)	(8)	(9)	(10)	(11)	(12)	(13)	(14)	(15)
2.3	15.5	7.1	0.4	3.6	4.1	10.9	16.2	22.0	28.1	15.3	14.5	12.1	16.9	12.0
0.1	0.8	0.3	0.0	18.6	1.9	5.0	7.3	6.3	11.8	6.3	6.9	6.2	6.2	6.4
2.6	4.6	0.1	0.0	13.2	9.1	13.1	13.3	19.2	13.3	3.0	11.6	13.6	9.4	14.1

Note and *Source:* Same as Table 6.4.

market replacement of Taiwanese products might have increased China's export by as much as nineteen percent in 1993. The same ratio in the E.C. market was 6.7 percent. Export replacement is especially significant in Taiwan's traditional export markets.

The estimated amount of Taiwanese export replaced by Chinese products in these three markets is about nine billion U.S. dollars, which is less than the estimated fifteen billion U.S. dollar export of Taiwanese firms in China. It shows that Taiwanese firms in China may also have replaced the markets of other countries, or created new markets, or sold the products in China's domestic market, or the production of Taiwanese firms in China was overestimated. However, since most of the manufacturing plants set up by Taiwanese firms in China are big or even much bigger than the plants they used to have in Taiwan, and some Taiwanese firms in China are newly established firms, the total output would certainly be much higher than the amount of Taiwanese exports replaced by China.

The massive replacement of Taiwan's exports by China may not be so harmful to Taiwan, because China has to import machinery and intermediate products from Taiwan to produce its exports. This new export demand would probably compensate for Taiwan's loss in the traditional exports. At least in the case of Taiwanese firms in China, this new demand is an important source for the upgrading of Taiwan's export and industrial structure.

Lin and Chung (1992) estimate that the ratio of Taiwanese products in the intermediate inputs and machinery of Taiwanese firms in China may be as high as 71.4 percent and eight-five percent, respectively. Lee (1994) also estimates that the direct demand of Taiwanese products by Taiwanese investments in China in 1993 was about twelve billion U.S. dollars, which is fourteen percent lower than the highest estimate of Taiwan's export to China made by the Taiwan's Mainland Affair Committee. Although the actual export of Taiwan to China induced by Taiwanese investment may be lower than this estimate, it is evident that the demand from Taiwanese firms is the major reason for the growth of export from Taiwan to China.

Partly due to the purchase by Taiwanese firms in China, and partly due to the fact that Taiwan has a higher comparative advantage in capital-intensive and skill-intensive products than China, Taiwan's export to Hong Kong and China was concentrated on producer goods in recent years. In 1993, the ratio of consumer goods in Taiwan's total export was 24.8 percent. However, consumer goods accounted only for 9.2 percent of Taiwan's export to Hong Kong and China. On the other hand, the ratio of intermediate products in the export of Taiwan to Japan and the United States was only 35.2 percent and 37.9 percent, respectively, in 1993, but this ratio was 71.1 percent in

Taiwan's export to Hong Kong (Wu, 1994). The shares of food, textile, leather, paper and printing, chemical materials, and chemical products in Taiwan's exports to Hong Kong and China were at least fifty percent higher than their respective shares in Taiwan's total export. The share of machinery was almost fifty percent higher. The influence of Taiwanese investment must be an important reason for this changing trade structure.

CONCLUSION AND PERSPECTIVES

The investment from Taiwan in China in the past few years was the combined result of the structural changes in Taiwan, policy changes in China, and export growth of China. In addition to the capital inflow relating to Taiwan's investment in China, Taiwan's investment also created foreign exchange revenue for China through an increase in trade. The export of Taiwan to China created by these investments was also higher than the estimated amount of Taiwanese export replaced by China in the Japanese, U.S., and E.C. markets. Taiwan's new exports to China are concentrated in producer goods rather than the traditional exports of Taiwan. Therefore, investment in China is also good for the structural change in Taiwan. It is also widely expected that because Taiwanese have family ties in China and Taiwanese firms are smaller than firms from other countries, Taiwanese investment would have a high-technology and information-diffusion effect in China.

However, the potential for China to replace Taiwan's traditional low-human-capital or labor-intensive products and consumer goods is declining. The mutually beneficial experience of the past few years may not continue in the near future. In addition, some Taiwanese firms are planning to engage in the production of producer goods so they can serve their traditional "downstream" firms directly in China or can occupy a larger share in the growing Chinese market. Many Taiwanese firms that have already invested in China are also trying to use more local inputs to reduce their tariff and transportation costs. In short, the trade and investment relationship between Taiwan and China is changing from one of a complementary nature to a competitive nature.

The liberalization of Chinese economy and the establishment of legal systems in China will reduce the comparative advantage of Taiwanese businessmen in China. Taiwanese firms, especially the smaller ones, may find it harder to conduct business in China in the coming years owing to the competition of investors from other countries. In addition, China's interest in Taiwanese investments is also declining. Since 1990, Taiwanese investment has been encouraged by the Chinese authorities and has become a major source of China's foreign capital. Recently, however, labor-intensive production and smaller Taiwanese firms have been discouraged. Moreover, some privileges given to Taiwanese investments in the past have been removed, partly owing to the anxiety of China to join GATT. Meanwhile, many Taiwanese firms have also been discouraged by the unpredictable changes in China's policies, including the large economic advantage demanded by Chinese officers.

Although the population of ASEAN countries is less than that of China, Taiwanese investment in ASEAN countries is only slightly less than Taiwan's investment in China. The development of Taiwan's trade with ASEAN countries is also similar to that between Taiwan and China. Though the market of China is attractive and the language and customs of China are quite familiar to the Taiwanese, China is not the only choice for Taiwanese firms. Unless China opens its domestic market and improves its legal environment and political attitude very soon, the eagerness of Taiwanese businessmen to trade and invest in China may gradually decline.

REFERENCES

Chen, Pochih, 1994, "Foreign Investment in the Hong Kong–Taipei China–Southern China Growth Triangle," in Mintang, Myo Thant, and Kazasu, Hiroshi (eds), *Growth Triangles in Asia*, Oxford: Oxford University Press, pp.74–93.

Chen, Pochih, Schive, Chi and Chu, Cheng Chung, 1994, "Export Structure and Exchange Rate Variation in Taiwan: A Comparison with Japan and the United States," in Ito, Takatoshi, and Krueger, Anne O. (eds), *Macroeconomic Linkage*, Chicago: University of Chicago Press, pp. 227–243.

Chen, Pochih, Schive, Chi and Wu, Chung Chi, 1991, *Report on the Multi-Classifications of Tradable Commodities of the Republic of China* (in Chinese), Taipei: National Taiwan University.

Kan, Chak-Yuen, 1994, *The Emergence of the Golden Economic Triangle—Mainland China, Hong Kong and Taiwan* (in Chinese), Taipei: Lifework Press.

Kao, Chang, 1995, *Economic Reform in China and the Cross Strait Economic Relations* (in Chinese), Taipei: Wu Nan Book Publishing Company.

Lee, Yu-chun, 1994, *Further Studies on the Influences of Outward Investment on the Manufacturing Sector of Taiwan* (in Chinese), Taipei, Taiwan Institute of Economic Research.

Lin, Li-chuen, and Chin Chung, 1992, *Research on Taiwanese Firms' Trade and Investment in China* (in Chinese), Taipei: Chung Hwa Institute of Economic Research.

Wu, Ching Tai, 1994, *Report on the Research and Upgrading Indicators of the Manufacturing Sector* (in Chinese), Taipei: Taiwan Institute of Economic Research.

7

Foreign Exchange Markets in China: Evolution and Performance

CLEMENT YUK-PANG WONG and
KENNETH W. K. LO

INTRODUCTION

Exchange rate black markets exist in many developing countries owing to the imposition of exchange controls on current and capital accounts transactions. Typically, exchange controls are used to defend an overvalued fixed exchange rate, to preserve foreign exchange reserves, and to insulate the domestic economy from foreign economic shocks. As a consequence, some of the foreign exchange is diverted and sold illegally in the foreign exchange black market. The excess demand of foreign exchange is reflected in the amount by which the black market exchange rate exceeds the offical rate, or the "black market premium." Marcus (1992) argues that parallel markets are rarely the cause of economic problems in a country, but rather the consequence and a symptom of those problems. The exchange rate was usually pegged by the central bank, and only authorized agents were licensed to transact. Since the demand for foreign exchange is high, the supply of hard currencies is either sold illegally or diverted to t' ·under-ground network. The selling price is always higher than the off in order to meet the excess demand.

Various economic distortions result from the emergence o black market. Exchange control leads to an overvalued curr· exports expensive, and imports are encouraged. A high blar mium weakens the effectiveness of capital controls, causes a deterioration in the balance of payment, and increases the cost of defending the exchange rate policy (Banuri, 1989). Agénor and Delbecque (1991) argue that if the economic agents, such as exporters, realize that there is a limited amount of foreign reserve in the central bank, they will increase the diversion of export receipts from the official to the black market. Substitution between domestic and foreign currencies will become inevitable since domestic residents are aware of their currency depreciation, and avoid inflation tax (Agénor, 1991, 1992). The presence of a large black market premium will continue to erode the effectiveness of government policies.

Recent empirical studies (Dornbusch et al., 1983; Canto, 1985; Koveos and Seifert, 1986; Huizinga, 1991; Kamin, 1993; Abdel-Mahmoud and Abdel-Rahman, 1994; Phylaktis and Kassimatis, 1994) on the foreign exchange black markets in the less well developed countries conclude that the size of the black market premium is largely the result of: a) excessive money growth; b) high expectation on devaluation; c) high anticipated inflation rate; and d) low degree of law enforcement.

Since China started her economic reform about two decades ago, the foreign exchange market has undergone major changes as the economy underwent a transition from a rigidly planned to a market-oriented one. China's exchange rate system has changed from a fixed exchange rate regime with strict capital controls in the prereform period to a managed float exchange rate system in the postreform period. Current account convertibility is expected to take place before the end of the 1990s.[1] Similar to most developing countries that maintain capital controls, a sizable foreign exchange black market exists alongside the official foreign exchange market. However, the experience of China is rather unique in that an officially sanctioned swap foreign exchange market was established in the reform period to satisfy the growing demand for foreign exchange that came with the rapid economic growth. Despite the existence of the swap market, however, the wide arrays of capital and trade restrictions led to the emergence of a foreign exchange black market in China until the unification of the exchange rate in 1994.

FOREIGN TRADE AND EXCHANGE REFORM: 1978 TO 1993

The development of the foreign exchange market in China is intertwined with its trade reform and open door policy. In the prereform period, the allocation of foreign exchange was completely determined by the state-controlled foreign trade plans. All foreign exchange earnings from exports must be remitted to and all foreign exchange needed for imports must be purchased from the Bank of China, which is the foreign exchange bank of China. The overvalued Renminbi (Rmb) in the prereform period did not serve any economic function but was merely a price to calculate the domestic currency profits and losses. Most foreign trade corporations (FTCs) incurred domestic currency losses from exports and imports. These losses were subsidized by the state budget. By 1986, the amount of fiscal subsidies to FTCs exceeded two percent of Gross Domestic Product (World Bank, 1994, pp.25–26).

China started to decentralize its foreign trade in 1984 by allowing market forces to direct foreign trade patterns. This gradually reduced the state's fiscal burden, and the percentages of exports and imports under the mandatory trade plans were gradually reduced while those outside the plans increased. The FTCs were given more autonomy in their production decisions and became responsible for their domestic currency profits and losses. A foreign trade contract system was introduced in 1988, under which provincial governments must sign a contract with the Ministry of Foreign Economic Relations and Trade (MOFERT) for a fixed amount of foreign exchange earnings including the amount to be turned over to the state and the amount of fiscal subsidies. In 1991, the government eventually abolished the entire export trade plan and substantially reduced the scope and size of the import trade plan. Fiscal subsidies to exports were completely eliminated, and those to imports were reduced.

Reforms in the foreign exchange system have been closely related to its foreign trade reform. The Renminbi started to depreciate in the postreform period from a level around Rmb 1.5 per U.S. dollar in 1979, but the initial depreciation was not large enough to cover the costs of earning foreign exchange needed by exporting enterprises, and fiscal subsidies given to these enterprises continued to grow. Effectively, this imposed an export tax on the exporters, thereby reducing their incentive to export, and drove up the exchange rates in the swap and black markets. Figure 7.1, which has been plotted in logarithm form, summarizes the movements of the black and official market exchange rates, and the major events that occurred during the period 1974–1993.

In an effort to reduce the trade subsidies, a dual exchange rate system was adopted in 1981. This included the official exchange rate for noncommodity trade and a further depreciated internal settlement rate for commodity trade (set at Rmb 2.8 per U.S. dollar) (see Sung, 1991, p. 47, Table 3.1). The internal settlement rate was abolished in 1985 when it merged with the official exchange rate at Rmb 2.84 per U.S. dollar (see Figure 7.1).

Figure 7.1
The Black and Official Market Exchange Rates (log)

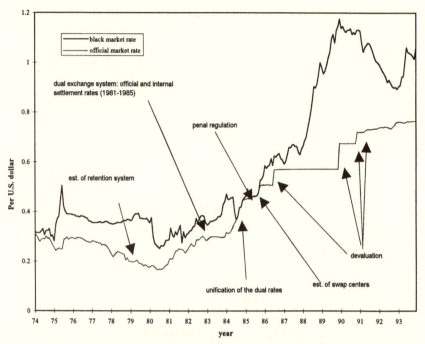

The second stage of the dual exchange rate system was introduced in 1986 with the establishment of the foreign exchange adjustment centers (FEACs), or swap centers. The Chinese government decentralized the administration of foreign exchange in 1979 by granting foreign exchange retention quotas to enterprises. These quotas represented the portion of foreign exchange earnings that enterprises were entitled to purchase from the Bank of China at the official exchange rate. By 1986, however, these retention quotas could be traded in the local FEACs where enterprises could "adjust" their foreign exchange needs. Since the price of these quotas was determined according to market conditions, the swap market had effectively become an officially sanctioned "free" foreign exchange market.

The introduction of the foreign exchange retention system has indeed helped to offset part of the adverse effects on trade and welfare from the overvalued official exchange rate. The incentive to export improved as exporters could sell their foreign exchange earnings in the swap market at a higher price than that in the official foreign exchange market. Wang (1993) documents the overvaluation of the official exchange rate and shows that the swap rate depreciated faster than the official rate (see Table 7.1).

Table 7.1
Renminbi Exchange Rate Indices and Changes

Interval	Nominal Rate (Rmb / 100 U.S. dollars)	Swap Rate (Rmb/100 U.S. dollars)	Real Effective Rate Index	Nominal Effective Rate Index
1980–1982	149.84 - 189.25	164.82 - 318.00	60.10 - 74.30	65.61 - 71.95
	(-20.82%)	(-48.16%)	(+23.63%)	(+9.66%)
1982–1985	189.25 - 293.67	318.00 - 393.67	74.30 - 100.00	71.95 - 100
	(-35.56%)	(-19.22%)	(+34.59%)	(+38.99%)
1985–1987	293.67 - 372.21	393.67 - 472.21	100 - 145.79	100 - 163.20
	(-21.10%)	(-16.63%)	(+45.79%)	(+63.20%)
1987–1988	372.21 - 372.21	472.21 - 600.00	145.79 - 132.62	163.20 - 174.12
	(+0.00%)	(-21.30%)	(-9.03%)	(+6.69%)

Source: Wang, L., 1993, *The Devaluation of Renminbi and Exchange Rate Policy*, Beijing: The People University of China Press, pp.147-148.

THE FOREIGN EXCHANGE BLACK MARKET

Foreign exchange transactions in China have been subjected to legal restrictions on usage and an official price ceiling. Various kinds of trade restrictions such as tariff, licensing procedures, and foreign trade plans created the incentives to smuggle and fake invoices in order to satisfy excess demand for the imported goods.[2] The demand for foreign exchange to finance this illegal trade further stimulated the development of the foreign exchange black market. Another source of demand for foreign exchange that could not be satisfied by the official and swap markets derives from capital account transactions. In times of acute inflation, demand for foreign exchange for portfolio diversification rises in order to hedge against the inflation tax from holding domestic currency (Agénor, 1992). In addition, economic upheavals and political instabilities could lead to capital flights and increase the demand for foreign currency. The rapid investment boom, coupled with the persistent trade deficit, and a high inflation rate for a prolonged period have increased the demand for foreign exchange tremendously. The increase in the capital flight to GNP ratio reflects a large outflow of capital from China.[3]

Although the establishment of the FEACs could alleviate the shortage of foreign exchange, they could not solve the problem entirely. The FEACs were local organizations with membership restricted to local enterprises only. Access to FEACs to purchase foreign exchange was subjected to approval and was limited to foreign exchange needs that conformed with the government's priority list. Therefore, while the official exchange rate remained overvalued, the excess demand for foreign exchange could only be satisfied from the black market where the exchange rate is truely market-determined.[4]

The currency supplied to the black market came from various sources: overinvoicing of imports, underinvoicing of exports, smuggling of exports, and remittance from overseas Chinese to their relatives in China (see Grosse, 1994; Wahba, 1991). As Figure 7.2 shows, the size of the black market premium became larger and exhibited a greater degree of volatility in the postreform period. Black market sanctions first appeared in 1980. The principal penalties for violations of foreign exchange controls were: a) compulsory exchange of the foreign currency; b) confiscation of the foreign currency; c) fines; and d) punishment as determined by the judicial authorities.[5]

Two major policies were enacted in the early 1980s to restrict black market activities. First, foreign exchange certificates (FECs) were issued to tourists and business visitors in specific locations. This policy reduced

Figure 7.2
The Black Market Premium (log)

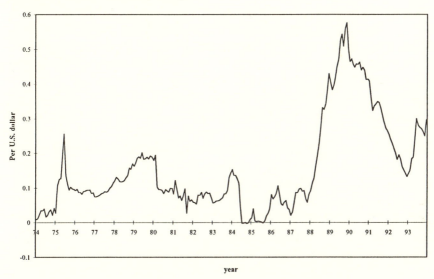

the supply of foreign exchange to the black market, but a black market for FECs was created instead. Second, foreign exchange deposits were introduced to absorb some of the foreign exchange into the banking system. Black market activities started to grow in 1983–1984 when the economy experienced double-digit growth, and imports grew by forty-six percent and 105 percent in 1984 and 1985, respectively. Between 1984 and 1986, the accumulated current account deficit reached 16.4 billion U.S. dollars and the international reserves declined by 4.42 billion U.S. dollars (Shanghai Asian Research Center, 1993, p. 29). Money supply grew at thirty to forty percent and inflation exceeded ten percent for the first time in 1985. Reports suggested that there were more than twenty black market locations with regular dealing in Beijing alone, and the total transaction amounted to 2.15 million U.S. dollars in 1988.[6]

There was a drastic increase in black market transactions in the 1988–1990 period. China's inflation exceeded eighteen percent and exerted a depreciation pressure on the Renminbi. The swap market rate increased from Rmb 5.7 per U.S. dollar to Rmb 6.5 per U.S. dollar between 1987 and 1988. The depreciation of the black market exchange rate was even greater. When the government tightened the money supply in 1989, the swap market exchange rate appreciated to Rmb 5.9 per U.S. dollar as many enterprises were forced to sell their foreign exchange in the swap market, but the black market exchange rate experienced a huge depreciation during this period, suggesting that the demand for foreign exchange to hedge against inflation remained strong. Moreover, the aftermath of the Tiananmen Square incident in 1989 also triggered massive capital flights and contributed to the depreciation in the black market. It was not until 1992 and 1993 that the black market premium narrowed when the official exchange rate was gradually depreciated and the swap market was further liberalized. The foreign exchange retention ratios were substantially increased to approximately eighty percent in 1991 as a result of the abolition of the export plan.

A comparison between the official, swap, and black market exchange rates is given in Figure 7.3.[7] The swap market exchange rate initially depreciated more than the black market rate until the first half of 1988. The differential between the swap and black market exchange rates accelerated to an all-time high of Rmb 9.1 per U.S. dollar in the fourth quarter of 1989, though it slowly declined to Rmb 0.69 per U.S. dollar in the fourth quarter of 1992. It appears that the swap market could not meet the demand for foreign exchange in times of extreme economic pressure, probably owing to the restrictive institutional structure and exchange controls in the swap market.[8]

DYNAMIC BEHAVIOR AND METHODOLOGICAL ISSUES

The dynamic relationship between the official and black market exchange rates has received considerable attention in recent years (Dornbusch et al., 1983; Phylaktis, 1991; Phylaktis and Kassimatis, 1994). The relationship between official and black market rates can be examined by looking at the long-term cointegration, causality relationship and the dynamic behavior. The existence of a long-term relationship implies a black market premium consistent with the prediction of the portfolio-balance model (Dornbusch et al., 1983; Macedo, 1982; Frenkel, 1990). The causality relationship can provide useful information about the role of the currency black market in the exchange rate policy. The other issue of concern is the efficiency of the currency black market. It may not be efficient because of its clandestine nature and fragmented market structure.

The following procedure for the estimation and investigation of the relationship between the black and official exchange rates is applied: 1) a structural equation is constructed to show that the black market exchange rate is driven by the official rate, or there is a one-to-one relationship between the two market rates; 2) the unit root test is applied to see if the two series have the same order of integration, and the cointegration technique is employed to test the long-term equilibrium relationship; and 3) a

Figure 7.3
Official, Black, and Swap Market Exchange Rates (log)

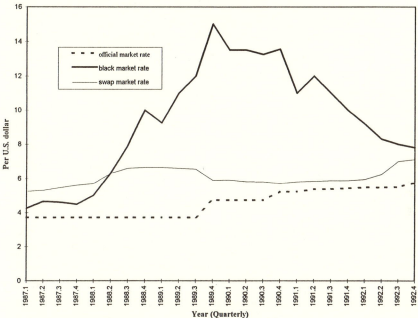

Year (Quarterly)

causality test is applied to examine the causation between the black and official exchange rates.

The long-term relationship between the official and the black market exchange rates can be represented by:

$$BMR_t = \alpha_0 + \alpha_1\,OMR_t + \mu_t \qquad (1)$$

where BMR_t and OMR_t are the black market and official market rates at time t respectively, and μ_t is the disturbance term, which is assumed to be a white noise. If there exists a long-term relationship between the two exchange rates, they will not drift apart from each other and the disturbance term will be a stationary process. The parameters, α_0 and α_1, are tested against the null hypothesis of the vector, $(0, 1)'$, to see if the black market rate may drift away from the official market rate, and whether there is a one-to-one relationship between the two market rates.[9]

In order to examine the comovement of the two exchange rates, the cointegration technique is used to test the long-term equilibrium (see Granger, 1983, 1988; Engle and Granger, 1987). A cointegrated series implies the existence of market inefficiency due to the existence of unexploited opportunities. The error-correction vector explains the process of an immediate overshooting and then the eventual reversal to the long-term equilibrium level. Three tests are used to investigate the degree of integration: Dickey-Fuller (DF), Augmented Dickey-Fuller (ADF), and Phillips-Perron (PP) Unit Root tests (see Dickey, 1976; Dickey and Fuller, 1979, 1981; Phillips, 1987; Perron, 1988; Banerjee, Dolado, Galbraith, and Hendry, 1993). If the two rates are integrated in the same order, the residual of the linear combination of the two series is stationary. The cointegration technique is carried out by using the residual-based ADF approach proposed in Engle and Granger (1987) and the Johansen's full maximum likelihood (FIML) approach (Johansen, 1988, 1989; Johansen and Juselius, 1990). If cointegration between the two series is found, an error-correction mechanism (ECM) can then be applied by using the Granger Representation Theorem.

To test the persistence of the random walk component in the black market series, a technique called the "variance ratio" test (Cochrane, 1988; Lo and MacKinlay, 1988, 1989) is employed. This test is preferred to the Dickey-Fuller test because the disturbances are not always identical and independent, and can help to find out whether black market rate fluctuations are permanent or not. The random walk carries the permanent component of a change while the stationary series (deterministic trend) carries the temporary part of a change. If the fluctuation is temporary, the shock today will ultimately be reversed in the long-term (Cochrane, 1988, p. 898). Suppose a series is a random walk with drift such that:

$$Y_t - Y_{t-1} = \delta + \varepsilon_t \tag{2}$$

The variance in its k-differences grows linearly with the difference of k. If the series follows a random walk, it must be the case that the variance of the k-differences is k times the variance of its first difference. That is:

$$\text{Var}(Y_t - Y_{t-k}) = \text{Var}(Y_t - Y_{t-1}) \cdot k \tag{3}$$

If we let $\text{Var}(Y_t - Y_{t-k})$ be σ_k^2 and $\text{Var}(Y_t - Y_{t-1})$ be σ_1^2, the null hypothesis of testing a random walk is:

$$H_0 = \sigma_k^2 / \sigma_1^2 = 1, \text{ against} \tag{4}$$

$$H_1 = \sigma_k^2 / \sigma_1^2 \neq 1 \tag{5}$$

Sims' (1972) test uses a distributed lag regression:

$$X_t = \sum_{i=-\infty}^{\infty} \beta_i X_{t-i} + v_t \tag{6}$$

where $\beta_t = 0$ for all $i < 0$ if X does not cause Y. For testing whether X "Granger-causes" Y, one should first compute a two-sided distributed lag of X on the past, present, and future value of Y, and then test the leads of Y.

The black market data are the month-end figures, obtained from the *World Currency Yearbook* for the period of 1974M1 to 1993M12. The official rates are obtained from the CD-Rom, *International Financial Statistics*. All quotations are against the U.S. dollar and the series is in logarithmic form.

EMPIRICAL RESULTS

The series of black and official rates are first checked for stationarity by using three types of unit root tests, namely the Dickey-Fuller (DF), Augmented Dickey-Fuller (ADF), and Phillips Perrons (PP) tests.[10] The tests include a constant and a trend term. For the ADF and PP tests, the assigned optimal lag is 14 (see Schwert, 1987).[11] The statistics of DF$\{\gamma\}$, ADF$\{\tau_\tau\}$, and PP$\{\tau_p\}$ are tested against the null hypothesis [H_0: $\alpha_2 = 0$, $\alpha_5 = 0$, $\rho_{10} = 1$]. The two F-test statistics, Φ_2 and, Φ_3, are used to test the hypothesis of zero drift and non-zero drift, respectively. The null hypothesis of a unit root cannot be rejected at the ten percent level for both variables (see Table 7.2). Since, Φ_2 and Φ_3 are not statistically significant, both BMR and OMR follow a random walk with no drift. The null hypothesis of a unit root in the first difference is rejected in all three tests for both variables. Therefore, the BMR and OMR are integrated at order 1, implying that the levels of the two series are not stationary.[12] Cointegration does not exist at the five percent level; the only exception is that a ten percent significant level is found in the ADF tests (see Table 7.3).

The Johansen's residual-based approach test (Cheung and Lai, 1993) is applied in order to justify the rejection of no cointegration (see Table 7.4). A maximum of eight lags is used to test whether the results are sensitive to lag specification. In all cases, we cannot reject the null hypothesis of no cointegration at the five percent or ten percent levels.

The lack of cointegration between the official and the black market exchange rates has two implications. First, it casts doubts on the validity of the portfolio-balance model to explain the movement of the black market

Table 7.2
Autoregressive Unit Root Tests of Black Market and Official Rates

(Level)						
Variable	DF		ADF		PP	
	γ	τ_r	Φ_2	Φ_3	$Z(\tau_\rho)$	$Z(\Phi_3)$
BMR	-1.4649	-2.3395	2.5761	3.2269	-1.7168	1.8312
OMR	-2.3146	-1.9386	2.4795	2.1922	-2.2947	4.6268
(First Difference)						
BMR	-14.041*	-2.9067	2.9269	4.3836	-14.517*	105.58*
OMR	-14.745*	-3.1822*	3.4942	5.2259	-14.883*	110.88*

Note: * denotes significance at ten percent level. The ten percent asymptotic critical value of DF $\{\gamma\}$ is (-3.13), the values of ADF $\{ \tau_r, \Phi_2, \Phi_3 \}$ are (-3.13), (4.03), and (5.34), and the values of PP $\{ Z(\tau_r)$ & $Z(\Phi_3) \}$ are (-3.13) and (5.34), respectively. (See Davidson and MacKinnon, 1993).

Table 7.3
Residual-Based (ADF) Approach of Cointegrating Regression Tests of Black Market and Official Rates

Regressand	Regressor	DF	ADF	PP
BMR	OMR	-1.8350	-3.1178*	-2.3845
OMR	BMR	-1.6843	-3.1647*	-2.2462

Note: * denotes significance at ten percent asymptotic level. The critical values of DF, ADF, and PP are (-3.36) and (-3.04) for five percent and ten percent level, respectively. (See MacKinnon, 1990.)

exchange rate in China. This is in sharp contrast to the findings of Phylaktis and Kassimatis (1994) that a long-term relationship exists between the official and black market exchange rates in a sample of Pacific Basin countries. Second, it provides evidence for a weak form of market efficiency.

To test if the black market exchange rate is characterized by a random walk process, we investigate the persistence (permanent) effect on the change of BMR using Cochrane's (1988) variance ratio approach. Using Equation (3), we first lag the k-differences up to 180. Since the data are month-end figures, the total 180 lags represents the time span of fifteen years, which is large enough to capture the permanent component of the random walk. Table 7.5 shows that the values of the variance ratio initially

Table 7.4
Results of Johansen Test on Black and Official Exchange Rates

Lag	Null	Alter.	Stat.	Null	Alter.	Stat.
		λ_{max}			Trace	
1	$r=0$	$r=1$	3.7368	$r=0$	$r\geq1$	5.0550
	$r\leq1$	$r=2$	1.3182	$r\leq1$	$r=2$	1.3182
2	$r=0$	$r=1$	4.2051	$r=0$	$r\geq1$	5.6416
	$r\leq1$	$r=2$	1.4365	$r\leq1$	$r=2$	1.4365
3	$r=0$	$r=1$	4.1018	$r=0$	$r\geq1$	4.9974
	$r\leq1$	$r=2$	0.8956	$r\leq1$	$r=2$	0.8956
4	$r=0$	$r=1$	5.7603	$r=0$	$r\geq1$	6.6617
	$r\leq1$	$r=2$	0.9014	$r\leq1$	$r=2$	0.9014
5	$r=0r$	$r=1$	6.8349	$r=0$	$r\geq1$	7.7990
	≤1	$r=2$	0.9641	$r\leq1$	$r=2$	0.9641
6	$r=0$	$r=1$	5.8312	$r=0$	$r\geq1$	6.6647
	$r\leq1$	$r=2$	0.8335	$r\leq1$	$r=2$	0.8335
7	$r=0$	$r=1$	6.8713	$r=0$	$r\geq1$	7.5506
	$r\leq1$	$r=2$	0.6793	$r\leq1$	$r=2$	0.6793
8	$r=0$	$r=1$	5.3937	$r=0$	$r\geq1$	6.1055
	$r\leq1$	$r=2$	0.7118	$r\leq1$	$r=2$	0.7118

Note: Alter. = Alternative. Stat. = Statistics. A trend variable is included in the VAR.

The ninety five percent and ninety percent critical values for λ_{max} and trace statistics are as follows (see Osterwald-Lenum, 1990):

null	λ_{max} 95%	90%	Trace 95%	90%
$r=0$	14.069	12.071	15.410	13.325
$r\leq1$	3.762	2.687	3.762	2.687

Table 7.5
Variance Ratio Test on Black Market Exchange Rates

k	Variance Ratio	Standard Error	k	Variance Ratio	Standard Error
1	1.0000	(0.0747)	95	1.7379	(1.6243)
5	1.3473	(0.2269)	100	1.6656	(1.6254)
10	1.5376	(0.3702)	105	1.5797	(1.6087)
15	1.7394	(0.5186)	110	1.4802	(1.5722)
20	1.9614	(0.6829)	115	1.3223	(1.4645)
25	2.0961	(0.8253)	120	1.2017	(1.3876)
30	2.1439	(0.9357)	125	1.0819	(1.3024)
35	2.1832	(1.0416)	130	0.9127	(1.1457)
40	2.1312	(1.1106)	135	0.7909	(1.0356)
45	2.0721	(1.1494)	140	0.6657	(0.9095)
50	1.9970	(1.1829)	145	0.5500	(0.7846)
55	1.9342	(1.2178)	150	0.4713	(0.7026)
60	1.9491	(1.2994)	155	0.3923	(0.6117)
65	1.9806	(1.3938)	160	0.2819	(0.4603)
70	1.9906	(1.4749)	165	0.1933	(0.3311)
75	1.9788	(1.5405)	170	0.0949	(0.1707)
80	1.9083	(1.5581)	175	0.0595	(0.1127)
85	1.8306	(1.5654)	180	0.0752	(0.1504)
90	1.7752	(1.5878)			

Note: The standard errors of the variance ratios (σ^2_k/σ^2_1) are computed as $(4k/3T)^{.5} \; d^2_k/d^2_1$, whereas k and T are the number of lags and observations; and d^2_k/d^2_1 are the estimates of σ^2_k and σ^2_1, respectively (see Cochrane, 1988).

moved upward (i.e., VR > 1) as k increased, but then shifted downward after sufficient lags were applied. The size of VR was reduced by fifty percent when k was approximately equal to 145 (i.e., about twelve years). The conclusion is that the movement of BMR is largely driven by the random walk component, which is very persistent. The random walk component falls after the first 110 lags. The variance ratio estimation of the BMR indicates that VR was greater than 1 in the first 120 lags, but after 150 lags, the value of VR declined by fifty percent. The random walk shock is therefore very persistent and large. This test further supports the previous conclusion on the nonexistence of cointegration and provides a stronger argument on the movement of the black market rate.

Traditional causality tests are valid only when the change of the original variable is not cointegrated. Since the validity and the interpretation of the causality test are highly sensitive to the lag specification (Thornton and Batten, 1985), Schwert's (1987) approach is used to determine the number of lags. Table 7.6 shows the causality result that BMR unidirectional causes OMR. Change in the BMR does have a feedback effect on the Chinese authorities to reconsider their foreign exchange policy.

The empirical results lead to several conclusions. First, the overvaluation of the official rate was due largely to the restrictive exchange rate policy. Second, as China exposed herself to world trade and economic reforms, demand for foreign currencies rose. The black market rate is determined by free market forces. The movement of the BMR leads the OMR, and the government's response to changes in the official rate was based on changes in the BMR.

However, the situation changed when unification of the exchange rate took place in 1994. In addition to the large black market premium, there were other pressing reasons for the Chinese authority to unify the foreign

Table 7.6
Causality Test on Black and Official Market Exchange Rates

Direction	Statistical Significance	Causality
BMR ---> OMR	$F(14, 180) = 5.22713$	Yes
OMR ---> BMR	$F(14, 180) = 0.32786$	No

Note: " ---> " denotes causality direction from left to right. The results indicate the F-statistical test at five percent significance level. The number of lags is fourteen (see Schwert, 1987).

exchange rate. One obvious reason is the large import bill since the late 1980s. There was also political pressure from the international community when China applied for entrance to the World Trade Organization, and from overseas countries whenever China seeks bilateral trading relationships. The unification helps China pave her way to the international community.[13]

UNIFICATION OF THE EXCHANGE RATE SYSTEM

On January 1, 1994, China took a major step toward current account convertibility by unifying its official and swap market exchange rates. The official exchange rate was depreciated by fifty percent from Rmb 5.8 per U.S. dollar to Rmb 8.7 per U.S. dollar at the end of 1993. Three months later, designated foreign exchange banks (DFEBs) were established in major cities with Shanghai as the headquarters to replace the foreign exchange adjustment centers. By the end of 1994, the interbank foreign exchange system had 303 members from twenty-six cities, with a cumulated transaction volume of 40.7 billion U.S. dollars from April to December 1994 (World Bank, 1994).

Under the new regime, the foreign exchange retention system is abolished and domestic enterprises are now required to sell all their foreign exchange earnings to and purchase foreign exchange from the DFEBs at the exchange rates quoted by the banks. These exchange rates are based on the rate set by the People's Bank of China, according to the supply and demand conditions in the previous trading day. The DFEBs must keep a certain percentage of their foreign exchange assets, and any surplus or shortfall must be eliminated by trading with other DFEBs or the Central Bank (*Asiamoney*, 1994).

The new interbank market has improved the efficiency of foreign exchange allocation in several aspects. First, it allows the exchange rate differentials to be eliminated quickly. Second, elimination of the administered official exchange rate means that the swap market rate has expanded to reflect all legal foreign exchange transactions. Third, elimination of the retention quotas has led to the hoarding of foreign exchange.

Movement of the Renminbi since the unification has been steady and has exhibited a gradual and mild appreciation against the U.S. dollar. In the first three months of 1994, the Renminbi did not deviate more than 0.2 percent from Rmb 8.7 per U.S. dollar. After the establishment of the interbank market in April 1994, the Renminbi started its steady appreciation from Rmb 8.6847 to Rmb 8.4462 per U.S. dollar in December 1994. Figure 7.4 plots the official and black market rates since unification.

Figure 7.4
Postunification Exchange Rate Movements

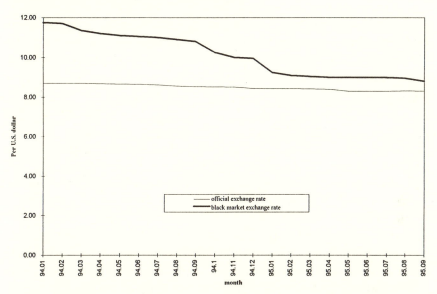

Several factors contributed to the appreciation since April 1994. The most important factor is the massive capital inflows triggered by the unification. The new foreign exchange system has tightened the control of the central bank on foreign exchange circulation in the country. Under the new system, the foreign currency accounts of most enterprises are abolished. As a result, billions of U.S. dollars held by enterprises must be channeled back to the DFEBs. Limited by the foreign exchange balance ratio set by the Central Bank, the DFEB had to sell this foreign exchange in the interbank market, causing the Renminbi to appreciate. Another source of capital inflow came from the increase in foreign direct investment due to optimism about the Chinese economy. Finally, the interest rate differential between the domestic and U.S. interest rates also led to possible capital inflows.

The improvement in trade balance and the more restrictive credit policy imposed after the unification are additional factors. The one-time depreciation of fifty percent has improved the competitiveness of Chinese exports. Exports in 1994 grew by thirty-two percent to reach 121 billion U.S. dollars and the trade balance turned from a deficit in 1993 to a surplus in 1994. Finally, even though the monetary growth rates in 1994 remained high, the tightening of credit extended to many state enterprises has forced them to sell foreign exchange in the interbank market in exchange for domestic currency, contributing to the appreciation of Renminbi.

A major problem caused by the massive capital inflow, however, is the loss of control over the base money. In an effort to slow down the appreciation of the Renminbi, the People's Bank of China was forced to purchase foreign exchange from the DFEBs, and this increased the supply of base money in the process. As a result, China s international reserves rose from twenty billion U.S. dollars at the end of 1993 to over fifty billion U.S. dollars at the end of 1994. Monetary policy in China has become more dependent on external conditions.

CONCLUDING REMARKS

The existence of a positive black market premium suggests that the official rate is overvalued. This will hamper domestic capital mobilization. Moreover, the high demand for foreign exchange through the black market would severely undermine the creditability of economic policies. The existence of the currency black market also reduces the effectiveness of monetary policy to curb the high inflation. Excess money supply would be transmitted through the banking system if the curb market is active.

The various restrictions in the preunification period had exerted a great pressure on the official exchange rate, resulting in a positive black market premium in China. Empirical work shows that the BMR was determined by the free market and influenced the movement of the OMR. The unification of the exchange rate system in 1994 was an important step in China's foreign exchange reform. The falling black market premium after the unification suggests that the level of black market activities has subsided. The black market premium has steadily declined from Rmb 3.05 per U.S. dollar at the beginning of 1994 to Rmb 0.4812 per U.S. dollar in September 1995.

The new system does have several implications on the black market. First, it tightens the Central Bank's control over foreign exchanges as all foreign exchanges must be redirected to the banking system. Enterprises can no longer hold on to their retention quota, thus preventing them from diverting these quotas to the black market for profit making. Second, the abolition of the Foreign Exchange Certificate helped to reduce black market activities. Third, the more efficient allocation of foreign exchange under the new system has also curbed black market activities by relaxing the tight supply situations of foreign exchange in some areas.

Under the unified system, the authorization process of acquiring foreign exchange for normal current account transactions has been abolished. However, most of the restrictions on the uses of foreign exchange under the FEAC system remain. Therefore, the degree of current account convertibility has not increased significantly. The success of the foreign exchange market reform depends very much on the speed and scope of liberalization in current account transactions. The other crucial factor is the determination to pursue stable macroeconomic policies. Excessive growth in the money supply and imprudent management in the fiscal budget would subject the Renminbi to depreciation pressure and rekindle black market activity again. Further liberalization of the exchange rate is expected. Although full convertibility of the current account will take place in 1996 at the earliest, China's repeated commitment to world trade and her intention to play a bigger role in international organization has meant that the Renminbi has to become an internationally acceptable currency.

NOTES

1. *South China Morning Post*, November 14, 1995, Hong Kong.

2. The general tariff rates in China ranged from three percent to 180 percent, depending on the nature of the imported goods and their categories. In addition, a regulatory tax ranging from twenty percent to eighty percent was applied to some imports. (See *World Currency Yearbook*, 1988–1989, New York.)

3. The construction of capital flight has been suggested by Edwards (1989). The estimation of capital flight increased from Rmb 4.86 billion in 1987 to Rmb 52.44 billion in 1992. The following table shows the changes. Negative sign represents capital outflow from the country.

Year	1986	1987	1988	1989	1990	1991	1992
Rmb (billion)	-12.11	-4.86	-3.28	-6.63	-33.44	-34.81	-52.44

One popular method is to divert foreign exchange before it even crosses the Chinese border. Silk (1988) argues that "it is possible when foreign exchange proceeds from a sale made outside China are diverted to a foreign bank account and substituted with Renminbi domestically."

4. Shanghai Asian Research Center (1993), *Issues on the Renminbi Exchange Rate Analysis*, Hong Kong: Joint Publishing (HK) Co. Ltd., p. 28.

5. The penalties are stated in Article 31 of the Provisional Regulations. See Brahm (1993) for details.

6. Brahm (1993), p. 44.

7. The sources of data are *International Financial Statistics, World Currency Yearbook,* and *World Bank* (1994).

8. For a thorough discussion on the Chinese foreign exchange system, see Tsang (1994).

9. Dornbusch *et al.* (1983) and Phylaktis (1991) used the portfolio balance model of black market rate and show how the expectation of future official

devaluation leads to an immediate jump in the black market rate (overshooting effect) and eventually reduces the premium as the realized official rate depreciates.

10. The regression equations are as follow:

DF:　$(1-L)Y_t = \alpha_1 + \alpha_2\,Y_{t-1} + \alpha_3(\text{time}) + \mu_t$

$\quad H_{0:}\ \alpha_2 = 0$ 　　　　　　　　　　t–ratio (γ test)

ADF: $(1-L)Y_t = \alpha_4 + \alpha_5 Y_{t-1} + \alpha_6(\text{time}) + \sum_{i=1}^{n} \alpha_7(1-L)Y_{t-i} + \mu_t$

$\quad H_{0:}\ \alpha_5 = 0$ 　　　　　　　　　　t–ratio (τ_τ test)

$\quad H_{0:}\ \alpha_4 = \alpha_5 = \alpha_6 = 0$ 　　　　F–test Φ_2 (zero drift)

$\quad H_{0:}\ \alpha_5 = \alpha_6 = 0$ 　　　　　　F–test Φ_3 (nonzero drift)

PP:　$Y_t = \psi_8 + \gamma_9(t - T/2) + \rho_{10}Y_{t-1} + V_{ct}$

$\quad H_{0:}\ \rho_{10} = 1$ 　　　　　　　　　$Z(\tau_p)$ test

$\quad H_{0:}(\gamma_9, \rho_{10}) = (0,1)$ 　　　　$Z(\Phi_3)$ test

We use only one of the three equations proposed by Phillips and Perron (1988) and Perron (1988).

11. Schwert (1987) sets up the optimal monthly lags by using the following formula:

$$k = \text{INT}\left\{12(T/100)^{2.25}\right\},$$

where k is the optimal lag number, T is the number of observations, and INT is the integer value.

12. It is claimed that the power of the DF test is low in rejecting the null hypothesis. In other words, it is easy to accept the series as a random walk. Therefore, Phillips-Perron's $Z(\tau_p)$ is preferred since it has a higher test power and is intended to correct the effects of heteroscedasticity and autocorrelation. For further details, see Campbell and Shiller (1991), Banerjee, Dolado, Galbraith, and Hendry (1993).

13. For a detailed discussion, see Jia (1994); Xu (1994); Sun (1994); Tao (1994); Yang (1994); and Hongkong Bank (1994).

REFERENCES

Abdel-Mahmoud, M. Abdel-Rahman, 1994, "Causality and Lag Structure Between Black Market Foreign Exchange Rates and Consumer Prices: A Case Study of Sudan," *Rivista Internazionale di Scienze Economiche e Commerciali*, 41(5): 423–447.

Agénor, Pierre-Richard, 1991, "A Monetary Model of Parallel Market for Foreign Exchange," *Journal of Economic Studies*, 18(4):4–18.

———, 1992, *Parallel Currency Markets in Developing Countries: Theory, Evidence, and Policy Implications*, Essays in International Finance, International Finance Section, Department of Economics, Princeton University, No.188, November.

Agénor, Pierre-Richard, and Bernard Delbecque, 1991, *Balance-of-Payments Crisis in a Dual Exchange-Rate Regime with Leakages*, Washington, D.C.: International Monetary Fund, March.

Asiamoney (1994), *Asian Currency Guide*, Supplement, pp 8–11.

Banerjee, Anindya, Juan J. Dolado, John W. Galbraith, and David F. Hendry, 1993, *Co-integration, Error-Correction, and the Econometric Analysis of Non-Stationary Data*, Oxford: Oxford University Press.

Banuri, Tariq, 1989, Black Markets, Openness, and Central Bank Autonomy, Helsinki: World Institute for Development Economics Research, Working paper No. 62, August.

Brahm, Laurence J., 1993, *Foreign Exchange Controls in China—A Strategic Guide for Corporate Survival*, Hong Kong: Longman Asia Limited.

Campbell, John Y., and Robert J. Shiller, 1991, "Cointegration and Test of Present Value Models," *Journal of Political Economy*, 95: 1062–1088.

Canto, Victor A., 1985, "Monetary Policy, 'Dollarization,' and Parallel Market Exchange Rates: The Case of the Dominican Republic," *Journal of International Money and Finance*, 4: 507–521.

Cheung, Yin-Wong, and Kon S. Lai, 1993, "Long Run Purchasing Power Parity During the Recent Float," *Journal of International Economics*, 34: 183–192.

Cochrane, John H., 1988, "How Big Is the Random Walk in GNP?" *Journal of Political Economy*, 96 October: 893–920.

Davidson, Russell, and James G. MacKinnon, 1993, *Estimation and Inference in Econometrics*, Oxford: Oxford University Press.

Dickey, David A., 1976, *Estimation and Hypothesis Testing for Nonstationary Time Series*, Ph.D. thesis, Iowa State University.

Dickey, David A., and Wayne A. Fuller, 1979, "Distribution of the Estimators for Autoregressive Series with a Unit Root," *Journal of the American Statistical Association*, 74: 427–431.

———, 1981, "Likelihood Ratio Statistics for Autoregressive Time Series with a Unit Root," *Econometrica*, 49: 1057–1072.

Dornbusch, Rudiger, Daniel V. Dantas, Clarice Pechman, Roberto De R. Rocha, and Demetrio Simoes, 1983, "The Black Market for Dollars in Brazil," *Quarterly Journal of Economics*, 98 February: 25–40.

Edwards, Sebastian, 1989, *Real Exchange Rates, Devaluation, and Adjustment: Exchange Rate Policy in Developing Countries*, Cambridge: MIT Press.

Engle, Robert F., and Clive W. J. Granger, 1987, "Cointegration and Error-Correction: Representation, Estimation and Testing," *Econometrica*, 55: 251–276.

Frenkel, Michael, 1990, "Exchange Rate Dynamics in Black Markets," *Journal of Economics*, 51 (2): 159–176.

Granger, Clive W. J., 1983, *Cointegrated Variables and Error-Correction Models*, Discussion Paper, University of California, San Diego.

————, 1988, "Some Recent Developments in a Concept of Causality," *Journal of Econometrics*, 39: 199–211.

Grosse, Robert, 1994, "Jamaica's Foreign Exchange Black Market," *The Journal of Development Studies*, 31(1) October: 17–43.

Hongkong Bank, 1994, "China's New Foreign Exchange Management System," *China Briefing*, 46 February: 1–3.

Huizinga, Harry, 1991, "Law Enforcement and the Black Market Exchange Rate," *Journal of International Money and Finance*, 10: 527–540.

International Currency Analysis, 1990, *World Currency Yearbook 1988–1989*, Brooklyn, New York.

Jia, Chunxin, 1994, "Monetary Policy Theory and Evaluation of the Monetary Control of the Recent Years," *Finance and Trade Economics*, Institute of Finance and Trade Economics, Chinese Academy of Social Science, 4: 27–32.

Johansen, Soren, 1988, "Statistical Analysis of Cointegrating Vectors," *Journal of Economic Dynamics and Control*, 12: 231–254.

————, 1989, *Likelihood Based Inference on Cointegration: Theory and Applications*, Lecture notes, Seminario Estivo di Econometria, Centro Studi Sorelle Clarke, Bagni di Lucca, Italy.

Johansen, Soren, and Katarina Juselius, 1990, "Maximum Likelihood Estimation and Inference on Cointegration—With Application to the Demand for Money," *Oxford Bulletin of Economics and Statistics*, 52 May: 169–210.

Kamin, Steven B., 1993, "Devaluation, Exchange Controls, and Black Markets for Foreign Exchange in Developing Countries," *Journal of Development Economics*, 40: 151–169.

Koveos, Peter E., and Bruce Seifert, 1986, "Market Efficiency, Purchasing Power Parity and Black Markets," *Weltwirtschaftliches Archiv*, 122: 313–326.

Lo, Andrew W., and A. Craig MacKinlay, 1988, "Stock Market Prices Do Not Follow Random Walks: Evidence from a Simple Specification Test," *Review of Financial Studies*, 1: 41–66.

————, 1989, "The Size and Power of the Variance Ratio Test in Finite Samples: A Monte Carlo Investigation," *Journal of Econometrics*, 40: 203–238.

Macedo, Jorge Braga de, 1982, "Exchange Rate Behavior with Currency Inconvertibility," *Journal of International Economics*, 12: 65–81.

MacKinnon, James G., 1990, *Critical Values for Cointegration Tests*, University of California San Diego Discussion Paper, 90–4.

Marcus, Robert, 1992, "Parallel Markets in Foreign Exchange: The Experience in Latin America," *World of Banking*, 11(2) March/April: 4–7.

Osterwald-Lenum, Michael, 1990, *Recalculated and Extended Tables of the Asymptotic Distribution of Some Important Maximum Likelihood Cointegration Test Statistics*, Unpublished manuscript.

Perron, Pierre, 1988, "Trends and Random Walks in Macroeconomic Time Series: Further Evidence from a New Approach," *Journal of Economic Dynamics and Control*, 12 June-September: 297–332.

Phillips, Peter C. B., 1987, "Time Series Regression with a Unit Root," *Econometrica*, 55: 277–301.

Phillips, Peter and Pierre Perron, 1988, "Testing for a Unit Root in Time Series Regression," *Biometrica*, 75 June: 335–346.

Phylaktis, Kate, 1991, "The Black Market for Dollars in Chile," *Journal of Development Economics*, 37: 155–172.

Phylaktis, Kate, and Yiannis Kassimatis, 1994, "Black and Official Exchange Rates in the Pacific Basin Countries: An Analysis of Their Long-Run Dynamics," *Applied Economics*, 26: 399–407.

Schwert, G. William, 1987, "Effects of Model Specification on Tests for Unit Roots in Macroeconomic Data," *Journal of Monetary Economics*, 20 July: 73–103.

Shanghai Asian Research Centre, 1993, *Issues on the Renminbi Exchange Rate Analysis*, Hong Kong: Joint Publishing (HK) Co., Ltd.

Silk, Mitchell A., 1988, "Economic Crime in China," *China Business Review*, January-February: 25–29.

Sims, Christopher A., 1972, "Money, Income, and Causality," *American Economic Review*, 62: 540–552.

Sun, Mingchun, 1994, "On Influences of Reform of Exchange Control System on Monetary Polices in China," *Economic Research Journal* (*Monthly*), (8), August: 52–56.

Sung, Yun-Wing, 1991, *The China-Hong Kong Connection: The Key to China's Open-door Policy*, Cambridge: Cambridge University Press.

Tao, Shigui, 1994, "Issues Relating to the Establishment of Inter-Bank Foreign Exchange Markets," *International Trade Journal*, (6): 63–64.

Thornton, Daniel L., and Dallas S. Batten, 1985, "Lag-Length Selection and Tests of Granger Causality Between Money and Income," *Journal of Money, Credit, and Banking*, 17 May: 164–178.

Tsang, Shu-ki, 1994, *The Chinese Foreign Exchange System at a Crossroads*, BRC Papers on China, Business Research Centre, School of Business, Hong Kong Baptist College, Series No. CP94006, March.

Wahba, Sadek, 1991, "What Determines Workers' Remittances?" *Finance and Development*, December: 41–44.

Wang, Liang, 1993, *The Devaluation of Renminbi and Exchange Rate Policy*, Beijing: The People University of China Press.

World Bank (1994), *China: Foreign Trade Reform*, The World Bank, Washington, D.C., 1994.

Xu, Tianwei, 1994, "A Preliminary Study of the Impact of the Change in Exchange Rates on Comparative Advantage," *International Trade Journal*, (4): 7–11.

Yang, Fan, 1994, "Repercussions and Prospects of the Reform in RMB Exchange Rates," *International Trade Journal*, (4): 47–51.

8

Official Flows to China: Recent Trends and Major Characteristics

KWANG W. JUN and SAORI N. KATADA

INTRODUCTION

For its rapid economic growth and accelerated modernization of the past decade and a half, the People s Republic of China's (China) development efforts have been supported by the increased amount of external finance. Official Development Finance (ODF) and its concessional component, Official Development Assistance (ODA), have been major contributors to China's economic development. External financial flows have provided additional resources for China's poverty reduction, infrastructure, development, and productive projects and facilitated expansion of foreign direct investment from abroad as well as international trade. Furthermore, official financial flows through bilateral donors and multilateral development organizations have provided China with access to advanced technologies and management expertise, and improved markets.

OVERALL TREND IN OFFICIAL FINANCIAL FLOWS TO CHINA

China began to receive official financial flows—from both bilateral donors and multilateral sources—in 1979. Following the changes in the Chinese government's development strategy, from relative isolationism to active pursuit of economic development using dual engines of domestic production incentives and increased access to foreign financial resources, China acknowledged its need for external development assistance. The country started converting itself from aid provider to aid recipient, and its first step was participation in the United Nations Development Program (UNDP) (Freeney, 1991).

A few bilateral donors—Federal Republic of Germany (1.3 million dollars in grants) and Japan (2.6 million dollars in grants)—provided ODA in 1979, as well as some United Nations specialized agencies (total of 12.6 million dollars). But the total amount of official flows in China remained insignificant until a couple of years thereafter. In 1980, net financial flows from official creditors, including nonconcessional official lending from all sources, totaled only some 200 million dollars.

Many donors started providing various types of official finance to China after the country joined the IMF and the World Bank in April 1980, and in May 1980, respectively. Official flows, measured by both ODF and ODA, increased steadily after the mid-1980s.[1]

Both ODF and ODA net flows have experienced a gradual upward movement, but they remained far below the 2 billion dollar a year level until 1987. However, the full effect of China's access to official creditors was not visible until the mid-1980s. The rise in official flows to China was further facilitated by its membership with the Asian Development Bank (ADB) in March 1986, and China received its first loan of 133.3 million dollars the year after its ADB membership. However, after 1987, both nonconcessional and concessional flows surged to reach a total above 2 billion dollars in 1989.

The upward trend suffered a setback following the Tiananmen Square incident in June 1989. Following the postponement of bilateral aid from major donors to China, the decision on June 26, 1989 by the United States for example, international financial institutions (IFIs) such as the World Bank and ADB suspended some of the new loans and credits to China which were already approved.[2] Ongoing projects were implemented without major disruptions, but there were some delays in inflows of new funding to the country. Such pressure had repercussions on aid disbursements from other bilateral donors like Japan (Freeney, 1991; Lardy, 1994). Although the situation improved by December 1989, credits closely related to basic human needs (BHN) from the International Development Association (IDA, the soft credit window of the World Bank) were the only portion committed from IFIs during the FY1990 (July 1989–June 1990). The drop in net flows from 1989 to 1991 reflects these interruptions in IFI s lending activities.

The most recent dramatic increase in official flows came in 1993, when multilateral nonconcessional lending (net) reached 1.1 billion dollars including a record high of 732 million dollars from IBRD. Bilateral nonconcessional flows also doubled from the previous year, 1992, to reach 1.9 billion dollars between 1992 and 1993.

The importance of official flows within the total financial flows has diminished in recent years due to the dramatic surge of private capital inflow in China after 1991. Nevertheless, ODF still constitutes thirty percent of total resource inflows (gross disbursement basis) to China in 1993, and ODF provides thirty-nine percent of net inflows (gross disbursement minus principal payments) in the same year. A critical difference between the more recent situation and the one in 1989, when ODF constituted thirty-six percent of total disbursement, lies in the composition of ODF. In 1989, only twenty-four percent of ODF was nonconcessional; on the other hand, nonconcessional official flows accounted for sixty-three percent of ODF in 1993. The amount of ODF to China captures about nine percent of total ODF in the world in 1993, compared with a three percent average during 1984–1988.

Despite the declining proportion of the concessional component of official flows to China, the absolute amount of ODA to the country still

Figure 8.1
ODA and ODF: Net Flow Trend, 1980–1993

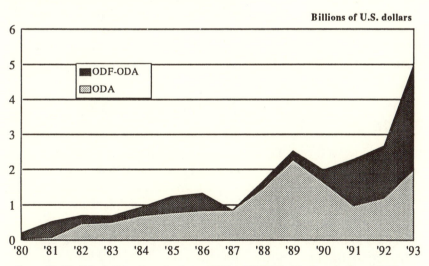

Source: The World Bank, Debtor Reporting System (DRS) and OECD, Creditor Reporting System (CRS).

Figure 8.2
Proportion of Official Flows in the Total Financial Flows
(disbursement basis), 1984–1993

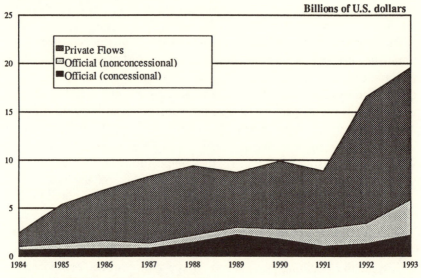

Source: The World Bank (DRS) and OECD (CRS).

makes it a leading ODA recipient in the world. According to the OECD/DAC report, China received 3.28 billion dollars in ODA (including technical cooperation grants) in 1993. This makes China the largest ODA recipient for the year, surpassing Egypt, the largest ODA recipient in the previous year. In addition, China is a major concessional fund recipient from many multilateral channels such as IDA (top), UNDP (second), UNICEF (eighth), UNFPA (top), and IFAD (top).

TERMS AND SECTOR DISAGGREGATION OF ODF TO CHINA

Official loans (excluding grants) to China have been extended at fairly stable and low interest rates (measured at the time of commitment). Figure 8.3 illustrates the lending rates and commitment level by multilateral lenders between 1984 and 1993. Both the new commitment and the lending rates provided by IFIs declined substantially in 1990. This was largely attributed to the fact that after the Tiananmen Square incident, only IDA credits for BHN purposes were committed during the first half of that year. The drop also reflected the subsequent suspension of new commitments by ADB.

Figure 8.3
Interest Rates and Commitment Level of Multilateral Loans, 1984–1993

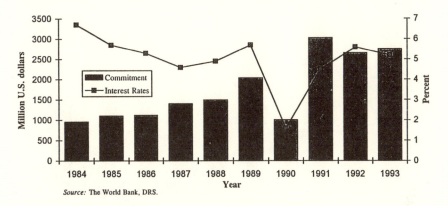

Source: The World Bank, DRS.

Year-to-year variation in bilateral aid flows after the 1989 incident was not as profound as in the case of multilateral flows. The level of official financial flows from bilateral donors has increased to a more or less steady pace since 1987. A surge in commitment occurred in 1993, much of which came from nonconcessional lending and export credits (see Figure 8.4).

During the 1991–1993 period, interest rates charged to China's new borrowing declined significantly, reflecting low international interest rates due to the slowing down of economic growth in the OECD countries. As China improved its creditworthiness and increased its access to private financing with interest rates more comparable to official loans, Chinese borrowing from private sources naturally increased.

Sector disaggregation of official flows to China shows a steady shift away from mining to social and economic infrastructure building (see Figure 8.5). The major components of official lending in the 1992–1993 average include social service (15.5 percent) and transportation (23.7 percent). The energy sector is becoming another important category owing to China's growing infrastructure needs, and the share of official flow to this sector increased from nineteen percent in 1992 to thirty-seven percent in 1993.[3] The sector allocation of official financial flows to China is roughly consistent with that to low-income countries in the aggregate where 21.5 percent was allocated to the energy sector and sixteen percent to the social service sector. The development projects in China have been aimed at reducing poverty in China and, at the same time, providing a social and economic infrastructure to enhance its productive capacity and foster its comparative advantage.

Figure 8.4
Interest Rates and Commitment Level of Bilateral Official Lending,
1984–1993

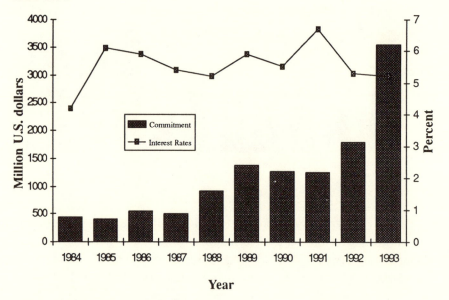

Source: The World Bank, DRS. Some committed portion of 1993 has no detailed lending information.

The sectoral composition of the concessional and nonconcessional flows shows marked differences (see Figure 8.6).[4] As Figure 8.5 illustrates, an average of twenty-five percent of the concessional lending was provided to the social service sector in the 1990s. Poverty-targeted and social sectors such as social services, education, and agriculture have received more than two-thirds of concessional lending since the late 1980s. In nonconcessional lending, the predominant share of the energy sector has diminished in recent years, as private financing (especially foreign direct investment—FDI) has replaced official financing for enclave and industry sector projects.

MAJOR SOURCES OF ODA TO CHINA

Information on ODA is systematically updated by OECD's Development Assistance Committee (DAC) where the member countries review their ODA performance periodically and compile statistics of ODA flows.[5] The multilateral organizations—the UN special agencies, the World Bank, and regional development banks such as the ADB—are contributors of ODA from the recipient point of view.[6] In addition, some emerging aid donors

Figure 8.5
Sectoral Disaggregation of Concessional Official Loans, 1984–1993

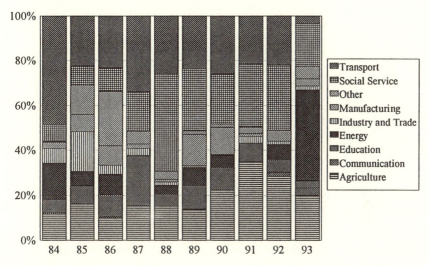

Source: The World Bank, DRS.

are found in the developing world, such as South Korea and Turkey. Oil-producing Arab countries and regional multilateral financial institutions affiliated with them have also contributed aid to developing countries, including China.

Concessional flows to China have been channeled mainly through several major ODA contributors over the past decade. Japan has been by far the largest bilateral ODA contributor to China, providing more than half of the country's bilateral ODA for 1990–1993. During the same period, IDA provided twenty-six percent of total ODA, accounting for seventy-nine percent of total multilateral concessional flows to China. This trend has been fairly consistent over time.

ODA consists of two types of transactions: grants, which can be divided into pure grants and technical cooperation grants, and official concessional loans. The mix of grants and concessional loans varies across the donors; some (such as the Nordic countries and the United Kingdom) provide only grants and others (such as Japan and Germany) include a significant portion of concessional loans. In general, soft windows of IFIs provide credit on a concessional basis (IDA and Asian Development Fund), whereas UN agencies as well as the European Union tend to concentrate on extending grants. In China, the composition of ODA (gross disbursement) was quite stable for the ten-year period from 1983 through 1992, with grants and

Figure 8.6
Sectoral Disaggregation of Nonconcessional Official Loans, 1984–1993

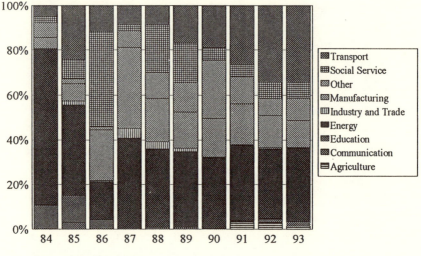

Source: The World Bank, DRS.

concessional loans splitting ODA about 30:70. Technical cooperation grants comprise slightly more than half of all grants.

Bilateral Donors

Japan's prominence as a bilateral ODA donor to China has been consistent since the beginning of China's borrowing from official sources among industrial countries in the early 1980s. Japan's dominance waned slightly in the first two years of the 1990s, partly in the aftermath of the Tiananmen incident. However, the ratio of Japanese ODA contributions to China recovered in 1992 and 1993 (see Table 8.1).

The major part of Japanese ODA to China is comprised of concessional loans (77 percent of Japan's gross ODA to China in 1992) extended by the Overseas Economic Cooperation Fund (OECF) and the Japan International Cooperation Agency (JICA). The former provides concessional official loans in Japanese yen, and the latter provides grants and technical assistance. OECF has extended three aid packages since 1979 totaling over ¥1.6 trillion (about ten billion dollars equivalent). Aid pledges to establish these packages have been made periodically as a "gift" during the visits of Japanese prime ministers to China. Prime Minister Masayoshi Ohira pledged ¥330 billion (1.4 billion dollars) for the 1979–1983 period. The

Table 8.1
Top Five Bilateral Donors to China, 1985, 1991, and 1993 (ODA number in millions of U.S. dollars)

1985	ODA (%)	1991	ODA (%)	1993	ODA (%)
Japan	387.9 (68)	Japan	585.3 (47)	Japan	1350.7 (60)
Germany	97.6 (17)	France	138.5 (11)	Germany	247.8 (11)
Australia	17.3 (3)	Germany	107.1 (9)	Spain	140.1 (6)
Canada	15.5 (3)	Austria	97.2 (8)	Italy	135.5 (6)
Italy	14.4 (3)	Spain	84.6 (7)	France	102.6 (5)

Source: OECD/DAC, CRS.

second package of ¥470 billion (2.7 billion dollars) was offered by Prime Minister Yasuhiro Nakasone during his trip in 1984 to cover the 1984–1989 period, and ¥810 billion (6.7 billion dollars) was pledged by Prime Minister Noboru Takeshita in 1988 for the period between 1990–1995.[7] These concessional loans have been used for the construction of physical plants (fertilizer, power), railroads, ports and highways, and telecommunication facilities.[8]

Multilateral Donors

Multilateral institutions are also important ODA donors. The UNDP has always been the largest multilateral grant funding organization, and its grant fund is often used for technical cooperation to support China's technical advancement, in conjunction with its modernization programs. The UNDP carries out five-year country programs based on its Indicative Planning Figures (IPF) to allocate its resources. China joined the list of UNDP's IPF recipients from the IPF-3 (1982–1986) with sixty million dollars, and its allocation has steadily increased to 135.9 million dollars (IPF-4, 1987–1991) and to 177.3 million dollars (IPF-5, 1992–1996) (Freeney, 1991). The UNDP's share of multilateral ODA to China has been around five percent in the 1990s. The European Development Fund is another important contributor of grants and technical cooperation to China.

As for concessional credits, IDA has been by far the most prominent donor to China. In 1993, IDA contributed eighty-four percent of multilateral ODA, far surpassing the next largest donor UNDP (four percent). Another IFI with a soft lending window is the ADB, which established its Asian Development Fund (ADF) in 1974. Although China (and India) are not qualified for the ADF because of their late entrance to the organization, China received a modest amount of 16.3 million dollars ODA from ADB for technical assistance for the purpose of project preparation in 1993.

NONCONCESSIONAL OFFICIAL FLOWS TO CHINA

Two major components of nonconcessional lending by official creditors to China have been: (1) development loans and credits at nonconcessional terms; (2) official export credits.[9] In addition, IMF has provided standby loans for China's balance-of-payments adjustments and other foreign exchange needs.

Nonconcessional Long-Term Lending

Nonconcessional official lending is still an important source of long-term development financing for China. A generous grace period (and long maturity) is useful to support China's much-needed infrastructure building and long-gestation projects.

There are only a few bilateral donors that provide nonconcessional official lending to the country, and the only significant amount of this type of financial resource comes from Japan. The Export-Import Bank of Japan has pledged over ¥1.7 trillion (ten billion dollars, using average yen dollar exchange rate between 1979 and 1994) total direct loans for energy resources development in China. Three memoranda were exchanged between the Ex-Im Bank of Japan and the Bank of China in 1979 (¥420 billion), in 1984 (¥580 billion), and in 1992 (¥700 billion) for the oil and coal development projects.

IFIs have been major contributors of nonconcessional loans for China. IBRD, the largest contributor of such loans, has provided a total net flow of more than two billion dollars in the four years 1990–1993. This is about one-third of total net flows of nonconcessional lending to China over the same period. ADB also provides a sizable nonconcessional lending to China. Its gross disbursement to China exceeded 1.1 billion dollars in 1994, and this amount makes China the largest borrower of ADB loans for the first time since China joined the organization in 1986. China is followed by the traditionally large borrowers, Indonesia (748 million dollars) and Pakistan (407 million dollars).[10]

Officially Supported Export Credits

China has been one of the most important markets for export credit agencies (ECAs) in recent years, and there has been competition among them to capture large export markets of China's expanding economy. According to the Berne Union, an association of ECAs, the amount of export credit support commitment outstanding to China by the third quarter of 1994 reached 35.7 billion dollars (of which 5.4 billion dollars was short-term), making the country the largest export credit recipient among developing countries.[11] New commitments in the first nine months of 1994 amounted to eight billion dollars. China's share of export credit commitment to developing countries has doubled during the 1990s from six percent in 1991 to twelve percent in 1994.

The increase in export credits supported by official creditors helped facilitate exporters and exporters' banks to actively engage in trading with China. The rapid increase in China's trading volume has been well documented: Chinese exports rose from 62.1 billion dollars in 1990 to 91.8 billion dollars in 1993, and its imports increased from 53.4 billion dollars to 104 billion dollars in the same period.

The largest contributor of export credit to China in 1994 was Japan's Export-Import Insurance Division, Ministry of International Trade and Industry (EID/MITI) with eight billion dollars worth of outstanding commitment, followed closely by French Campaignie Française d' Assurance pour le Commerce Extérieur (COFACE) with 7.8 billion dollars. Export Credit Agencies from Germany, the United States, and the United Kingdom are other major official financiers.

IMF Standby Loan

The IMF supports, among others, the promotion of foreign exchange stability and the alleviation of temporary balance-of-payments problems. Since its entrance to the IMF in 1980, China has turned to IMF resources several times in response to its domestic economic difficulties and trade deficit. The most recent case took place in November 1986 when the IMF approved a twelve months standby first credit tranche arrangement for up to SDR 597.7 million (717 million dollars).[12]

WORLD BANK LOANS AND CREDITS TO CHINA

The World Bank Group, consisting of IBRD/IDA (the World Bank), International Finance Corporation (IFC), and Multilateral Investment Guarantee Agency (MIGA), has been actively involved in China's development plans. Since China became a member of the World Bank, and later joined the latter two organizations, its access to the pool of development capital has increased, directly through IBRD and IFC loans and IDA credits, and indirectly through China's improved technical capacity (training and technical assistance) and economic and physical infrastructure, and MIGA guarantees.

China and the World Bank

The World Bank's program in China for the past decade was largely threefold: formal economic sector works providing comprehensive coverage of issues in specific sectors or policy areas; well-prepared investment projects, supporting productivity gains, technological modernization, and institutional development objectives; and lending programs in support of well-defined sector reform objectives.

Earlier economic studies produced by the World Bank provided a basic policy framework for Chinese officials, and the policy dialogue between China and the World Bank has been exceptionally strong and constructive. The World Bank's various economic and sector works, with their objectivity and relevance, have been well received by Chinese authorities. Member developing countries receiving the World Bank loans and credits for development projects can be categorized in three groups: IBRD only, Blend (of IBRD and IDA), and IDA only.[13]

With its GNP per capita of 490 dollars (in 1993), China belongs to the Blend group, and that status has always been the same since China joined the World Bank in 1980. Thus, China has had access to both IDA credits and IBRD loans since the Bank's first commitment for the University Development project was made in 1981 (100 million dollars from IBRD and 100 million dollars from IDA). The cumulative project portfolio is well balanced, both geographically and sectorally.

The amount of IBRD loan and IDA credit commitments to China, as well as their disbursements, has increased significantly over the past ten years (see Figure 8.7). For 1994, China received the largest commitment from the IBRD of 2.9 billion dollars, far surpassing the second largest recipient, Mexico (with 2.1 billion dollars). This 2.9-billion-dollar allocation to China accounts for eighteen percent of IBRD loans committed in 1994. China also

Figure 8.7
Share of China's Borrowing from the World Bank, 1985–1994

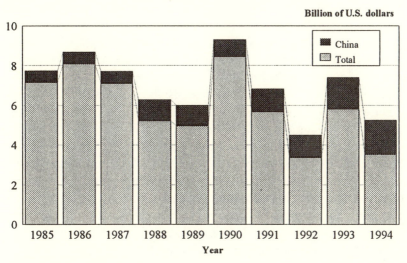

Source: The World Bank, DRS.

has the second largest IDA credit commitment of 1.1 billion dollars after India (with 1.4 billion dollars), and this IDA credit allocation to China is about fifteen percent of the total IDA commitment for the same year. Although China is a large IDA credit recipient, IDA credit as proportion of its GNP is significantly low (0.21 percent), even compared with smaller and poorer countries in sub-Saharan Africa. China ranked 54th out of 58 recipients of positive net IDA disbursements.

The implementation status of the World Bank development projects in China has been robust, reflecting a combination of strong local administrative capability and the powerful sense of borrower ownership that has consistently characterized the Bank-supported programs in China. Most Bank projects have been successfully implemented, and no major problems have been identified as generic to a significant number of operations.

Experiences with China's project implementation suggest areas, both China-specific and in general, where performance can be enhanced still further. These include: the quality of projects on entry; the role of the government in implementation and supervision; and the implementation of technical assistance and institutional development components.

From the negligible level of 100 million dollars in 1981, IBRD loan commitment increased to over 1.2 billion dollars in 1989, and after a temporary setback from commitment suspension in 1990, the commitment came back up to the previous level of 1.3 billion dollars in 1991. In 1994, the annual commitment to China has increased to 2.9 billion dollars, the record amount of IBRD commitment for a single year to a single country. In recent years, the World Bank has been particularly active in three areas in support of reform plans implemented by the Chinese government: (a) physical investment to avoid infrastructure bottlenecks for China's rapid reform and development; (b) a housing and social security reform; and (c) labor redeployment, following reform of states-owned enterprises.

The increase in IDA commitment has also been noteworthy. IDA credit did not experience a drop in commitment in 1990, because IDA money continued to be committed to China to provide basic human needs as indicated earlier. In recent years, the commitment of IDA credits has seen some decline from its highest level in 1991 (1.3 billion dollars), partly owing to China's rapid economic growth that has enabled the country to broaden its access to the external private capital directly. Given the limited availability of IDA resources, priority of IDA credits in China is focused on projects directly in support of the social sectors, the development of the poorest regions, and environmental protection and pollution control.

The growth in net disbursements of both IBRD loans and IDA credit has been steady, although slower than that of commitment, largely due to the time lag between them. The IBRD net disbursement to China in 1994 was 1.1 billion dollars, the largest yearly amount since the Bank's lending relationship with China started in 1981. Meanwhile, the IDA net disbursement declined slightly between 1993 (865 million dollars) and 1994 (671 million dollars).[14]

IBRD loans and IDA credits have been used to implement different types of development projects; in that sense, the complementarity between the two resources is fairly clear and that trend has been stable over time (see Figures 8.8 and 8.9) on a disbursement basis. The two figures suggest that China received more credits from the IDA for social service and agriculture sectors. A heavy concentration of IDA activities in these two sectors, which relate closely to basic human needs, has not changed, despite the significant increase in the total amount of IDA credit disbursement over time. The share of IDA credits allocated to the social service sector has fluctuated above forty percent of its total gross disbursement, and the share to agriculture has stabilized at around twenty-three percent since the late-1980s.

For IBRD, sectoral concentration is found in economic and infrastructure sectors and industry sectors such as energy, manufacturing, and transportation. This concentration has been most prominent since the late 1980s. During 1992–1993, transport and manufacturing sectors have gained in importance relative to the energy sector. In order to avoid an infrastructure bottleneck, substantial new investment is required in the infrastructure sector in the years

Figure 8.8
Sectoral Disaggregation, IDA Disbursement, 1984–1993

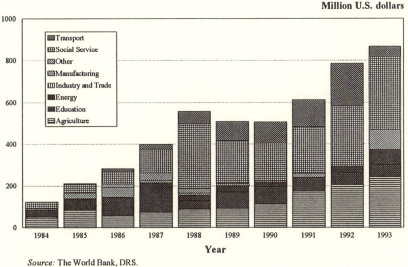

Source: The World Bank, DRS.

Figure 8.9
Sectoral Disaggregation, IBRD Disbursement, 1984–1993

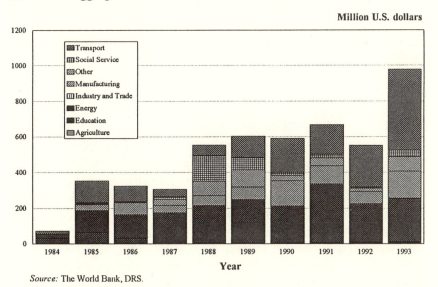

Source: The World Bank, DRS.

to come. Effective new mechanisms to facilitate domestic resource mobilization need to be further developed, although much progress has been made. The progress is reflected in better internal resource generation in the railways and the power sectors, as well as rapid commercialization of ports.

Environment, which is sometimes not included in the traditional sector disaggregation, has been the fastest-growing area of concentration in the Bank's lending program to China. Investment operations have addressed the amelioration of environmental conditions, especially in the field of water pollution in cities and provinces. These programs include significant technical assistance to strengthen local environmental management agencies and promote corporatization of local public utilities such as water supply and sewage treatment, to ensure a financially sustainable basis for their operations.

China and Other Organizations in the World Bank Group: IFC and MIGA

IFC was founded in 1956 with the aim of furthering economic development by encouraging the growth of productive private enterprises in member countries. IFC provides loan and equity financing for private sector projects to mobilize additional capital for companies. IFC's country assistance for China focuses on three principal objectives: (a) promotion of a more favorable foreign investment framework, (b) serving as a catalyst to the expansion of private sector investment, and (c) acceleration and deepening of financial and capital markets. To respond effectively to the rapid development of the Chinese economy and the growing IFC activities within the country, IFC opened its first representative office in Beijing in October 1992.

IFC's operations in China have strong emphasis on supporting joint ventures between foreign investors and Chinese enterprises, and IFC plays an advisory role in helping China structure these transactions and arrange financing on a project risk basis without guarantees from state banks. The first IFC financing for China was a fifteen-million-dollars loan to finance the Guangzhou Peugeot Automobile Company in 1985. The IFC loans to China grew very slowly in the late 1980s; two small additional loans were made in FY1988, and another two in FY1989. However, with China's rapid economic growth, increased investor confidence in the country, and the expansion of outside and intra-regional investment in Asia, IFC's activities in China have considerably increased since the early 1990s. In addition, IFC's active involvement in supporting and encouraging private investment in infrastructure projects has increased as the Chinese government announced new policies to encourage foreign participation in infrastructure development (see *IFC Annual Reports*).

MIGA was established in 1988 with a mandate to increase the flow of productive investments to developing member countries by (a) guaranteeing (or insuring) investments in developing countries made by private investors against specific noncommercial risks; and (b) advising and assisting these countries' effort to attract and retain such investment. China had first coverage by MIGA in FY 1993 for 0.5 million dollars for a joint venture between Nonfluid Oil of the United States and Shandong Yantai Glass Factory. Since then, China received cumulative maximum liability coverage of 57.7 million dollars by the end of 1994, 45.6 million dollars of which was committed during the second half of 1994.

CONCLUSION

The amount of official flows to China has increased significantly over the past fifteen years. The benefits of these official flows, both concessional and nonconcessional in terms, have been reflected in the way that China has improved its basic economic conditions, physical and social infrastructure, and technical expertise needed for its modernization. The official flows appear to have provided the foundation for large-scale inflows of private capital in recent years. However, China still requires significant improvement in social as well as physical infrastructure. This continues to make the role of official flows, which are conducive to long-term projects, crucial and an integrated part of China's foreign exchange sources.

Also, from the donor's perspective, China, with its over-one-billion population, has been an important recipient country. China is the leading recipient of ODA, as well as other official flows from Japan. More than thirty percent of net disbursements in 1994 from IBRD and IDA combined went to China. Active dialogue between donors and Chinese authorities and the strong accountability and ownership of the Chinese government for their development projects have contributed to this large inflow of official capital to China.

Improved creditworthiness has helped reduce China's reliance on official flows in recent years. Nevertheless, official flows—from both bilateral and multilateral sources—will continue to be a stable source of external development financing for China and contribute to China's economic and social development plans for the foreseeable future.

NOTES

1. Note that ODA is a concessional component of ODF. The differences between these two types of official financial flows, both undertaken by the public sector of the OECD/DAC member governments, OPEC member countries, and

multilateral development institutions such as the World Bank, Asian Development Bank (ADB), and the United Nations agencies, are as follows:

(i) Official Development Assistance (ODA) consists of loans or grants to developing countries that are undertaken by the official sector, both bilateral and multilateral, with the promotion of economic development and welfare as the main objective. It is concessional and conveys a grant element of at least twenty-five percent.

(ii) Official Development Finance (ODF) consists of ODA plus nonconcessional finance to developing countries from official bilateral and multilateral sources. These includes official export credits and other nonconcessional official lending.

2. "World Bank on China Aid," *New York Times*, June 27, 1989, p. 43.

3. Data from 1993 figures of the World Bank Debtor Reporting System. The sector disaggregation of the concessional flows excludes the sector information of grant flows.

4. The numbers exclude lending from multiple lenders, which does not have any sector breakdown.

5. The OECD/DAC members include Australia, Austria, Belgium, Canada, Denmark, Finland, France, Germany, Ireland, Italy, Japan, Luxembourg, The Netherlands, New Zealand, Norway, Portugal, Spain, Sweden, Switzerland, the United Kingdom, the United States, and the Commission of the European Union. In the analysis of donors' contribution of ODA based on OECD/DAC data, ODA includes technical cooperation grants, other grants, and concessional official lending. ODA also have to have development objectives, thus military aid is not included.

6. From donors' point of view, these organizations are recipients of aid, because these bilateral donors contribute financial resources to them from the donors' budget.

7. All conversions were done by taking the average of yen-dollar exchange rate over the specified period: 1979–1983 ($1=¥230.6), 1984–1989 ($1=¥175.89), and 1990–1995 ($1=¥120.29). During the third package, commitments for new projects were suspended after the June 1989 incident, but they resumed in November 1990.

8. Japan's ODA, *Annual Report*, 1993.

9. Donor breakdown of nonconcessional official lending is available from the OECD/DAC.

10. News Release from Asian Development Bank (No. 2/95), January 6, 1995. This amount includes a small portion of technical cooperation grants.

11. The Berne Union is an international association of export credit agencies. It works for international acceptance of sound principles of export credit insurance and foreign investment insurance, and it provides a vital forum for the exchange of information, experience, and expertise of forty-three member countries and IFIs (including the World Bank and the IMF).

12. IMF *Annual Report*, various issues.

13. The World Bank has two windows of developing country lending. The first and largest one is through IBRD loan facility, which provides market-term long-term loans of fifteen to twenty years' maturity and with a three-to-five-year grace period. On the other hand, IDA, the soft window of the World Bank, provides highly concessional long-term loans, with virtually no interest payments, of thirty five to forty year maturity and ten-year grace period to the countries whose GNP per capita is less than 1,345 dollars; however, operational cutoff for IDA eligibility is 835 dollars GNP per capita (as of September 1994 according to the World Bank Atlas methodology). In addition to the GNP per capita criteria, creditworthiness and other factors (the size of certain small island economies) are considered to determine IDA eligibility.

14. For the World Bank fiscal year 1994 (July 1993–June 1994), net disbursements for IBRD and IDA were 781 million dollars and 863 million dollars, respectively.

REFERENCES

Freeney, William R., 1991, "China's Relations with Multilateral Economic Insititutions," in Joint Economic Committee of Congress of the United States (ed), *China's Economic Dilemmas in the 1990s: The Problems of Reforms, Modernization and Interdependence*, Vol. 2, U.S. Government Printing Office, Washington, DC: 795–816.

Lardy, Nicholas R., 1994, *China in the World Economy*, Institute for International Economics, Washington, DC.

9

Commodity Futures Markets in China

DAVID WALL and WEI JIANG

INTRODUCTION

China introduced economic reforms in 1978, first in agricultural produce and then in other consumer items. Markets for intermediate products, factors of production, and services came later and are less well developed. Markets in derivatives are normally seen as a feature of highly developed capitalistic economies with sophisticated institutional arrangements for facilitating the operation of the instruments of capitalism. The period 1988–1994 saw a phenomenal growth in trade in derivatives managed by a rapidly growing number of brokers operating on a large number of newly established exchanges in China, and on a growing number of exchanges outside China.

Of the four basic derivatives—forward contracts, futures contracts, options, and swaps—only forward and futures contracts are allowed to be written in China.[1] Enterprises that are explicitly permitted to do so can trade in all forms of derivatives on overseas exchanges and many individuals and enterprises trade, illegally, on "informal" futures markets throughout China.

THE ROLE OF FUTURES MARKETS IN A SOCIALIST MARKET ECONOMY

The Government's Perspective

The first proposals for the establishment of commodity exchanges in China on which forward and futures contracts could be drawn up and traded were made in the late 1980s. On February 10, 1988, Premier Li Peng wrote to Ma Hong, the President of the State Council's Development Research Centre, calling on the Centre to carry out a study of futures markets in foreign countries.[2] Things moved quickly. On March 25, 1988, Li Peng issued a policy statement calling for the reform of the commercial system in China and for the development of wholesale commodity markets and the experimental introduction of futures contracts.

To support the introduction of futures contracts, a joint research group involving the State Council's Development Research Centre, the State Committee for Economic Reform, and the Ministry of Commerce was established. The group studied the operation of futures exchanges abroad, mainly in the United States. It issued a report in 1990 in which it argued that there was indeed a role for futures contracts in commodity markets in China, and that such markets would have three important functions: 1) they would provide a mechanism to replace state control over the allocation of commodities; 2) they would establish a means of price discovery; and 3) they would provide a means of risk management (Sun, 1994).

The futures markets study group also emphasized the importance of the price discovery function of futures markets in China. This is because enterprises increasingly have to arrange production and manage stocks and costs in response to market forces, which they did not have under the planned economy. Futures markets are seen as providing a practical pricing tool for these new market players. This is particularly important in an economy in transition in which many sectors are to some degree shielded from the forces of international competition and in which domestic prices are not guided by world market prices.

The third argument was that they could provide a means for state-owned enterprises (SOEs) to manage the risks associated with their entry into the market economy. They argued that in the move toward a market economy enterprises sometimes have to base their decisions on prices (both current and expected), which for some commodities and factors may give ambiguous or unclear signals because of their volatility. In such situations futures and forward contracts allow them to reduce business risks by locking in the costs of future input requirements and/or the prices of their future output.

The State Council accepted these arguments in favor of allowing futures markets to be established in China and agreed to the proposal that four markets should be set up. The Government was moved by the claims that such markets would ease the process of moving toward a more market based economy.

Enterprise Perspective

While the allocation mechanism, price discovery, and risk management roles of futures markets were all accepted by the Government as providing the logic for the introduction of futures markets into China, enterprises and individuals are more directly attracted by the risk management role. They are also attracted by three other functions of futures markets. These are the inventory management role, the arbitrage role, and the speculative role. While the risk management function justifies the existence of futures markets, traders attracted by the other three roles are needed if they are to operate effectively and efficiently. The increased activity attracted by these secondary functions of futures markets adds important liquidity to the markets. If all four motives for trading on futures markets are adequately balanced, the price volatility that justified their creation can be modified.

Risk management in the form of entering into forward or futures contracts to cover market risks, i.e., risks of price changes or marketability, is known as hedging. Those who currently hold property rights carry the risk that the price of the item will fall and those who wish to acquire property rights in the future carry the risk that prices might rise. Such risks may be laid off by entering into a forward or futures contract. In this way both buyers and sellers can lock in to a known future price.[3]

Another reason to enter into futures contracts is inventory management. The cost of capital tied up in margin payments needed to secure futures contracts is less than the cost of maintaining stocks, particularly as warehousing is a specialized activity and different locations and firms will have different competitive advantages in maintaining stocks of commodities. Risk and inventory management are the primary reasons why principals in a market see advantages in operating with futures and forward contracts. The price volatility which encourages such management practices, and the effect these practices themselves have on price structures, attract, however, other players into the futures and forward markets: arbitrageurs and speculators.[4]

The arbitrage argument is less obvious and straightforward. Under the "law of one price," prices for the same commodity should be identical in all markets. In practice they often vary between markets (other than for reasons of taxes, tariffs, transport costs, etc.) because of imperfect information. Arbitrageurs can profit by buying in one market and selling in another. Price gaps between futures contracts can occur if different participants in the market have different expectations as to changes in market conditions. The future is always uncertain; people have different degrees of optimism and pessimism, and this is reflected in their market activity.

CHINESE FUTURES MARKETS

The Exchanges

The report of the study group on futures markets concluded that four markets on which futures contracts could be traded should be established in China, on an experimental basis. The markets that the group proposed should be established included one for wheat contracts in Zhengzhou, one for corn in Changcheung, one for rice in Wuhan, and one for pork in Mianyang. Only the Zhengzhou market was established. The Zhengzhou commodity exchange was set up in October 1990, with an organization structure and regulations modeled on those of the Chicago Board of Trade (CBOT).

After the establishment of the Zhengzhou Commodity Exchange, futures exchanges in China mushroomed for a period of three and a half years until the government introduced its rectification measures in the spring of 1994. It was, however, nine months after the Zhengzhou exchange was set up before the second exchange opened. This was the Suzhou Raw Materials Exchange, opened in June 1991. Two more exchanges opened in 1991 and then 15 in 1992 and 21 in 1993. Altogether 40 exchanges (listed in Table 9.1) had been opened by the end of 1993 by provincial or municipal governments, usually in conjunction with central government ministries or agencies.[5]

The exchanges spread over a wide area in China, from Dalian in the north to Hainan in the south, Shanghai in the east, and Chengdu in the west (see Table 9.1). The main concentration is, however, in Shanghai where all the state level exchanges in China were operating at the end of 1993. Total trade on the forty exchanges approached one trillion Renminbi in 1993, more than half of which, around Rmb 500 billion, was conducted in the Shanghai exchanges. The greatest share of the trade was in the Shanghai Metal Exchange (SHME) where trade in 1993 was worth Rmb 388.9 billion, more than a third of all trade on commodity exchanges in China. In 1993 the SHME became the third largest metal futures market in the world, after the London Metal Exchange and the Chicago Board of Trade. On the Shenzhen

Table 9.1
Commodity Futures Exchanges in China, December 1993

Exchange	Sponsoring Agencies	Contracts Traded	Date Set Up
Zhengzhou Commodities Exchange	Ministry of Domestic Trade Henan Provincial Government	Grains	Oct. 1990
Suzhou Raw Materials Exchange	Ministry of Raw Materials Committee for National Restructuring	Steel	June 1991
Beijing Jinpeng Cooper Exchange	China Non-ferrous Metal Corporation	Cooper	Sept. 1991
Chengdu Wholesale Market for Meat	Ministry of Domestic Trade Sichuan Provincial Government	All types of meat	Sept. 1991
Shenzhen Non-ferrous Metals Exchange	China Non-ferrous metals Corporation Shenzhen Municipal Government	Copper, aluminum, lead, zinc and tin	Jan. 1992
Shanghai Wholesale Markets for Meat Products	Shanghai Municipal Government	Meat and meat products (W)	May 1992
Southwest Wholesale Markets for the Means of Agro-production	Sichuan Province Corporation for the Means of Production for Agriculture Sichuan Province Managing Bureau for Industry and Commerce	Means of production for agriculture	August 1992
Hainan Futures Exchange	The Regional Committee for Agricultural Reform in Hainan Province	Watermelons	Sept. 1992
Zhengzhou Markets for Agromachinery	Ministry of Raw Materials Henan Provincial Government	Agromachinery Gauze	Sept. 1992

Table 9.1 (continued)

Zhengzhou Wholesale Market for Building Materials	National Building Materials BureauMinistry of Raw Materials Henan Provincial Government	Building materials	Sept. 1992
Zhongyuan Trading Market for Gauze	The Commercial Committee of Henan Province The Spinning Committee of Henan Province	Gauze	Sept. 1992
Shanghai Petrochemical Exchange	China Petrochemical Corporation Shanghai Municipal Government	Gasoline (W) Diesel oil (W)	Oct. 1992
Qing-Huangdao Wholesale Coal Market	China Coal Corporation for Internal Distribution	Coal	Nov. 1992
Tianjin Trading Market for Copper and Iron Furnace Inputs	China Metallurgical Ministry Tianjin Municipal Government	Steel, coke, pig iron	Dec. 1992
Tianjin Trading Center for Petroleum Products	China Petrochemical Corporation	Petrochemicals	Dec. 1992
Beijing China Wholesale market for Building Materials	China Building Materials Industrial Machinery	Building materials	1992
Yantai Chemical Raw Materials Market	Ministry of Raw Materials Shandong Provincial Government	Chemical products	1992

Exchange	Authority	Commodity	Date
Shanghai Means of Agroproduction Exchange	Ministry of Domestic Trade Shanghai Municipal Government	Carbamide (Fo), sugar (Fo), potassium chloride (Fo), ammonium phosphate (Fo), plywood (Fo)	Feb. 1993
Nanjing Petroleum Exchange	China Petroleum Ministry Jiangsu Provincial Government	Crude oil	March 1993
Shanghai Industrial Chemicals Exchange	Ministry of Industrial Chemicals	Natural and synthetic rubber (Fo), plastic (Fo), carbamide (Fo), methanol (Fo), polyvinyl chloride (Fo)	March 1993
North East Caol Exchange	Inner Mongolia Coal Corporation	Coal	March 1993
Beijing National Chemical Trading Market	Ministry of Industrial Chemicals Beijing Municipal Government	Chemicals	April 1993
Shanghai Petroleum Exchnage	China Petrochemical Corporation China Gas Corporation Shanghai Municipal Government	Crude oil (Fu), diesel oil (Fu), gasoline (Fo)	May 1993
South China Commodity Exchange	Ministry of Agriculture Guangdong Provincial Government	Rubber	May 1993

Table 9.1 (continued)

Shanghai Cereal and Oil Exchange	Ministry of Commerce Shanghai Municipal Government	Sugar (Fu), corn (Fu), rise (Fu), wheat (Fu), soybeans (Fu), soybean and rapeseed oil (Fu)	June 1993
Shanghai Automobile Exchange	Ministry of Internal Trade Shanghai Municipal Government	Automobiles (Fo)	Sept. 1993
Shanghai Building Materials Exchange	The National Bureau of Building Materials Shanghai Municipal Government	Cement (Fu), plywood (Fu), wire rod (Fu)	Nov. 1993
Beijing Petroleum Exchange	China Petrochemical Ministry Beijing Municipal Government	Petroleum	1993
Da Zhongshi Agricultural Products Market	Ministry of Agriculture Beijing Da Zhongshi Market	Agricultural products	1993
Beijing Commodities Exchange	Beijing Planning Committee China Consulting Center for Futures Markets	Agricultural products, metal products, chemical products, fabric products	1993
Shenzhen International Futures Exchange	Shenzhen Trading and Development Bureau of the SHenzhen Municipal Government	Nonferrous metals	1993

Sichuan Nonferrous Metal Exchange	The Raw Material Bureau of Sichuan Provincial Government	Nonferrous metals	1993
Southwest Market for Petrochemical Products	The Chongqing First Commercial Bureau The Managing Bureau for Industry and Commerce in Chongqing	Petrochemicals	1993
Sichuan Hauxi Futures Exchange	Chengdu Huaxi Shareholding Corporation	Grains, vegetable oils	1993
Shenyang Wholesale Petroleum Market	Shenyang Oetroleum Corporation	Crude oil	1993
Harbin Petroleum Exchange	China petroleum and Gas Corporation	Crude oil	1993
Gansu Nonferrous metals Exchange	The Raw Materials Bureau of Gansu Province	Nonferrous metal	1993

Note: W = wholesale market. Fo and Fu = forward and futures contracts, respectively.
Source: Jiang (1994) and Sun (1994).

Metals Exchange (SME) the total trading volume in 1993 was Rmb 2.5 billion.[6]

Not all of the so-called futures exchanges actually traded standardized futures contracts. For example, of the ten exchanges in Shanghai at the end of 1993 only four traded standardized futures contracts (two of those also traded forward contracts), four traded only forward contracts, and two were in reality only wholesale markets with neither futures nor forward contracts being traded. Of the total trade on the SHME in 1993, twenty-eight percent was in standardized futures contracts. It was fourteen percent on the Shanghai Petroleum Exchange (SPEX) and 100 percent on both the Shanghai Cereal and Oil Exchange (SCOE) and Shanghai Building Materials Exchange (SMBE).[7]

Table 9.1 gives an indication of the range of products for which futures and forward contracts are, or were, traded on the exchanges at the end of 1993.[8] Four features relating to the range of contracts traded stand out. The first is that in some cases futures contracts in the same commodity are traded on several exchanges. For example, copper futures contracts are traded on seven exchanges, and futures in crude oil and/or its derivatives are traded on six, and coal, grains, and steel on three each. The second is that the range of products involved includes some for which China is import-dependent, such as copper and timber, for which there has to be some correlation between domestic and international prices, and others for which China is more or less self-sufficient, such as coal and oil, where that form of market discipline is absent. The third feature is that several of the products traded, for example, coal, oil, and steel, were still subject to significant production and distribution controls in 1993. The fourth feature is that some contracts cover products not normally traded on futures exchanges, such as watermelons (storage problems) and plywood and automobiles (homogeneity and storage problems).

The Players

Because of the minimum size of most contracts traded in China, the demand for futures and forward contracts comes mainly from SOEs and collective enterprises. On some exchanges the minimum contract size is such that the margin payment is not a major barrier to entry and many individuals invest as private persons in contracts on those exchanges, for example the Shanghai Building Materials Exchange and the Shanghai Cereals and Oil Exchange.[9] The bulk of the value of the trade on all exchanges is, however, accounted for by the large SOEs, including subsidiaries of central ministries and departments. Despite this major role being played by the SOEs, it is still widely believed in China that much trade on the futures exchanges is purely speculative in motive—the exchanges are often compared to casinos. There are, however, indications that some of the trade on most of the exchanges is for hedging purposes and that on some exchanges hedging accounts for a significant share of business. As far as inventory management and arbitrage are concerned, present conditions on the exchanges in China are such that the possibilities to undertake and benefit from such activities are limited. We will draw on experience in the Shanghai exchanges to throw light on these issues.

The general impression that the futures markets in Shanghai, as in the rest of China, are highly speculative is partially based on a misunderstanding. The speculation ratio is often exaggerated because only those who actually take delivery of physicals when the contracts expire are considered to be real hedgers, and this "going physical" as a share of total trading dropped dramatically as the exchanges became established. When the SHME was opened in May 1992, physical delivery accounted for eighty-six percent of total dealing. It dropped to twenty-six percent at the end of the same year, and further to an average of 4.6 percent in 1993. The record low physical delivery ratio of 1.8 percent occurred in September 1993. This is close to the ratios found in mature futures markets, where they range from one percent to three percent (Yu, 1994). SCOE, SPEX, and SBME also now have a ratio of around five percent. This ratio is higher than those in London or Chicago futures markets but it does not necessarily imply high levels of speculation. Hedgers in the Chinese market have learned to offset their contracts before expiration and let winnings and losses on the spot market be fully or partially canceled out by those on the futures market. This makes it difficult to tell hedgers from speculators. There is, however, some evidence that there are some successful hedgers on the Shanghai exchanges. For example, China's largest metal trading company—the Shanghai Metal Materials Company—now purchases eighty percent of its metal needs from the SHME, using futures contracts to lock into fixed prices. They also use futures contracts to economize on capital, as only five percent of the total value of the metal is tied up, as the margin deposit, until delivery is taken. The Shanghai Electrical Cable Company is also a large consumer of nonferrous metal. Within two months of the founding of SHME, the company reduced its operating costs by more than Rmb 10 million by hedging in the futures market. China's largest steel company—Baoshan Steel Company—also successfully uses the futures market both to lock in prices and to reduce funds tied up in stocks (Xu, 1993).

Another indication that risk management plays a significant role in trade on the SHME is its record of price movements. In 1988, before any futures exchanges were set up, the prices of both ferrous and nonferrous metals jumped. However, in 1993 prices of nonferrous metals were stable; the price index in October 1993 was 99.29 compared to one year earlier, while that of ferrous metals was as high as 227.82. The difference has been attributed to the establishment of the futures market for nonferrous metals. The reduced price volatility is also encouraged by the arbitrage activities which the major players engage in between the SME and SHME and between those exchanges and the London Metal Exchange.

The member companies of various exchanges are usually of four types: producing, consuming, trading, and financial companies. The motive of the first two should be primarily hedging. Among the fifty-five founding member companies of the SHME, twenty nine are involved in domestic trade and distribution, seventeen are producers, and nine are foreign trade or financial companies. In SPEX, the founding members were thirteen crude oil producers, fourteen oil processors, ten oil traders, and seven financial companies, most of whom are among the top 500 enterprises in China (Yang, 1993).

Although the hedging and arbitrage activities on the SHME, and its closer link to world markets, appear to have successfully reduced price volatility, the market prices of products for which there are futures contracts traded on other exchanges, such as agricultural products or building materials, are just as volatile as ever. There are two basic reasons why speculation may dominate in these exchanges. The first is that underlying markets remain subject to nonmarket forces. And the second is that arbitrage processes that can reduce the attractions of speculation cannot currently operate effectively in many Chinese commodity futures markets. The physical, or cash, markets for those products, other than nonferrous products, traded on other futures markets, mainly primary and intermediate goods, are not yet well formed in China. Enterprises do face price risks if they produce or consume these goods or related ones, but many of these risks are not market risks. The so-called "*guanxi*" (relationship) system plays an important role in the buying and selling of these goods, especially among large SOEs (most exchange member companies fall into this category), when these goods are in overall shortage.[10] Even prices for standardizable or homogeneous products can be "personalized" and vary markedly and unpredictably, depending on who the transacting agents are. Such price risks cannot be offset by trading in futures market. In addition, government policies, rather than market factors, are still the most important determinant of many prices. For example, the first futures contracts opened in SPEX shortly after its establishment in March 1993 were crude oil and gasoline futures with expiration in October. The prices of these contracts followed an upward trend until July 5 when the central government announced the introduction of macroeconomic austerity measures. Following this announcement the crude oil price dropped from Rmb 1,553 per ton the day before to Rmb 1,503. That of gasoline fell from Rmb 2,799 per ton to 2773, and then further to Rmb 2,689 the next day. Such large changes had never before been experienced in SPEX.

The experience of the SCOE provides another example of the effect of government intervention on price volatility. This occurred after the State Council held a conference on ways of stabilizing the prices of cereal products on December 25, 1993. The major prices on the SCOE dropped by the full permissible limits for the next three consecutive trading days. A more recent case is the State Securities Council's ban on trade in coal, steel rod, and sugar futures after October on April 22, 1994, although forward contracts in both could continue to be sold. Traded contracts of sugar futures on the SCOE dropped to 490 transactions from 2,525 just one trading day earlier; the futures price of steel rod with a delivery date in January was Rmb 3,690, while July prices dropped to Rmb 3,285 (Wu, 1994). Shanghai Coal Exchange and Shanghai Means of Agri-production Exchange were the poorest in performance in 1993, with average daily trading of only Rmb 9.64 million and Rmb 7.39 million. The Coal Exchange experienced a blank month, i.e., there was no single transaction, in June 1993 (Liu *et al.*, 1994). The principal reason is that the products traded in these exchanges, coal, agricultural chemicals, and so forth, are mainly allocated by the government rather than by market forces. SPEX, which used to be among the top three exchanges, faced the same problem early in 1994, when the government raised the plan-allocated share of trade in oil; trading on SPEX had to be suspended from mid-May.

The second indication that activity on many of China's futures exchanges is predominantly speculative in nature is that prices in futures markets often diverge significantly from "fundamentals." It is quite common in some futures exchanges for prices there to be totally different from those in the underlying cash markets. On the SBME, for example, there used to be two major trading contracts, one for steel rod and the other for plywood. After the government ban on the former, trading in the latter saw a thirty percent to forty percent rise. Plywood futures became subject to pure speculation with little or no relation to the underlying market in physicals and prices followed an independent path. The plywood traded on the exchange is mainly imported from Indonesia and Malaysia. The CIF Shanghai price early in 1994 was about Rmb 51 per piece and the retail price in the cash market around Rmb 54. The futures price was, however, driven up to as high as Rmb 73 in mid-January 1994 and was quickly driven down to less than Rmb 50 by the end of April, which means reexport, if possible, would have been profitable. SBME and SCOE are thought to be more speculative than other exchanges in Shanghai because the value of a contract is relatively small on these two exchanges. The low minimum entry price (the minimum initial margin requirement at five percent is only Rmb 2,500) attracts many private individuals and small enterprises to participate in small trading. These participants are neither producers (nearly all the customers in SCOE are urban people rather than peasants) nor big consumers (individual consumption of grain or plywood is very limited); speculation is their main motive. Such exchanges and ancillary offices are reminiscent of casinos, with crowds of punters in front of large quotation screens placing bets.

Speculation-generated price volatility can be sustained because the process of arbitrage, which would limit it, cannot be operated effectively. This is because the transaction costs of cross market arbitrage for most market players are prohibitively high. Any attempt to arbitrage large price disparities in and out of the futures market involves a process of cash delivery, which would prove impossible for most individuals and enterprises. The first problem is to ensure the availability of transport. Shanghai Coal Exchange was frustrated by transportation problems, even before its trading was banned. When first established in December 1992, the Exchange was considered to be adequately backed by transport capacity. However, the first month's trading volume of Rmb 250 million fell to less than Rmb 90 million over the period January to April 1993 because of shortfalls in transport facilities. As a result, in 1993, the Coal Exchange ran at a loss in debt because its transaction fee revenue did not cover the basic costs (Liu *et al.*, 1994). Trade in futures contracts on the Exchanges was banned in April 1994. Similarly, six months after Zhenzhou Cereal Wholesale Market was set up, 74.7 percent of the railway carriages applied for by market participants could not be fulfilled (Wang, 1993). The Yunnan Tin Corporation once had to organize special truck teams to run eight consecutive days and nights from Gejiu city (Yunnan province) to Shanghai in order to honor its contract when railway transportation failed it. While this story is often related (Xu, 1993; Hu, 1993) as an example of the credit-worthiness of Shanghai futures markets, the fact is that most companies could not mount such an exercise. Warehousing is another problem limiting arbitrage possibilities. Only the SBME has its own delivery warehouses (Liu *et al.*, 1994). Other exchanges usually stipulate warehouses of some member companies as exchange-approved ones, but the companies who own the storehouses can explicitly or implicitly refuse to accept materials from other sources for storage in their depots, except for some companies that have "special cooperation relations" with them.

There is a third reason why China's futures and forward markets tend to be speculative in nature. This is what can be called the moral hazard problem which arises out of the fact that property rights in China are poorly defined and most enterprises are still SOEs without well-specified trading objectives. SOEs are the biggest group of both producers and consumers operating on the futures and forward markets, but they are not responsible for their own winnings and losses and do not respond to normal management incentives. They have a sluggish response to the risks associated with price movements, which makes them less interested in the risk management function of futures and forward markets. For example, prices of cereal goods in China are highly volatile. The "cobweb cycle" can be accurately applied to the Chinese situation (Tian, 1993). The per kilo price of round-grained rice in 1985, for example, was Rmb 0.68; it surged to Rmb 1.80 in 1988, and then dropped back to Rmb 1.00 in 1991 (Song, 1993). The price saw another fifty percent hike in late 1993 (Yang, 1994). The cereal futures market has not, however, been fully utilized to offset such risks. China lacks both the large-scale farmers of Western countries and the great commercial enterprises, such as *Sogo Shosa* of Japan.

Agricultural producers are too small in scale (which is the result of the family responsibility system) to enter the futures market, and enterprises engaged in circulation and distribution are owned by different authorities (central and local) and are asked to play dual roles in commodity allocation. As market-oriented institutions they are expected to be profit maximizers; and as government agents they set market stabilization objectives compatible with state macroeconomic policies. If they enter the futures and forward markets at all, these enterprises do so with these dual objectives in their minds and few can tell whether any losses they make are due to management inefficiency or to government policies. Whichever is the real or main cause, however, their losses will eventually be compensated by the state fiscal subsidies. In Shanghai, at least, companies can deduct losses from futures trading from their pretax profits (Zhu, 1993). It is the state, rather than the enterprises and their managers, who are bearing the risks. Managers in SOEs do benefit from working in profitable enterprises, however, and as they risk nothing, but could gain, by speculating on futures and forward markets, if they can do so they will.

This section has presented some reasons why enterprises that have risk management or inventory management and arbitrage motives for using futures and forward contracts may be unable or unwilling to use them. It has also suggested reasons why the speculative motive may attract more players into the markets than would be the case in normal situations; a communist planned economy in transition to a socialist market economy is not a normal situation. When the speculative motive dominates, it is possible that the futures and forward markets cannot operate efficiently and effectively as the players will be more concerned with second guessing each other's behavior than with seeking out the market consequences of changes in underlying fundamentals in the cash markets. In that case the futures and forward markets may generate destabilizing market signals rather than equilibrium prices.

CRITERIA FOR EFFICIENCY IN FUTURES MARKETS

Criteria for Efficiency

Experience in mature futures markets has shown that if futures and forward markets are to operate efficiently, various criteria must be met. These criteria relate to the trading practices of the markets; the relationship between derivatives and physical markets; the liquidity of the markets; the competitiveness, or openness, of the markets; confidence in the markets; and the management of the rules and regulations established to govern practices on the markets.

The first requirement of an efficient market is that the trading practices it uses to establish prices and transfer property rights must work efficiently, i.e., quickly and cheaply. Although the actual trading practices vary somewhat from exchange to exchange, typically deals are made through brokers who instruct members of the exchange as to their clients' requirements. There must be: a) a quick, secure, low-cost system for moving orders from clients through brokers and exchange members into the dealing procedure, whether trading pit or computer, and on through the registration and clearing processes; b) quick, secure, low-cost methods of providing information about deals to actual and potential market participants; and c) a quick, secure, low-cost way of establishing the *bone fides* and creditworthiness of clients and brokers, of effecting margin and other payments, and of delivering secure property rights.

Second, for derivatives markets to work effectively there must be well-established and highly liquid markets in the underlying physicals on which they are based. As most of those who take short positions, in the derivatives markets do not own and maintain stocks of the items in which they have taken that position, they have to be completely confident that they can deal in a cash, or spot, market to meet their obligation without being subject to a squeeze—i.e., their entry into the cash market will have no effect on prices in that market. To support trade in futures and forward contracts the associated spot market must be in a commodity that can be easily and reliably graded, be storable in freely accessible warehouses, and have access to an adequate and efficient transport system. The grading, storage, and transport network must be supported by an adequate commercial infrastructure of inspectors, merchants (stockholders), agents, financiers, and suppliers of commercial services such as insurance.

Third, markets in futures and forward contracts must be liquid if they are to be run efficiently. In other words, buyers and sellers of contracts must be able to conduct their business on the market as and when they wish to at the prevailing market price. Membership of the exchanges should be large enough to cope promptly with the business they receive.

The fourth criterion is that they should be competitive and that all players in the markets should be on an equal footing. The markets should be open in the sense that any enterprise or individual who meets the requirements of the market should be able to buy and sell contracts on it. No enterprise or individual should be allowed to hold a monopoly or monopsony position in the market and thereby be able to corner or squeeze it. Nor should insider trading be allowed. And when market members and brokers take positions on their own account they should not take those positions until after they have dealt with any or all of their clients' business.

Fifth, participants in futures and forward markets should be confident that any money held or handled by their brokers, members of the exchange, and the exchange itself and its clearing house are secure and that the property rights conferred by the contracts are secure. To some extent the latter is outside of the competence of the exchanges as it depends on the exchanges operating in the context of an adequate national law on property rights and commercial law governing their exchange. The exchanges can, however, take steps to ensure that participants in the exchanges are well-established and reliable entities. The same applies to brokers and members of the exchanges. In addition, exchanges must ensure that the obligations of their members and their brokers are adequately covered by a system of guarantees and indemnity funds to cover against unforeseen defaults.

Finally, rules and regulations are needed to ensure that the above criteria for the efficiency of futures and forward markets are met. Also, there should be some form of surveillance to ensure that the set of rules and regulations is comprehensive and that they are complied with. The governments of the countries in which the exchanges are located must either establish the rules and regulations under which they operate (the American system) or ensure that the market itself maintains an adequate system of self-regulation (the

UK system). In both cases there has to be an adequate underlying commercial law and enforcement mechanism.

THE EFFICIENCY OF CHINA'S FUTURES MARKETS

Trading Practices

The most common trading practice in Western exchanges is the open-outcry, pit-based system. In the case of China, the futures markets have fully computerized trading. It has been argued that this is not appropriate for Chinese conditions (World Bank, 1994, p. 98). Computer-based trading is a cumbersome procedure which slows down the markets considerably (because of the need for constant typing in of complicated orders and codes and slow feedback), as compared with the open-outcry procedures of most Western markets. It also raises the specter of computer failure, a not infrequent occurrence. The costs of trading are also, unnecessarily, raised by collecting all of the traders onto a trading floor instead of allowing them to trade via the screens in their office and telephone links.

Computer-based trading is a highly capital-intensive technology which is not necessarily appropriate in a labor-abundant country. This raises the costs of trading on the exchanges—and the costs of trading on the exchanges in China are a large multiple of the costs of trading on Western exchanges. Exchange commissions on contracts range between 0.1 and 0.15 of the value of the contracts as compared to 0.0005 percent on the London Metal Exchange, for example. Such costs will mean that Chinese exchanges will not be able to compete with foreign exchanges once their clients are able to operate on them when capital account convertibility is introduced, which the government has promised to do within five years.[11]

Screen-based, or computer, trading also makes it difficult for local account traders, or locals, to emerge. Locals provide futures markets with an important source of liquidity by moving in and out of the market quickly during the trading sessions, making profits from "marrying" initially disparate bids and offers. Market makers always clear their positions every day. Screen trading slows the trading process down and removes the face-to-face contact which allows skilled market makers to judge market trends. The absence of profitable opportunities for short-term trading which is the result of screen-based trading prevents the emergence of liquidity-generating local traders.

A second practice that limits the efficiency of the markets, in this case by effectively financially prohibiting the use of the futures markets for inventory management, is the requirement of two margin payments to cover a "spread" (for example, buying a near contract and selling an identical contract for a later date). The margin is fixed for all commodity futures contracts on all Chinese exchanges at five percent. For comparison, in the London Metal Exchange only one margin is charged on a spread and its rate is not fixed but is determined by price volatility and associated risks. In an example provided by the World Bank (1994) the same spread on a twenty-five-ton copper lot in March 1993 would have required a margin deposit of 5,000 U.S. dollars in China's metals exchanges as against 1,000 U.S. dollars on the London Metal Exchange. For aluminum the same ratio was 150 U.S. dollars in London compared to 2,250 U.S. dollars in China. In an efficient market, rational inventory management will ensure that the time profile of forward prices reflects the cost of holding inventories, but excessive margins on spreads will prevent such inventory management techniques from being used optimally and this potential source of efficiency is lost.

Cash Market

For futures and forward markets to work properly there has to be a fully operational and competitive cash market. It has already been argued that such markets do not exist in China. In the case of copper, China's position in the world market means that the world market itself can act as the cash market within which offset trade and arbitraging can take place, within the limits set by China's trade and industrial policies. This is not the case for other markets. We have already shown that they cannot operate efficiently because of inadequate transport and warehousing facilities. We also pointed to government intervention as a constraint on the essential competitiveness of cash markets. Another reason for their inability to support futures trade efficiently is the dominance of some large players in the cash markets.

For a market to be efficient, individual traders should not have any power over market price setting. In most of China's futures markets, however, this is not the case. In most exchanges trading volume is not large enough for the market to be efficient. Companies that need or provide the underlying physical structure usually regard the futures exchanges as the last-resort market, because they usually have well-established channels for real buying and selling which are determined by "*guanxi*." At the going prices, traders cannot necessarily buy or sell the amount they want to, or if they can they may drive the price significantly up or down. This gives those participants, the large SOEs which produce or consume the traded products, a large degree of monopoly or monopsony power. As already noted, the SHME fares best in this regard because of its links to the international market and this supports its relatively high trading volume.

"Market squeezing" by big traders is a common occurrence in many of China's futures markets (Zhao *et al.*, 1993). When the delivery date is near, traders with sufficient storage capacity or large net spot positions often deliberately keep large open interests, either in long or in short position. Then those small traders who still have open positions are forced to choose between offsetting at very unfavorable prices or taking cash delivery, which can be even more difficult or loss making. Natural, noncompetitive advantages usually determine who wins and who loses in China's futures market. These natural advantages include: production, which accounts for a considerable proportion of the total output of the traded products; a monopoly of specialized information; and long-term and special *guanxi* with producing or distribution companies.

Taking SPEX as an example, large oil-producing companies (usually at the provincial level) were the big winners; if relatively small players whose spot business has nothing to do with the traded product traded profitably, this was mainly a matter of luck. A large oil field–owning company was a member of SPEX. As its oil was traded on the exchange it naturally possessed important inside information relating to output, demand, and possible new government policies, and so forth, which was denied most other traders in the same market.

In such situations, where market manipulation becomes possible, there are strong speculative incentives for those traders who can relatively easily arbitrage between the futures market and the spot market. In such situations the degree that prices can be pushed away from efficient levels is asymmetric, and market squeezing usually takes place in the form of irrationally low prices. When prices are driven up to an excessively high level, many big producers will be attracted to the futures market and take short positions; on the other hand, excessively low prices can stay for a relatively long time, because end users are usually individuals or small companies who cannot utilize the futures market and benefit from low prices. Furthermore, in a general economic background of austerity when money supply is tight, few companies have sufficient cash to make purchases from the futures market, especially since the use of bank guarantees was banned early in 1994. According to an informal survey, in several major futures markets in China about three quarters of the participants are consistent losers and the remaining quarter consistently winners (Ni *et al.*, 1993).[12]

Markets can be successfully squeezed in China because of the persistence of excess demand for most of the primary and intermediate goods that are traded in the futures markets. To operate effectively futures markets are supposed to operate in an economy with frequent price fluctuations but without systematic shortages or gluts. If shortage is a chronic phenomenon and price movements in cash markets are monotonously in the same direction, the techniques of futures markets are irrelevant. After fifteen years of reform, buyers' markets exist for most consumers' goods. For raw materials and energy products, however, it is still a classic shortage economy. In this situation, neither sellers nor buyers have much interest in hedging. Their attention is focused on such questions as: "What *guanxi* do I have that I can use to get the materials I want?" and "How should I trade the goods now in great demand for something else that I urgently need but which is in short supply?" In fact, the *guanxi* system provides a significant incentive *not* to place trade through competitive markets. The use of agreed overinvoicing by buyers and underinvoicing by sellers generates a cash margin which can be shared by the participants. A private-sector network of well-connected commission agents has sprung up to broker such trades.

Liquidity

Chinese commodities futures markets are not liquid. We have already noted the absence of locals and the prohibition of the use of bank guarantees for margin purposes. A further problem is that trade has spread over a large number of "protected" exchanges. By the end of 1993, there were more futures exchanges in China than in the United States, United Kingdom, Japan, and Germany combined. In Henan province alone, ten exchanges were set up within a very short period of time (Cai and Li, 1994). In countries with a long history of the development of futures markets, such as the United States or Britain, futures trading is highly concentrated in a few exchanges. More than seventy-five percent of agricultural futures contracts in the United States are traded on the Chicago Board of Trade, and almost 100 percent of energy futures contracts are traded on the New York Mercantile Exchange. The London Metal Exchange accounts for ninety percent of world nonferrous metal futures trading (Grossman and Chang, 1992; London Metal Exchange, 1994). Concentration of trading is necessary to ensure that there is sufficient liquidity in the futures markets and authoritative pricing. This is especially true during the early stages of the development of future markets, as now in China. There have been suggestions for the establishment of a comprehensive futures exchange such as the CBOT in Pudong, East Shanghai, and in the spring of 1994 the government announced plans to concentrate futures trading in a smaller number of exchanges, but the realization of these plans will depend on a compromise of interests being reached among the different "stripes" and "blocks".

The liquidity-reducing segmentation of markets, both futures and cash markets, is due to the rise of the "tribal economy," complete with blockades and protection measures and interprovincial smuggling.[13] The futures markets have been introduced against this background. Futures markets are not private-sector institutions. Usually a futures exchange is jointly set up by a central ministry or bureau which originally administered the production and distribution of the traded products and relevant bureaus of provincial or municipal governments. For example, SHME is cosponsored by the central Ministry of Internal Trade, the Shanghai Materials Bureau, and the Shanghai Municipal Government. Each "stripe" (central ministry or administrative bureau and its local offices) and block (regional government) wants to set up its own futures exchange. As already noted, many futures markets for the same product were set up in different regions or even in the same region because they belong to different provinces, cities, or different ministries or bureaus. Crude oil and petroleum were traded on six exchanges and coal and steel were traded on three each. As of October 1994, copper continued to be traded on seven exchanges.

Competitiveness

The segmentation of futures trade in China across many exchanges and the dominance of large state enterprises in that trade restrict the competitiveness of trade on the exchanges and therefore the efficiency and effectiveness with which they can carry out their functions. Competition on Chinese futures exchanges is also restricted by prohibitions on membership by foreign companies and by restrictions on international trade and currency convertibility.

Futures exchanges have to be competitive markets and this can be ensured by allowing risk to be spread internationally and price-smoothing arbitrage possibilities to be globalized.[14] So far, however, no foreign company has been allowed to take up membership in any futures exchanges.[15]

The competitive effect of international openness on the exchanges is also restricted by China's trade policy. Not many member companies on the exchanges nor many of their clients have import or export rights. Most foreign trade in primary or intermediate goods is effectively or actually under state control, so international arbitrage is not easy even when price differences are large. There are a few successful cases, such as the China Metal and Minerals Import and Export Corporation and the China Nonferrous Metals Import and Export Corporation, that have branches or agencies in London which can place orders in London futures exchanges via brokerage firms; or such as the China International Futures Corporation (CIFCO), which is itself a member of the Chicago Board of Trade, the Chicago Mercantile Exchange, and the New York Commodity Exchange. But even for them, arbitrage is no easy task, for they must go through two cash delivery processes in and outside China to get the profits from price disparity. High transaction costs and export-import restraints cut deeply into profits. So even for SHME, whose prices closely follow international prices, there still exist price disparities. One study has been made of the comparative movements in the price of copper contracts between SHME and New York Commodity Exchange (COMEX). This examined the period November and December 1992 (Liu, 1993). After adjustments for the exchange rate and location factors, differences ranged from a peak of 14.77 cents/pound to the lowest gap of two cents/pound. For half of the observed trading days, price differences surpassed five cents/pound.

If China's futures markets are to benefit from links with international markets, the foreign companies will have to be allowed to become members of its exchanges. The London Metal Exchange once excluded foreign members, yet today over ninety percent of its members are foreigners or joint ventures (Zhen and Peng, 1993; London Metal Exchange, 1994). The delay in China arises mainly from the fear that foreign companies with strong financial international expertise and rich experience may dominate the domestic futures market. Even in the more developed and mature Shanghai stock market, this fear has led to domestic and nondomestic participants being separated into different markets, i.e., the A share market and B share market. But it should be noted that when the Shanghai futures market is really internationally linked, no players will have the power to systematically beat the market; this can be inferred from the performance of different futures markets in Shanghai. The SHME, the most internationalized exchange among all exchanges in China, is also the one that most nearly approaches full competition. But this problem is closely related to the currency convertibility problem and the problem of trade controls.

The effectiveness of opening up China's futures markets to foreign members and to competition through foreign trade will depend on improvements in the convertibility of the Chinese currency, the Renminbi (Rmb). From January 1994, China began a new foreign exchange era, with a single exchange rate and a managed flexible exchange rate system. The Rmb currently only enjoys conditional convertibility on the current account, however, and none on the capital account. If foreign companies want to become members of Chinese futures exchanges or plan to make big deals in Chinese futures markets, they may face currency problems. While those foreign companies can easily buy their Rmb investment funds by converting hard currencies, it is unlikely to be so easy to convert back their investment proceeds into their own currencies and even more difficult to send their trading profits home.

Security

The institutional features of all of China's futures exchanges are modeled on Western exchanges, in particular the CBOT and LME. As a result the financial safeguards for participants on the exchanges are similar to, but not the same as, the security arrangements on Western exchanges.

In the first instance applicants for membership of the exchanges must pass tests of financial status. The trading positions of the members are then monitored by Management Committees, or internal supervisory committees of the exchanges' councils, which are themselves supervised by the local authorities and the local branches of the People's Bank of China. All of the exchanges control the daily range of price fluctuations. They all operate a standard margin system, the margin being an unvarying five percent for all commodity futures in all exchanges. Positions are marked to market every day through internal settlement divisions which also act as clearinghouses taking on the counterparty risk for members' trades. All of the exchanges operate an internal guarantee fund to protect members against each other's possible default. The method of financing the fund varies from exchange to exchange. In the case of the Shanghai Metal Exchange the fund is financed by an initial deposit of members of Rmb 200,000 and twenty percent of the Exchange's annual revenue. By the middle of 1994 the fund stood at Rmb 100 million. In the case of the Beijing Commodity Exchange the initial deposit is Rmb 300,000.

A weakness of the Chinese exchanges is that none of them appears to operate a fidelity fund to protect clients against their brokers' default. There is an awareness of this gap, but so far no plans to fill it.

The Regulatory and Legislative Framework

At the present time there is no national legal framework governing the operation of futures exchanges in China. Each exchange has developed its own regulatory code which is supervised by a Council and Management Committee. Although all of the exchanges have modeled themselves on Western exchanges, mainly the CBOT, they have not established identical systems of regulatory supervision. And all exchanges are partially or completely "owned" by ministries or provincial or municipal governments and therefore are subject to their authority. It was the lack of a central authority with an enforceable national legislative framework which allowed the industry to grow without control and the number of exchanges and brokerage firms to mushroom. The legal vacuum also allowed a large number of nonstate informal, illegal brokers to establish themselves and also a large industry based on overseas futures markets to develop.

Without legislative backing the State Administration for Industry and Commerce was unable to impose a national regulatory framework on the industry. National legislation is currently under preparation, in a committee established by the China Securities Regulatory Commission (CSRC), but progress is slower than expected and the draft laws were not expected to be published until mid-1995. In the meantime the CSRC is attempting to assert central authority over the industry using the medium of administrative "circulars," which it issues with State Council approval. Until such circulars are backed up by enforceable laws their effectiveness depends on the CSRC's ability to obtain compliance by approval of the State Council and, by implication, of the Chinese Communist Party.

In the absence of a legislation-enshrined central regulatory system the CSRC issued, in June 1994, a State Council–approved circular aimed at bringing the futures industry under central government discipline. The "Circular on Resolute Prohibition of the Blind Development of Futures Markets" contained six new administrative orders.

The first determined that only thirty-three of the existing exchanges will be allowed to continue to trade and that most of these will be restricted to wholesale trade. The circular set out four criteria that commodity markets must meet if they are to be allowed to trade in futures contracts. The first is that an exchange must have more than fifty members. The second is that its daily turnover in the January-April 1994 period should have been more than Rmb 100 million. The third criterion is that futures contracts must account for more than ninety percent of trading volume. And the fourth criterion is that futures exchanges will have to be located in the major cities. In September 1994 it was announced that the number of futures exchanges would be limited to fifteen; the fifteen to be allowed to operate as futures exchanges were not announced, but they are believed to include three in Shanghai and one each in Beijing, Shenzhen, Guangzhou, Tianjin, Chungqing, Zhengzhou, Hainan, Suzhou, and three other cities as yet unidentified. The exchanges refused permission to trade futures contracts will be allowed to continue in business as wholesale or cash markets.

The second order forbids Chinese enterprises from taking part in futures trading on foreign exchanges. There is an exception for banks, which are allowed to hedge currency positions, and authorized trading companies, which are allowed to hedge positions they hold in internationally traded commodities. Both exceptions are subject to specific approval of each contract and to the contracts being traded on exchanges with which the

Chinese State Securities Regulatory Committee has signed a coregulation agreement.

The third order prohibits trade in all index futures (mainly stock exchange indices). It also prohibits domestic trade in currency futures until a management act is published by the State Foreign Exchange Management Bureau and CSRC. Trade in treasury bond futures will continue to be allowed, but only in a few authorized exchanges.

The fourth order covers the reregistration of brokerage companies. Only 144 of the 300 to 500 previously operating have been reregistered.[16] No Sino-foreign joint venture brokerage has been reregistered and no new ones will be allowed. All brokerage firms that had been allowed to trade on foreign exchanges will now only be allowed to trade on domestic exchanges (if they have been reregistered).

The fifth order states that SOEs and institutions can only trade in futures that are related to their cash market business. All SOEs that are making losses are prohibited from trading futures contracts.

Finally, the sixth order sets up a new three-tier management structure for the industry: self-discipline of futures exchanges; self-management of the futures industry; and government regulation via legislation and enforcement.

The June 1994 circular joins the two existing measures governing registration of brokers and foreign exchange trading and a (forthcoming) temporary arrangement governing Means of Production Exchanges.[17] Together, these measures represent national policy on the development and regulation of futures markets. They are all to be superseded by the new Law of Futures Trading currently being drafted by a group commissioned to do so by the CSRC.[18] When completed, which was expected by mid-1995, after approval by the State Council, it was to be submitted to the National People's Congress for enactment.

CONCLUSION

This chapter has shown that futures exchanges have established themselves as a significant element in China's socialist market economy. It has also argued that there are factors preventing them from achieving their full potential efficiency and effectiveness. Whether or not the administrative measures introduced by the Government in June 1994 will succeed in controlling the burgeoning trade in futures contracts, or simply force those that are now prohibited underground, is a moot point.

As the Chinese economy continues its process of transformation into a socialist market economy, increasing numbers of enterprises and individuals will want to take advantage of the risk management and inventory management roles of futures and forward markets, and this in turn will help attract arbitrageurs and speculators into the markets. In the short to medium run, however, the ability of the Chinese economy to run such markets on an efficient and effective basis is limited. This is partly because of the limited development of the institutional framework required by a market economy, partly because of the limited development of the physical infrastructure needed to sustain the cash markets essential for futures and forward markets, and partly because of the remaining controls and controllers in the economy. Taken together with the limited openness of the economy to the forces of international competition, the presence of these factors means that China's futures and forward markets have so far been on balance destabilizing—with the exception of the copper market, which is more closely connected with the world market. The balance of activity on the markets has been biased toward speculation, which has led to an increase in price volatility with an inflationary trend. The moral hazard problem peculiar to a communist economy in transition has meant that the substantial profits made by some players have attracted many more players into the markets whose only interest is gambling.

The use of the futures contracts for gambling has introduced a destabilizing element into the markets. The practice has also encouraged the growth of an informal futures industry on which extensive illegal trade takes place. It has also encouraged the use of futures contracts on overseas exchanges for speculative purposes, sometimes illegally. *The Financial Times* (June 24, 1994) reported large losses (unspecified in the article but widely believed to be in the order of forty to forty-five million U.S. dollars) incurred by Shanghai traders on the London Metal Exchange and which led them to default. The Government of China is, however, aware of these problems. It is this awareness, and awareness of the problems on domestic exchanges, which led the State Council to authorize the release of the "Circular on Resolute Prohibition of the Blind Development of Futures Markets" while waiting for the new "Law on Futures Trading" to be written.

In the short run, the Government hopes that the administrative measures that have been introduced will limit the potential for speculation. They limit the range of contracts to those commodities for which a cash market exists, or can be developed soon. They also limit the number of markets on which similar contracts can be traded, and the number of cities in which they can be established, in order to encourage economies of scale. They also ban speculative investments on foreign markets in order to reduce instability and to focus attention on the development of the domestic markets.

In the longer run, the Government needs to continue developing the infrastructure necessary to encourage the formation of a single national economy in order to ensure that futures markets can operate efficiently. It also needs to press ahead with the development of the comprehensive commercial law which is needed to provide the framework for legislation on trade in futures contracts. Finally, it should make preparations to encourage foreign enterprise specializing in this sector to bring their expertise to China in order to ensure that the most efficient trading practices are adopted and to improve the competitiveness and liquidity of the markets.

NOTES

The research on which this chapter is mainly based was carried out before the rapid development of trade in financial futures in Shanghai and Beijing in 1994; consequently little account is taken of that trade. Financial futures in China are the subject of a separate paper by the authors (see Wall and Jiang, 1995, *Futures and Derivatives Law Review*, Vol. 2 (1), pp. 13–42). The authors would like to thank the editor of *Futures and Derivatives Law Review* for reproducing this chapter.

1. Forward contracts are in the main agreements between parties with an interest in a physical commodity as producer on the one side and consumer on the other, although traders can and do act as intermediaries in many cases. They will be denominated in quantities specific to the interests of the parties involved and as such are often difficult to trade. Futures contracts are standardized contracts with respect to quantity, quality, and delivery point. They form the basis of trade on commodity, or futures, exchanges. Forward contracts always result in delivery. Most futures contracts do not. They are offset with an equal and opposite contract before maturity, or they may be written in cash settlement terms so that only the difference between the price set in the contract and the price in the market for the underlying physical commodity or financial instrument is settled between the buyer and the seller of the contract.

2. The State Council is, effectively, China's Cabinet.

3. However, having bought insurance against price falls, sellers (buyers) may now worry that they will be forgoing profits if the prices actually rise (fall). They can cover this risk of losing potential gains in many exchanges, but not yet in China, by buying an option on a futures contract giving them the option to buy (sell) the item at the same time that they have a commitment to sell (buy) it, with a locked-in price equal to or somewhat above (below) the price that they have a commitment to sell (buy). In this way the sellers and buyers of the contracts can be sure that their future income (loss) from the transaction will fall within a known range.

4. The four groups are not mutually exclusive; principals may arbitrage and speculate as main activities because they believe themselves to have superior knowledge of, or skills in operating in, the underlying markets.

5. Several more were opened early in 1994 but no details are available. For reasons discussed below they are unlikely to become proper futures markets.

6. For comparison, trade in financial futures (treasury bond futures) was only Rmb 216.28 million in 1993 (Lu, 1993), although this trade grew rapidly in 1994 following reforms in the financing of government expenditure and the clampdown in the commodity exchanges. The daily transaction value in treasury bond futures reached Rmb 1.2 billion (137.9 million U.S. dollars) on the Beijing Commodity Exchange on June 9, 1994, compared with the daily average of Rmb 300 million (34.5 million U.S. dollars) in March. The closest comparable figures on the Shanghai Stock Exchange were the May 1994 daily average of Rmb 990 million (113.8 million U.S. dollars) and the January/April daily average of Rmb 370 million (42.5 million U.S. dollars). Trade in treasury bond futures began on the Shanghai Stock Exchange in late 1992 and has since developed on ten other exchanges, five officially and five unofficially (*China Daily Business Weekly*, June 19–25, 1994). For further analysis of financial futures markets in China, see Wall and Jiang (*forthcoming*).

7. Data from Liu *et al.* (1994).

8. Trading in sugar and steel futures with delivery dates later than October 1994 was banned in June 1994.

9. The margin payment on the smallest contract in financial futures is only Rmb 500 and this has attracted millions of small investors to speculate in those contracts.

10. See Wall (1993) for a discussion of the *guanxi* effect in Chinese markets.

11. The introduction, by the Shanghai Municipal Government on January 1, 1994, of a 1.5 percent tax on transactions in all Shanghai exchanges except the SCOE will intensify pressure to be able to use foreign exchanges.

12. Several brokers on SPEX, SCOE, and SBME agree with this ratio.

13. For a comprehensive review of the factors preventing the development of a national market, see World Bank (1994).

14. Brokers in China feel that they need a period of learning before they have to compete with foreign firms. Lu Jian, President of China International Futures Co. Ltd (CIFCO), has called for at least five years' protection. He describes the Chinese industry as a "sampan" and the industry overseas as a "gigantic ship" and asks, "How can the gigantic ship be allowed to sail in China when the country has yet to dig the channel" (*Beijing Review*, 1994, Vol. 37, Issue 8). However, foreigners can, and to a limited extent do, enter the market and make deals through Chinese members; this is neither encouraged nor prohibited. It has not been prohibited mainly because it cannot be under the present clearing system. Exchange members normally open only one clearing account or margin account in each futures exchange, and clearing departments cannot tell from their accounts if

any dealing is for foreign customers. So the futures exchanges just watch the general safety and margin sufficiency of member companies and if the latter have foreign clients, that is up to the member companies themselves.

15. In April 1994 the Shenzhen Municipal Government announced (*China Daily Business Weekly*, April 24–30, 1994, p. 5) plans to allow Hong Kong–based brokerage companies to take up seats on the then two exchanges in Shenzhen.

16. The Chinese Securities Regulatory Commission estimates that 500 brokerage firms were operating at the peak, of which only 300 were registered (reported in the *Financial Times*, April 11, 1994). Fifty Sino-foreign joint ventures were reported to be operating at the beginning of 1994—now all threatened with closure.

17. "Temporary Measures for Registration Management of Futures Brokerage Companies" issued by the State Administration Bureau of Industry and Commerce on April 28, 1993 and the "Trial Measures for the Management of Foreign Exchange Futures Trading" issued by the State Foreign Exchange Administration Bureau on June 9, 1993. "Temporary Stipulations for Means of Production Exchanges" to be issued by the State Materials Ministry.

18. Traders and officials in futures markets worry about the proliferation of administrative orders and are anxiously awaiting the new legislation. After the publication of the six new regulations Chen Gongyan, vice-president of the Beijing Commodities Exchange, is reported as saying that "many exchanges are at a loss without detailed guidelines. . . . [we] hope that the government will publicly clarify its policies. We should rely more on laws and regulations, instead of administrative policies, to supervise the market" (*China Daily Business Weekly*, June 12–18, 1994, p. 1).

REFERENCES

Cai, Youcai, and Li, Xushen, 1994, "Severe Blindness in the Development of Futures Market in China," *Shanghai Economy*, January (in Chinese).

Grossman, W.D., and Chang, Qing, 1992, *Theoretical Policies and Administration of Futures Market*, Shandong People's Publishing House (in Chinese).

Hu, Yuezheng, 1993, "Current Situation and Operational Mechanisms in the Shanghai Metal Exchange," Speech at the opening ceremony of the Shanghai Petroleum Exchange.

Jiang, Wei, 1994, "The Efficiency of Shanghai's Futures Markets," Paper presented at the University of Sussex/Fudan University conference on Shanghai in the International Economy, Shanghai, September.

Liu, Huangsong, et al., 1994, "Existing Problems and Countermeasures of State Level Commodity Exchanges in Shanghai," *Shanghai Statistical Report*, Volume 3, January (in Chinese).

Liu, Xiaobing, 1993, "Feasibilities of Cross-Markets Arbitrage in Shanghai Futures Market," *Shanghai Economy*, March (in Chinese).

London Metal Exchange, 1994, *Profile*.

Lu, Yan, 1993, "Futures Heat—Problems and Countermeasures," *Journal of International Financial Introduction*, April (in Chinese).

Ni, Runting, *et al.*, 1993, "Development of Futures Markets—A Natural Choice for a Socialist Market Economy," Paper presented at Special Seminar on Futures Markets by the People's Bank of China (in Chinese).

Song, Hua, 1993, "Deep-Rooted Handicaps for Futures Market Development in China and Countermeasures," *Economic System Reform*, May (in Chinese).

Sun, Haiming, 1994, "The Futures Markets in China: A Retrospective," Mimeo, Chinese Economy Programme, University of Sussex, March.

Tian, Yuan, 1993, China's *Futures Market*, Guangdong Higher Education Press (in Chinese).

Wall, David, 1993, "Special Economic Zones in China: The Administrative and Regulatory Framework," *Journal of East Asian Affairs*, 7(1) Winter/Spring.

Wang, Benqiang, 1993, "Research on Several Problems in the Construction of Futures Markets in China," Economic System Reform, May (in Chinese).

World Bank, 1994 China: *Internal Market Development and Regulation*, Report No. 12291–CHI, Washington, DC, March.

Wu, Zheng, 1994, "Ban Dims Futures," Shanghai Star, April 26.

Xu, Xuewu. 1993, "Proposals for a Futures Market Experiment in Shanghai," *Research on Shanghai Economic System Reform*, 17, June (in Chinese).

Yang, Jinming, 1993, "The Establishment and Development of Shanghai Petroleum Exchange," Opening speech on the establishment of SPEX, May.

Yang, Peixin, 1994, "Checking the Price of Cereals and Oil—Another Step in Macro economic Control," *Shanghai Economic Research*, February (in Chinese).

Yu, Guocong, 1994, "One Year of Struggle and Progress Exploration of the Shanghai Metal Exchange," *China Futures*, March (in Chinese).

Zhao, Zhangsheng, *et al.*, 1993, "Meditation on Improvements of the Legal Framework of China's Futures Markets," *Research on Shanghai Economic System Reform*, 26, November (in Chinese).

Zhen, Yuanhen, and Peng, Gang, 1993, "The Way to Internationalise China's Futures Markets," *Special Zone Economy*, January (in Chinese).

Zhu, Zhongdi, 1993, "Retrospection and Expectation of Shanghai Futures Markets," Paper presented at the seminar Strategies for Shanghai Becoming an International Metropolis in the 21st Century, Shanghai, June (in Chinese).

10

The Stock Markets in China

KUI-WAI LI and KWOK-FAI WONG

INTRODUCTION

Between 1979 and 1993, China's annual average GDP growth rate was as high as nine percent. Combined with financial market liberalization, China has become an attractive location for manufacturing, export, and financial market development. Capital markets first began in 1984, and together with the stock market, the PRC government hopes that surplus personal savings and foreign funds can be directed to productive investments. With Deng's visit to southern China in 1992, China's economic reform momentum and free-market drive will remain. This could encourage foreign investors to invest in China stocks.

The PRC government began conducting the "shareholding experiment" in 1984. At the end of 1993, more than 2,000 companies and 17,000 employees were working in the securities industry. The value of stocks in 1987 represented about two percent of the market securities outstanding and the figure rose to eight percent in 1993 (see Table 10.1).[1] In terms of trading volume, shares represented 86.5 percent of the market transaction in 1993, increased from 7.2 percent in 1987 (Table 10.2).

Directives concerning the national standards for establishing limited liability companies were issued in 1992. They included the "Standards Opinion on Companies Limited by Shares" and the "Standards Opinions

Table 10.1
Composition of Financial Securities in China, 1985–1993

(100 Million Rmb)

	1985	1986	1987	1988	1989	1990	1991	1992	1993
Government Bond*	237.2	293.1	391.5	558.6	769.3	890.3	1,060.0	1,282.7	1,540.7
	98%	72%	68%	57%	59%	50%	47%	39%	42%
Finance Bond	5.0	30.0	60.0	85.0	75.6	89.9	123.1	170.1	
	2%	7%	10%	9%	6%	5%	5%	5%	0%
Enterprise Bond		83.7	86.4	115.0	146.4	195.4	331.1	653.9	653.9
		21%	15%	12%	11%	11%	15%	20%	18%
A-shares			10.0	35.0	6.6	4.3	29.5	114.6	37.4
B-shares							1.5	11.2	12.8
H-shares									40.4
Share Outstanding			10.0	35	41.6	45.9	76.9	202.6	293.2
			2%	4%	3%	3%	3%	6%	8%
Others			30.0	179.3	265.6	543.7	675.4	1,015.5	1,205.6
			5%	18%	20%	31%	30%	31%	35%
Total	242.2	406.8	577.9	972.9	1,298.5	1,765.2	2,266.5	3,324.8	3,693.5

Note: * Government Bond for 1981, 1982, 1983, and 1984 were 48.6, 92.5, 134.1, and 176.6, respectively. Date for bond issues were the year end outstanding figures whereas the shares were the new issues in that year.
Source: Yearbook of China Securities Market 1994, Beijing: Reform Publishing.

Table 10.2
Trading Volume of Marketable Securities in China (Rmb, ten thousand)

(Rmb 10 thousand)

	1987	1988	1989	1990	1991	1992	1993
Government Bond		242,085.0	212,600.0	1,159,353.0	3,701,728.0	10,825,742.0	8,305,649.2
		92%	92%	85%	74%	40%	10%
Financial Bond	1,200.0	6,958.0	4,611.0	4,622.0	78,147.0	350,192.0	222,477.0
	11%	3%	2%	0%	2%	1%	0%
Enterprise Bond	9,162.0	11,587.0	7,909.0	10,558.0	246,328.0	1,282,293.0	2,345,091.8
	82%	4%	3%	1%	5%	5%	3%
Stock	800.0	922.0	2,315.0	181,237.0	867,400.0	13,624,800.0	73,340,600.0
	7%	0%	1%	13%	17%	50%	87%
Others		1,285.0	2,725.0	10,157.0	133,280.0	1,167,882.0	532,172.3
		0%	1%	1%	3%	4%	1%
Total	11,163.0	262,837.0	230,160.0	1,365,927.0	5,026,883.0	27,250,909.0	84,745,990.2

Source: Yearbook of China Securities Market 1994, Beijing: Reform Publishing.

on Limited Liability Companies." On June 10, 1993, in order to permit China stocks to be listed overseas, an addendum to the "Standards Opinions" was issued. On July 1, 1994, the first companies law, the PRC Companies Law, became effective. On August 27, 1994, the "Mandatory Provisions for the Articles of Association of Companies Listing Overseas" was promulgated to perfect the regulation on overseas listing.[2] Subsequently, shareholding companies developed quickly and by 1993 there were more than 3,000 shareholding companies in the country and the total capital raised amounted to Rmb 28,335 million (Table 10.3).

THE STOCK FEVER

At the beginning, state enterprises were permitted to issue shares to their employees only. The first publicly traded stock in the PRC, the Tianqiao Department Store in Beijing, was introduced in July 1984. This was followed by the second marketable stock issue, Shanghai Fello, which was offered to the public in Shanghai in November. The PRC government intended to make Shanghai the country's primary financial center, and granted Shanghai the right to trade bonds and shares over-the-counter (OTC) in 1986.

However, domestic investors were not interested in stock investment before 1989 even though trading of securities in the PRC was carried out in the over-the-counter markets in various major cities, including Shanghai, Chongqing, Wuhan, Guangzhou, and Shenyang. It was only after March 1989 that the public started to realize the potential gains from stock investment and the stock market became active. In March 1989, the Shenzhen Development Bank, the first publicly traded stock in Shenzhen, distributed handsome dividends and rights issues to its shareholders. Its share price then rose rapidly. In May 1989, the share price of the Shenzhen Development Bank surged to Rmb 120, from around twenty Renminbi in 1988. This represented a huge profit to its shareholders.[3] "Stock fever" developed quickly in Shenzhen. As people believed that buying stocks was a "sure win" game, share prices surged. The demand for Shenzhen stocks soon came from various parts of China. At that time, however, there were only five securities traded in Shenzhen (Shenzhen Development Bank, Shenzhen Vanke Company, Shenzhen Gintian Industry Company, Shenzhen Shekou Anda Industry Company, and Shenzhen Champaign Industrial). As there was plenty of demand while supply was limited, share prices rose rapidly and black-market activities developed.

The Shenzhen government and the People's Bank of China (PBOC) were alarmed by the overwhelming public reaction. Actions were taken to

Table 10.3
Distribution of the Shareholding Companies (1993)

(Rmb 1,000)

City	No. of Firms	Book Value Issued	State Shares	Legal person Shares	Natural Person Shares		B-Shares
					Worker Shares	Public Shares	
Beijing	68	830,391	32,765	754,812	28,545	4,269	10,000
Tianjin	21	375,895	239,817	58,809	22,992	54,276	
Hebei	79	585,752	168,140	334,422	79,191		4,000
Shanxi	28	378,211	45,389	276,325	56,497		
Iner Mongolia	27	74,833	34,339	35,910	2,964	1,620	
Liaoning	228	2,263,000	904,000	925,000	403,000	27,000	4,000
Jilin	135	1,509,375	777,199	432,562	284,921	14,693	
Heilongjiang	86	683,756	258,745	302,816	122,195		
Shanghai	120	2,796,153	1,394,946	822,111	64,155	167,169	347,773
Jiangsu	115	916,130	393,056	434,433	57,316	31,325	
Zhejiang	126	814,785	130,376	573,291	73,359	35,559	2,200
Anhui	36	775,425	469,324	54,336	28,172	50,300	173,293
Fujian	43	305,429	147,596	118,880	6,571	27,002	5,380
Jiangxi	34	57,400	44,600	1,400	240	11,160	
Shandong	236	767,423	299,777	265,263	113,549	51,468	37,366
Henan	174	276,979	105,991	100,441	37,481	24,181	8,886
Hubei	176	812,544	257,414	415,381	139,750		
Hunan	98	487,568	132,207	264,920	78,111	12,330	
Guangdong	229	3,327,280	728,103	2,141,619	383,346	43,722	30,490
Guangxi	105	919,525	213,631	531,803	149,591	4,500	20,000
Hainan	96	1,572,780	92,667	1,234,550	232,537	13,026	
Sichuan	47	494,764	166,868	220,680	68,726	38,490	

Table 10.3 (continued)

Guizhou	20	154,164	30,639	94,267	22,998	6,260	
Yunnan	19	234,923	32,783	175,386	10,114	10,140	6,500
Tibet	0	0					
Shaanxi	24	238,818	78,631	110,221	34,441	15,525	
Gansu	11	70,972	11,900	37,114	6,918	15,040	
Qinghai	0	0					
Ningxia	8	22,053	711	16,060	1,942	3,340	
Xinjiang	22	67,757	9,928	40,632	12,697	4,500	
Chongqing	34	289,060	125,699	126,882	20,855	10,120	5,504
Shenyang	50	590,461	321,129	167,654	75,193	22,750	3,735
Dalian	83	545,750	95,113	310,362	133,181	7,094	
Harbin	26	156,748	59,945	65,554	14,615	16,635	
Wuhan	90	433,176	102,416	254,013	76,748		
Guangzhou	50	527,875	174,818	254,614	63,674	14,659	20,111
Xian	14	100,221	22,381	57,484	4,831	15,525	
Qingdao	30	162,585	50,184	84,403	13,998	14,000	
Ningbo	12	48,459	5,493	37,450	1,758	3,758	
Xiamen	13	99,684	26,597	56,676	5,246	4,995	6,171
Shenzhen	209	1,494,411	936,654	197,475	92,935	112,602	154,745
Chengdu	83	719,120	136,336	204,148	331,709	46,928	
Nanjing	20	134,273	70,361	49,483	9,430	5,000	
Changchun	39	305,932	145,221	99,398	61,313		
Jinan	21	111,197	45,015	28,813	13,036	21,932	2,400
Others	25	902,852	497,317	150,919	40,581	44,440	169,594
Total	3,210	28,435,889	10,016,221	12,918,772	3,481,422	1,007,333	1,012,148

Source: Yearbook of China Securities Market 1994, Beijing: Reform Publishing.

discourage speculation from May 28, 1990, onward. Regulations were also strengthened. All transactions were required to be conducted by authorized institutions in order to suppress black-market activities. Furthermore, a heavy transaction tax, a capital gain tax, and a daily maximum fluctuation of price were imposed. At the end of May 1990, daily price movement was restricted to ten percent. On June 18, 1990, the daily maximum price fluctuations were further limited to five percent. The Shenzhen authority introduced asymmetric price limits on June 28; prices were allowed to fall by five percent, but their upward movements were restricted to one percent.

These measures, however, were ineffective. Stock prices kept going up. After the introduction of the one percent upper limit in June 1990, stock prices of the five issues went up by more than three times in the subsequent five months. Black-market activities became more rampant. The authority soon found that the old measures were ineffective; extra and severe punitive measures were imposed on November 20, 1990. There were also "unintended" consequences. Panic selling started on December 20, 1990, as investors lost their confidence in the shares. The slump of the stock prices began and lasted for about eleven months.

As stock prices in Shenzhen fluctuated widely in 1990, stocks in Shanghai were rather quiet, and trading was inactive. The Jingan Index, which was introduced on December 2, 1987 with a base value of 100, went down by seventeen percent to 83 in December 1989. By June 1990, the Jingan Index, however, rebounded and broke through the 100 index level. In the middle of July 1990, the State Council finally permitted the opening up of the stock exchange. The Jingan Index surged to 155.49 on July 26, 1990.

During this period, more and more speculators transferred their funds from the Shenzhen to the Shanghai stock market. Determined not to repeat the Shenzhen experience, administrative measures were quickly adopted by the Shanghai authority. A three percent daily price limit was introduced and black-market activities were prohibited. However, these measures were not effective and the stock prices continued to rise.

The inflow of capital coming from the Shenzhen market pushed the authorities to revise the daily price limit downward to one percent on December 27, 1990. In January 1991, it was further narrowed down to 0.5 percent. But the Shanghai Composite Index continued to go up and closed at 292.75 at the end of 1991. People became very speculative and observed that the rising stock prices were regarded as an assurance of a good return.

China's stock markets entered the second stage of their development in 1991. The PRC government allowed foreign participation in the market. In 1991, Shanghai Vacuum Electron Devices successfully got the first permission to issue "special Renminbi shares," commonly known as the "B-shares" available only to foreigners. Shanghai Vacuum Electron Devices had its offering only on January 20, 1992, and was listed on the SSE on February 21. In December 1991, China Southern Glass offered 1.6 million of B-shares in SZSE.

In April 1992, the PRC officially gave the Shenzhen and Shanghai city governments more autonomy over local share issues. On October 9, 1992, the first N-share issued by Brilliance was listed in the New York Stock Exchange (NYSE). This move was regarded as a milestone in China's stock market history.

However, stock activities were volatile in 1992. Since April 1991, the Shenzhen Stock Exchange (SZSE) had relaxed its price limits, while the price limit was removed in May 1992. Fueled by the huge excess demands in the two exchanges, trading activities increased rapidly. The Shanghai Composite Index jumped sharply, and surged from 616 to 1,266 on May 21, 1992. Investors paid little or no attention to the fundamentals of the stocks.

Investors and speculators learned their lesson when low-quality stocks were suspended from trading. On July 7, 1992, the Shenzhen Champaign Industrial was suspended from trading.[4] That was the first time trading was suspended in the history of the PRC stock market. This incident aroused the discontent of the shareholders and the authority's attention to the quality of the listed company.

Another undesirable event that happened in 1992 was the outbreak of riots in Shenzhen. The riots were induced by the lottery system of initial public offerings (IPOs) in Shenzhen and caught the attention of the central government. Driven by a sharp increase of household savings and declining bank interest rates, domestic investors were eager to buy shares, especially those in the initial public offering. As there was huge demand for the IPOs, a lottery system was used to allocate the new issues to the applicants. Investors were required to buy the "application form," or so-called "lottery form." Each application form costed Rmb 100. Even though the lottery forms were distributed on August 9, long lines already appeared on August 7 at every selling center. It was estimated that over 400,000 investors rushed to Shenzhen and lined up overnight for the application forms. Lottery forms were quickly out of stock. Since most of the investors could not buy the application forms, black markets and bribery activities soon appeared, violence eventually broke out, and rioting began.[5]

In order to meet the huge demand, new stocks were listed. Although subsequent new listings were supplied on a large scale, stock prices in these two exchanges soon began to drop substantially. The Shanghai Composite Index slumped from its year high of 1,421 on May 25, to 702 at the end of September 1992, and dropped further to 393 on December 17, 1992.

It was not until the end of 1992 that stock prices rebounded and closed at 780, as investors expected handsome dividend payments from the listed companies. Both the Shanghai and Shenzhen Composite Indices reached their peak on February 15 (1,536) and February 22 (359), 1993, respectively. After these peaks, the indices slumped again.

To curb inflation, the PRC government started its austerity program in the summer of 1993; stock prices responded negatively and dropped. On July 21, 1993, the Shenzhen Composite Index was down to 203, while the Shanghai Composite Index dropped to 787 on July 26. Even though the indices rebounded on August 1993, they went down again in the following months. By the end of 1993, the market indices of Shenzhen and Shanghai closed at 238 and 833, respectively.

The year 1993 represented another step in China's stock market development. After the announcement of the China Securities Regulatory Commission (CSRC) that nine China companies would be listed on the Stock Exchange of Hong Kong (SEHK), Chinese companies started to raise capital in Hong Kong directly through the listing of the so-called H-shares in the SEHK. At the end of 1993, six H-shares were listed in the SEHK. Shanghai Petrochemical went further and issued its American Depository Receipt (ADRs) in the New York Stock Exchange and became the first Chinese company to secure a listing in the United States.[6] It was remarked that "if the first half of 1992 was the era of the B-share, 1993 became the era of the H-share" (*Euromoney*, December 1993).

The Shanghai and Shenzhen stock markets continued to decline in 1993. This was caused by the twofold impact of the domestic austerity measures and the rising number of new shares issued. Both the Chinese government and the People's Bank of China took further action to increase savings deposits, and a large amount of funds began to flow into the banking system in April 1994.[7] As a result, the indices of the Shanghai and Shenzhen stock markets reached their year low at 333 and 96, respectively, on July 29, 1993.

The declining price, however, was regarded as a positive sign from foreign investors' points of view as it pulled the markets "towards more sensible valuations" (Margolis, 1995). The authorities, however, were concerned about the decline and its impact on social stability. Rescue measures aimed at halting the slide were introduced. These measures included the delay of new A-share issues, the provision of credit to local brokers, and the suggestion of foreign participation in the A-share market. These measures were unexpected and the market reacted positively. Trading became active again. On September 12, 1994, the indices of Shanghai and Shenzhen markets rebounded to 1,019 and 225, respectively. The upward trend, however, did not last long; the two indices went down and closed at 562 and 125, respectively, at the end of 1994.

THE TWO EXCHANGES: TRADING SYSTEM, SETTLEMENT, AND PERFORMANCE

The Shanghai Securities Exchange (SSE) and the Shenzhen Stock Exchange (SZSE) were officially opened on December 19, 1990, and July 3, 1991, respectively.[8] The two exchanges were first regulated by the People's Bank of China (PBOC), but this power was later delegated to the State Council Securities Policy Commission (SCSPC) in 1992. The China Securities Regulatory Commission (CSRC) is responsible for the overall day-to-day supervision and administration of the two stock exchanges. The listed securities include debt instruments issued by the state, construction bonds, bonds issued by financial institutions, corporate bonds, corporate shares, and fund and other certificates with rights attached.

The A-shares are ordinary shares denominated and traded in Renminbi by domestic legal entities, enterprises, and individuals. Foreign investors, including Chinese in Hong Kong, Macau, and Taiwan, trade only the B-shares, which are settled in foreign currencies. Similarly, local investors are not permitted to acquire the B-shares.

By May 1995, 175 A-shares and 34 B-shares were listed in the SSE and 122 A-shares and 24 B-shares in the SZSE.[9] In the SSE, the market capitalization of the A-share and B-share was Rmb 232,077 million and 1,131.6 million U.S. dollars, respectively, on May 9, 1995. In the SZSE, the market capitalization of the A-share and the B-share was Rmb 87,281.2 million and 3877.2 million Hong Kong dollars, respectively. The highest ten stocks by market capitalization in the two exchanges and their market weighting are given in Tables 10.4 and 10.5. Not many A-shares are included in the 10 largest stocks as their total market weightings are less than forty percent. The top ten A-shares in the SSE represent only 32.5 percent of the total A-share stocks, whereas the corresponding weighting in the SZSE is only 24.5 percent. As there are fewer stocks in the B-share market, the corresponding weightings in the SSE and SZSE are 63.6 percent and 75.05 percent, respectively. As these indices are all value-weighted, the B-share indices are more sensitive to the changes in the value of the large stocks than the A-shares.

Table 10.6 gives the regulations, trading mechanisms, and settlement methods of the two exchanges. Both exchanges have a computerized order-matching system. A-shares in both exchanges are traded in Renminbi. The currencies for the settlement of B-shares in the SSE and the SZSE are

Table 10.4
Shanghai Securities Exchange: The Top 10 Stocks (market capitalization, May 1990)

Name	Thousand Renminbi	Percent of Total
A-Shares Market		
Shanghai Lujiazui Finance and Trade	9,967,100	4.30
Shanghai Wai Gaoqiao Free Trade Zone	9,675,000	4.17
Shanghai Petrochemical Co. Ltd.	8,327,700	3.59
Shenergy Co. Ltd.	8,169,300	3.52
Shanghai Oriental Pearl Co. Ltd.	8,099,942	3.49
Maanshan Iron and Steel Co. Ltd.	7,461,344	3.22
Yizheng Chemical Fibre Co. Ltd.	6,994,000	3.01
Shanghai Jinqiao Export Processing Zone	5,706,300	2.46
Shanghai Dajiang Group Stock Co. Ltd.	5,512,236	2.38
Shanghai Chloride Alkaline Chemical	5,487,115	2.36
Total of the Top Ten	75,400,041	32.5

Name	Million U.S. Dollars	Percent of Total
B-Shares Market		
Shanghai Lujiazui Finance and Trade	136,000	12.02
Shanghai Yaohua Pilkington Glass Co.	93,800	8.29
Shanghai Chloride Alkaline Chemical	75,936	6.71
Shanghai Outer Gaoqiao Free Trade Zone	72,267	6.39
Shanghai Jinqiao Export Processing Zone	70,928	6.27
Shanghai Diesel Engine Work Co. Ltd.	68,640	6.07
Shanghai Tyre and Rubber Co. Ltd.	57,460	5.08
Shanghai Shangling Electric Appliancant	55,720	4.92
Shanghai Dazhong Taxi Co. Ltd.	54,756	4.84
Shanghai New Asia Group Co. Ltd.	37,000	3.27
Total of the Top Ten	722,507	32.50

Source: Bridge Information System, Hong Kong.

Table 10.5

Shenzhen Stock Exchange: The Top 10 Stocks (market capitalization, May 1990)

A-Shares Market		
Name	Thousand Renminbi	Percent of Total
Shenzhen Development Co. Ltd.	3,965,835	0.05
Guangdong Electric Power Development	3,097,935	0.04
Shenzhen Baoan Enterprises Group Co.	2,559,200	0.03
Shenzhen Sez Real Estate Group Co. Ltd.	2,474,356	0.03
Anhui Wanneng Co. Ltd.	2,186,700	0.03
Changcheng Special Steel Co. Ltd.	1,581,403	0.02
Shenzhen Properties and Resources Development	1,540,263	0.02
Guangdong Macro Co. Ltd.	1,462,227	0.02
Xin Du Hotel Co. Ltd.	1,274,364	0.01
Shenzhen Nanshan Power Station Co. Ltd.	1,246,667	0.01
Total of the Top Ten	21,388,950	0.25

B-Shares Market		
Name	Thousand H.K. dollars	Percent of Total
Shekou Zhao Shang Harbour Service Holding	449,550	0.11
Shenzhen Konka Electric Group Co.	413,714	0.10
China Southern Glass Co. Ltd.	373,457	0.09
Tsann Kuen China Enterprises Co. Ltd.	362,600	0.09
Shenzhen Nanshan Power Station Co. Ltd.	318,226	0.08
Shenzhen China Bicycle Co. Holding Ltd.	291,073	0.07
Zhuhai Sez Lizhu Pharmaceutical Group	270,065	0.07
Shenzhen Sez Real Estate Group Co. Ltd.	205,000	0.05
Shenzhen Chiwan Wharf Holdings Ltd.	154,000	0.04
Shenzhen Properties and Resources Development	147,297	0.04
Total of the Top Ten	2,984,981	0.75

Source: Bridge Information System, Hong Kong.

Table 10.6

Comparison of Regulations, Trading Mechanisms, and Settlement Methods

	Shenzhen	Shanghai
Regulation		
Foreign Investment Restriction	* Can invest only in B-shares. * Individual/institutional owner not to exceed five percent of total B-shares outstanding. * Evidence of "foreign investor" status required. * No restriction on the remittance of the principal, profits, and income derived from B-shares.	
Withholding Tax	* Ten percent on income derived from dividends, and capital gains. Some companies issuing B-shares may qualify for PRC tax purposes as a joint-venture company, in which case dividends paid by the company are free of withholding tax.	
Trading		
Trading Hours	* Monday to Friday, 9:00 a.m. to 11:00 a.m.; 2:00 p.m. to 3:30 p.m. No trading of B-shares on China and Hong kong holidays.	* Monday to Friday 9:00 a.m. to 11:00 a.m.; 2:00 p.m. to 3:00 p.m. No trading of B-shares on China and New York holidays.
Trading Currency	* B-shares are quoted in U.S. dollars but settled in H.K. dollars.	* B-shares are quoted in Renminbi but settled in U.S. dollars.
Method	* Computerized order-matching system. * For B-shares, order must be placed through brokers approved by the PBOC. Foreign investors located outside of the PRC would trade through an authorized foreign broker, who will in turn deal through an authorized broker in the SSE and SZSE, respectively. * More than seventy overseas brokerage firms are engaged in B-shares. * Eleven have seats on the floor of the exchange.	* Fifty eight foreign firms are authorized to accept B-share orders. * Twenty have seats on the floor of the exchange.

Table 10.6 (continued)

Clearing and Settlement		
Depositories Clearing Agencies	* One central clearing agent/depository for each issue. Currently, three banks have been approved as depository/central clearing agent. * Securities movements are recorded on settlement day by book entry. Settlement information is electronically fed to the Shenzhen Securities Registrars Co. (SRC), the official registration agency for Shenzhen B-shares. * Shares are not available for trading prior to settlement of the trade. Sales of shares on a T+1 day basis.	* The Shanghai Securities Central Clearing and Registration Corporation (SSCCRC) is fully set up to function as a paperless central clearing house.
Clearing Fees and Stamp Duties	* 0.1 percent clearing fee based on value: minimum 185 Hong Kong dollars; maximum 625 Hong Kong dollars, for both buy and sell. * Levy 0.55 percent for B-shares * Stamp duty at 0.3 percent of the value of the trade.	* The SSCCRC charges a clearing fee of four U.S. dollars plus a depository fee of twenty U.S. dollars per investor account per annum. The SSCCRC also levies a remittance charge for fund transfers. * Cable fee: eight U.S. dollars per buy; ten U.S. dollars per sell. * bank fee: twelve U.S. dollars per trade.
Settlement Process	* The authorized clearing banks are: Citibank, Hongkong Bank, and Standard Chartered Bank. * Settlement is on a T+3 days basis.	* Funds for purchases must be remitted to the SSCCRC's settlement account with Citibank.
Registration	* Same-day registration is effected by the SRC on a T+3 day basis. * A registration fee of 0.3 percent of par value of the shares. * Shares are not available for trading prior to registration.	* Same-day registration is effected by the SSCCRC on a T+3 day basis. * A registration fee of 0.1 percent of par value of the shares.

Source: SBCI Securities and Jardine Flemming (1995 a, b).

U.S. dollars and Hong Kong dollars, respectively. For B-shares, orders must be placed through brokers approved by the PBOC. Foreign investors who want to trade the B-shares in the SSE and SZSE have to approach an authorized foreign broker, who in turn deals through an authorized local broker to trade the stocks. There are fifty-eight and seventy foreign firms authorized to accept B-share orders in the SSE and SZSE, respectively. Among them, twenty and eleven have seats on the floor of the corresponding exchanges, respectively.

As paperless trading systems are introduced in these two markets, all buyers and sellers must maintain accounts to keep track of their share transactions. The Shanghai Securities Central Clearing and Registration Corporation (SSCCRC) acts as the central clearinghouse for the SSE. In the case of SZSE, three banks (Citibank, Hong Kong Bank, and Standard Chartered Bank) are the authorized clearing banks, though in the future a central clearing corporation will be formed to replace these three clearing banks. Securities movements are recorded on the settlement day by the book entry system and the information is electronically fed into the Shenzhen Securities Registrars Company (SRC).

Since its opening, the SSE has launched the Shanghai Composite Index. The Shanghai A-share Index and the Shanghai B-share Index were also introduced. The SZSE also published its own market indices. Its composite index was launched on April 3, 1991, and the A-share and B-share indices were launched on October 6, 1992.[10]

Figures 10.1 and 10.2 depict the performance of price indices from the Datastream International Limited in May 1995.[11] The figures show that the A-share indices in both stock exchanges have fluctuated a lot since their introduction. Compared with the A-shares, the B-share indices seem to be more stable. The standard deviations of the daily return, which measures the dispersion of the A-shares index returns, for the A-share indices are two times greater than their corresponding B-share indices (3.532 percent versus 1.447 percent in the SZSE and 4.762 percent versus 2.009 percent in SSE). This suggests that SSE seems to be a more volatile market than the SZSE (4.762 percent versus 3.532 percent for the A-shares and 2.009 percent versus 1.447 percent for the B-shares). The maximum daily return of the A-share index in the SZSE was as high as 74.517 percent whereas the one for the SSE was 29.571 percent.

Table 10.7 shows the volatility of these markets by looking at the year high of the composite indices in the two exchanges from 1990 to 1995.[12] Defining the annual percentage range of these indices as the year high minus the year low and then over the average of the year high and low, we find that, between 1991 and 1994, the average annual percentage range for the

Figure 10.1
Stock Price Indices in the Shanghai Market

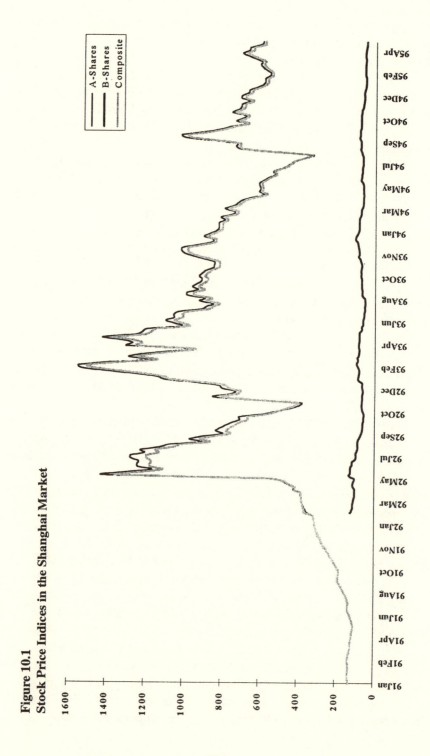

230

Figure 10.2
Stock Price Indices in Shenzhen Market

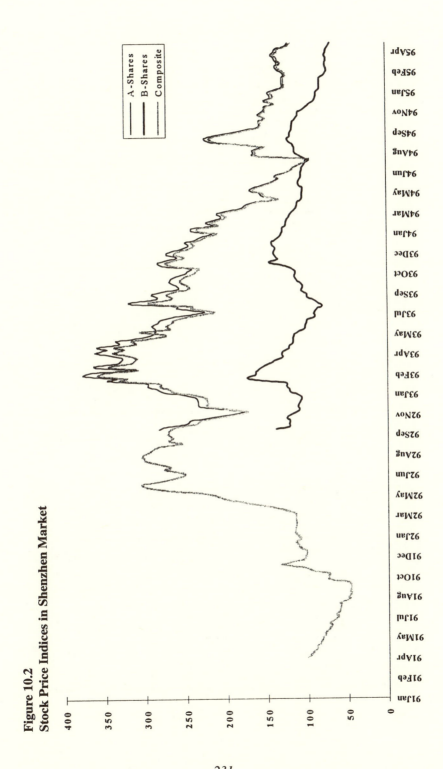

Table 10.7
Year High and Year Low Market Indices

	Shanghai					
	A-share Index		B-share Index		Composite Index	
	High	Low	High	Low	High	Low
1991					292.75	105.77
					94%	
1992	1,503.2	293.8	139.4	57.0	1,421.6	292.8
	135%		84%		132%	
1993	1,615.9	801.3	103.2	51.5	1,536.8	778.3
	67%		67%		66%	
1994	1,057.3	328.8	103.9	60.0	1,020.0	333.9
	105%		54%		101%	
1995 (May 10)	698.6	548.7	62.8	49.7	673.7	532.5
	24%		23%		23%	
	Shenzhen					
1991					136.9	45.7
					100%	
1992	283.8	169.0	142.0	105.7	312.2	107.1
	51%		29%		98%	
1993	379.1	214.9	185.5	80.6	359.4	203.9
	55%		79%		55%	
1994	249.7	95.26	142.9	85.7	242.7	96.6
	90%		51%		86%	
1995 (May 10)	146.8	118.3	86.7	65.8	143.4	115.3
	21%		27%		22%	

Source: Datastream International Limited, United Kingdom.

Shanghai Composite Index and the Shenzhen Composite Index was ninety-eight percent and eighty-four percent, respectively. It is difficult to assess the performance of the A-share and B-share indices, however, as they have different base years. In order to compare the performance of the A- and B-share indices, we recalculated the A-share and B-share indices and set them equal to one on the date of the introduction of the corresponding B-share indices. B-shares in the SSE have underperformed A-shares since their introduction. Even though the A-shares performed better than the B-shares, the A-shares market was more risky. The B-shares market in the SZSE, on the other hand, performed slightly better than the A-shares, but it still was far below the base level.

The price movements in the two markets are influenced by their local economic environments and investment climate. The situation becomes even more complicated as investors are divided into two groups: domestic investors and foreign investors. Clearly these two types of investors have their own information and investment objectives. Correlation coefficients are used to measure the linear relationship between the two variables. The A-share and B-share markets are, as expected, separate markets, and they show little relationship. The correlation ratios between the A-shares and the B-shares are only 0.0972 and 0.131 in the SZSE and the SSE, respectively. However, the A-share markets in the SSE and SZSE seem to be much more closely related. Their correlation coefficient is 0.563, whereas the ratio for the B-share markets is 0.184. It is clear that the China stock markets differ by the type of investors.

FOREIGN INVESTORS

Apart from the B-shares, foreign investors have the alternative of investing directly in China stocks. They can buy the so-called H-shares and N-shares. H-shares are the China stocks listed in the Stock Exchange of Hong Kong (SEHK) while N-shares are those listed on the New York Stock Exchange (NYSE).[13]

Attracted by its impressive growth, various China country funds were introduced (see Slade, 1995). Foreign companies rushed to open their representative offices in the China market. At the end of 1994, there were 301 foreign representative offices, 250 of which were foreign banks, four were finance companies, seven were investment companies, and forty were securities companies.[14]

However, there is a tendency for foreigners to buy the H-shares and N-shares rather than the B-shares listed in the SSE and SZSE. This is because the listing requirements of these well-established stock markets provide better confidence to foreign investors. The enthusiasm of the foreign investors for the China stocks can be seen by the oversubscriptions of the Initial Public Offerings (IPOs) of the H-shares in Hong Kong (Table 10.8). Oversubscriptions on a multiple scale are not uncommon.[15] In 1994, the IPOs of the H-shares accounted for about fifty-eight percent of all the IPOs in the SEHK.

When the China fever cooled down, however, foreign investors became more and more conservative in investing in the China stocks. They realized that the inherent level of risk is huge. The *Asian Wall Street Journal* (December 1, 1994) concluded that "not long ago financiers from around

Table 10.8
Initial Public Offerings (IPOs) of H-shares in Hong Kong

Company	IPO Closing Date	Capital Raised (H.K.$ Million)	No. of Times Sub- scribed
Tsingtao Brewery	July 2, 1993	889	111.0
Shanghai Petroleum	July 16, 1993	2,654	1.7
Guangzhou Shipyard	July 26, 1993	327	77.0
Beiren Printing Machinery	July 28, 1993	208	25.0
Maanshan Iron and Steel	Oct. 26, 1993	3,934	69.0
Kunming Machine Tool	Nov. 26, 1993	129	628.0
Yizheng Chemical Fibre	Mar. 17, 1994	2,380	6.0
Tianjin Bohai Chemical	May 6, 1994	408	1.0
Dongfang Electric Machinery	May 24, 1994	481	16.0
Luoyang Glass	June 24, 1994	913	1.0
Qingling Motors	Aug. 3, 1994	1,035	24.0
Shanghai Haixing	Nov. 4, 1994	1,577	14.0
Zhenhai Refining and Chemical	Nov. 18, 1994	216	7.0
Chengdu Telecommunication Cables	Dec. 2, 1994	448	6.0
Harbin Power Equipment	Dec. 8, 1994	1,122	1.4
Total		16,721	

Source: Compiled from various newspapers in Hong Kong.

the world considered China a honeypot. They found that it's mostly a grinding headache." For example, the subscription results of the Tianjin Bohai Chemical and the Luoyang Glass in mid-1994 were regarded as disappointing.

In addition, investing in the China stock market is not an easy task. Owing to the low degree of transparency and legal framework in the China markets, coupled with an inadequate information dissemination, foreign investors are discouraged.[16] Major international accounting practices are needed in China. These practices can assist mainland accountants to meet the International Accounting Standard (IAS). However, there is discrepancy between the Chinese accounting practices and the IAS, although it has been narrowed down (Price Waterhouse, 1995).

Can foreign investors benefit from the China stock markets? Judging by the outcomes, the answer seems to be "no". This is because the B-share indices of both the SSE and the SZSE have dropped below their base values. The B-share indices for the SSE and SZSE were only 65.746 and 50.577, respectively, on May 10, 1995. Experience showed that investing in the B-share market made the investors worse off.

Based on the International Finance Corporation (IFC) Investiables Indices, we computed description statistics for twenty-five emerging markets, including China, from November 11, 1993, to May 11, 1995.[17] We found that, on average, emerging markets in Asia, Europe, the Mideast, and Latin America all incurred losses during this period. The U.S. stock market, represented by Standard and Poor's 500 Index (S&P 500), rose.

China seems to be the loser among all the emerging markets. We used the date of November 11, 1993, as the base and recalculated the China and regional indices. We found that on May, 11 1995, the China index had the lowest level. Ranking twenty-five emerging markets by their mean returns, China was the second worst performance market in this period. When ranked by the standard deviation of the index return used as a proxy of risk, it is the lowest tenth. In additional to high return, investors will also demand a lower risk. It is well known that the China markets are highly volatile. However, foreign investors can benefit from these markets if they can reduce the risk level of their portfolio.

These emerging markets vary greatly in their correlation with the U.S. market, ranging from 0.27 (Poland) to -0.20 (Pakistan). China is situated in the middle of the range and had a correlation coefficient of -0.002. It seems that the China market did not correlate with the U.S. market at all. Investing in these markets, including China, therefore may be beneficial to U.S. investors as the China market provides an opportunity for them to diversify risk. On the contrary, the China stock market seems to be highly correlated with the Asia-Pacific emerging markets. Its correlation coefficient with Thailand was the highest, with 0.64. This was followed by Malaysia, Indonesia, and Philippines, with correlation coefficients of 0.44, 0.39, and 0.36, respectively.

CONCLUSION

During the last ten years, the PRC introduced a shareholding system and developed two modern stock exchanges. One is located in Shanghai and the other in Shenzhen. Other provinces have intentions to develop their own stock exchanges too. The history of the two exchanges suggests that the China stock markets are still in their early stage and investors are mostly speculative. Although the authorities gained experience quickly, the direction of future development will depend very much on the government's decision and ability to carry out reform smoothly, especially regarding trading regulations. It is perhaps correct for *Asiamoney* (Dec. 1994/Jan. 1995) to conclude that investing in the stock of the PRC "is a bet on the long-term prosperity of China."

NOTES

1. These figures were calculated from book value.

2. To have a better understanding of the development of the securities regulation framework, see Wu and Bang (1995).

3. When the Shenzhen Development Bank had its initial public offering in May 1987, it was, in fact, undersubscribed by about fifty percent. Other Initial Public Offerings had the same results. For example, Shenzhen Vanke, which offered its shares in December 1987, also suffered the same setback.

4. It has since become the Shenzhen Fountain Corporation.

5. Commenting on the riots in Shenzhen, the mayor of Guangzhou said, "It is not chaos, it's just like a baby learning to walk" (Li, 1994). Thus, as the stock exchanges developed and problems with the security industry appeared, the State Council Securities Policy Commission (SCSPC) and the China Securities Regulatory Commission (CSRC) were set up in October 1992 to regulate the stock markets. The SCSPC is responsible for policy making on securities issues which was held by the People's Bank of China. It reports to the State Council, the ultimate governing body of China's equity markets. Under the SCSPC, the CSRC is responsible for the day-to-day management of the securities industry and markets, and for preparing legislation and regulations.

6. For a better understanding of China's participation in the ADR market, see Sanford (1995).

7. The PBOC, for example, introduced a system of guaranteeing deposits of at least three years against the effect of inflation.

8. Since there was a stock exchange in Shanghai before 1949, people might say that it is reincarnated. Other provinces also developed their own trading centers. In addition to the SSE and SSZE, there are seventeen other exchange centers in the PRC. They are Fujian Stock Exchange Center, Fuzhou (Fujian Province); Guangzhou Stock Exchange Centre, Guangzhou (Guangdong); Shantou Stock Exchange Centre, Shantou (Guangdong); Hainan Stock Exchange Centre, Haikou (Hainan); Harbin Stock Exchange Centre, Harbin (Heilongjiang); Wuhan Stock Exchange Center, Wuhan (Hubei); Hunan Stock Exchange Centre, Changsha (Hunan); Nanchang Stock Exchange Centre, Nanchang (Jiangxi); Dalian Stock Exchange Centre (Liaoning); Shenyang Stock Exchange Centre (Liaoning); Xian Stock Exchange Centre, Xian (Shanxi); Qingdao Stock Exchange Centre, Qingdao (Shandong); Taiyuan Stock Exchange Centre, Taiyuan (Shanxi); Sichuan Stock Exchange Centre, Chengdu; Sichuan Chongqing Stock Exchange Centre, Chongqing (Sichuan); Tianjin Stock Exchange Centre, Tianjin (Tianjin); Zhejiang Stock Exchange Centre, Hangzhou (Zhejiang). A- and B-shares, however, are not traded in these markets. They concentrate on trading legal person shares over the counter. If these centers were linked to all the official stock exchanges, a strong national network would be formed (Pong 1995).

9. Sources come from the Bridge Information System.

10. Other institutions also published their own indices for the China stocks. For example, Credit Lyonnais Securities Asia Ltd. introduced its own CLSA China indices in 1991. This reflects the foreigners' interests in China stocks.

11. The data on the various indices (comprising the composite, A-share, and B-share indices and later IFC indices) come from Datastream International Limited, UK.

12. Our sample period covered up to May 10, 1995, and used the daily closing price to calculate these figures.

13. These stocks were the well-known Red-Chips in Hong Kong. A complete list of the Red-Chips is given in Law (1995).

14 See *China Financial Outlook* 1995, The People's Bank of China, Beijing.

15. It is, however, the smallest amount of capital raised (129 million Hong Kong dollars).

16. Moakes (1995) discussed the accuracy of the information released by Chinese companies.

17. The IFC Investiables (IFCI) indices were first released at the end of March 1993. We use these indices because they are "designed to measure more precisely the sorts of returns foreign portfolio investors might receive from investing in baskets of stocks that were legally and practically available to them" (*Emerging Stock Markets Factbook 1994*).

REFERENCES

Asiamoney, 1994/95, "More Caution Towards Red Equities," Dec. 1994/Jan. 1995, Hong Kong: Euromoney Publishing, p.67–68.

Emerging Stock Market Factbook 1994, Washington, D. C. : International Finance Corporation.

Euromoney, 1993, "The Rise of the Red Chip," December, London: Euromoney Publishing, pp. 23–27.

Law, C.K., 1995, "Red-Chips and H Shares in Hong Kong," in Philip Jay (ed.), *China Securities Handbook 1995–1996*, Hong Kong: Philip Jay Publishing Limited, pp. 45–47.

Li, Kui-Wai, 1994, *Financial Repression and Economic Reform in China*, Connecticut: Praeger Publisher.

Margolis, Richard, 1995, "The Progress and the Prospects of China s Securities Markets," in Philip Jay (ed.), *China Securities Handbook 1995–1996*, Hong Kong: Philip Jay Publishing Limited, pp. 27–29.

Moakes, Nick, 1995, "How Good Is the Information Released by Chinese Companies?" in Philip Jay (ed.), *China Securities Handbook 1995–1996*, Hong Kong: Philip Jay Publishing Limited, pp. 53–54.

Pong, Arthur, 1995, "Seventeen Securities Exchange Centres Waiting in the Wings," in Philip Jay (ed.), *China Securities Handbook 1995–1996*, Hong Kong: Philip Jay Publishing Limited, pp. 41–42.

Price Waterhouse, 1995, "A Review of Accounting Practices and Standards," in Philip Jay (ed.), *China Securities Handbook 1995–1996*, Hong Kong: Philip Jay Publishing Limited, pp. 23–25.

Sanford, Thomas D., 1995, "Depository Receipts: Chinese Companies Go Global," in Philip Jay (ed.), *China Securities Handbook 1995–1996*, Hong Kong: Philip Jay Publishing Limited, pp. 57–59.

SBCI Securities and Jardine Fleming, 1995a, "Trading Regulations: Shanghai B-share Market," in Philip Jay (ed.), *China Securities Handbook 1995–1996*, Hong Kong: Philip Jay Publishing Limited, pp. 81–83.

SBCI Securities and Jardine Fleming, 1995b, "Trading Regulations: Shenzhen B-share Market," in Philip Jay (ed.), *China Securities Handbook 1995–1996*, Hong Kong: Philip Jay Publishing Limited, pp. 89–91.

Slade, Nigel, 1995, "Four Ways of Investing in China Country Funds," in Philip Jay (ed.), *China Securities Handbook 1995–1996*, Hong Kong: Philip Jay Publishing Limited, pp. 61–63.

Wu, Y.W., and Elizabeth Bang, 1995, "Regulating Securities and Companies Law," in Philip Jay (ed.), *China Securities Handbook 1995–1996*, Hong Kong: Philip Jay Publishing Limited, pp. 37–39.

11
Risk, Return, and Price Linkage in China Stocks

MICHAEL C. S. WONG, WINSON S. C. LEUNG, and
KWOK-FAI WONG

THE MEASUREMENT OF RISK AND RETURN

In general, investors are risk-averse in their investment decisions. Return usually has two interpretations. First, it represents the expected return investors will obtain from an investment. Second, it refers to the actual return the investors obtain from the investment. Risk generally refers to the uncertainty on the deviation of the actual return from the expected return. We use the Modern Portfolio Theory (MPT) to estimate risk with historical returns in China's stocks markets (see Sharpe and Alexander, 1990, Chapters 6–8). To compare the performance of all the China stocks in our sample period, we first calculate the mean monthly return of stock j, $E(R_j)$:

$$E(R)_j = \sum_{1}^{n} R_{j,t} \tag{1}$$

where n is the number of months in the sample. Risk is measured by both standard deviation and beta. Standard deviation $SD(R_j)$ is generally used to measure total risk of a stock j, i.e.:

$$SD(R_j) = \sqrt{\sum_{1}^{n} \frac{[R_{j,t}-E(R_j)]^2}{n}} \qquad (2)$$

n is the number of months in the sample. Company risk (or unsystematic risk) can be eliminated by formulating investment portfolios. To a certain extent, these portfolios still face market risk, which is measured by the sensitivity of the portfolios' return to the return of the whole market. When the whole market performs very well, most of the stocks tend to have a very good performance. The performance of the whole market is affected by many fundamental variables, such as economic growth, inflation, and so on. A portfolio of a higher (lower) market risk means that its return is more (less) sensitive to the fundamental variables than the average return of the whole market. This sensitivity can be represented by the β_j in the following single-index regression model:

$$R_{j,t} = \alpha_j + \beta_j R_{m,t} + e_t \qquad (3)$$

where $R_{m,t}$ is the return of the whole market proxied by the average return of all listed stocks, e_t is a white noise, and α_j is a constant. We estimate β_j, the market risk, with the Ordinary Least Square method.

For the four different segments in the China stock market, Shanghai A-shares (SH-A), Shanghai B-shares (SH-B), Shenzhen A-shares (SZ-A), and Shenzhen B-shares (SZ-B), we use four respective proxies for the $R_{m,t}$. These are simply the mean returns of all the shares in the respective segments. This makes sense since the A-share and B-share markets are traded with different currencies and Shanghai and Shenzhen markets represent some regional difference in their business natures. Tables 11.1A to 11.1D display the $E(R_j)$, $SD(R_j)$, and β_j of all stocks in the four segments. It can be seen that most stocks have a negative mean monthly return in the sample period, indicating a bear market.

To compare the stocks' performance, we use three different measures: 1) the actual return, 2) the return-to-volatility ratio (ratio 1), and 3) the return-to-variability ratio (ratio 2). The actual-return measure is suitable for risk-neutral investors who do not care how much risk they have to take, while ratios 1 and 2 are suitable for those risk-averse investors who maximize their expected returns and minimize their risk in investment decisions. Ratios 1 and 2 are defined, respectively, as follows:

Table 11.1A
Risk and Return of Shanghai A-Shares

	Sample Period	Mean Return	Standard Deviation	Beta	Ratio 1	Ratio 2
Tsingtao Brewery Co Ltd	8/92-8/94	(0.0425)	0.2748	0.7944	(0.1546)	(0.0535)
Shanghai Yanzhong Industrial Stock Co Ltd	8/92-8/94	(0.0010)	0.3465	0.9551	(0.0029)	(0.0010)
Shanghai Vacuum Electron Devices Co Ltd	8/92-8/94	0.1396	0.6044	1.1105	(0.2309)	(0.1257)
Shanghai Xing Ye Housing Co Ltd	8/92-8/94	(0.0374)	0.4585	0.6622	(0.0816)	(0.0565)
Shanghai Erfangji Co Ltd	8/92-8/94	(0.0401)	0.2723	0.8306	(0.1474)	(0.0483)
Shanghai Light Industry Machinery Co Ltd	8/92-8/94	(0.0255)	0.3607	1.1448	(0.0708)	(0.0223)
Shanghai Jia Feng Co Ltd	8/92-8/94	(0.0282)	0.3462	1.0653	(0.0815)	(0.0265)
Shanghai United Textile Holdings Co Ltd	8/92-8/94	(0.0248)	1.2125	3.3263	(0.0204)	(0.0074)
Shanghai Special Shape Steel Co Ltd	8/92-8/94	(0.0256)	0.3583	1.1036	(0.0715)	(0.0232)
Jinbei Automotive Co Ltd	8/92-8/94	(0.0508)	0.2470	0.7179	(0.2056)	(0.0708)
China Textile Machinery Stock Co Ltd	8/92-8/94	(0.0263)	0.3130	0.9410	(0.0840)	(0.0280)
Shanghai Dazhong Taxi Co Ltd	8/92-8/94	(0.0127)	0.4394	1.2242	(0.0289)	(0.0104)
China First Pencil Co Ltd	8/92-8/94	(0.0305)	0.2988	0.8303	(0.1020)	(0.0367)
Shanghai Wingsung Stationery Co Ltd	8/92-8/94	(0.0280)	0.2516	0.5361	(0.1115)	(0.0523)
Shanghai Rubber Belt Co Ltd	8/92-8/94	0.0159	0.3390	1.0156	(0.0469)	(0.0156)
Shanghai Fengwa Ball Pen Co Ltd	10/92-8/94	0.0019	0.3287	1.0147	(0.0058)	(0.0019)
Shanghai First Provision Store Co Ltd	11/92-8/94	(0.0214)	0.3448	1.0288	(0.0621)	(0.0208)
Shanghai Lian Hua Fibre Corporation Ltd	11/92-8/94	(0.0206)	0.3405	1.0021	(0.0605)	(0.0205)
Shanghai Chlor Alkai Chemical Co Ltd	11/92-8/94	(0.0100)	0.3444	1.0283	(0.0292)	(0.0098)

Table 11.1A (continued)

	Sample Period	Mean Return	Standard Deviation	Beta	Ratio 1	Ratio 2
Shanghai Refrigerator Compressor Co Ltd	11/92-8/94	(0.0166)	0.7120	0.6692	(0.0233)	(0.0248)
United Agriculture Incorporation	11/92-8/94	(0.0186)	0.3516	1.0202	(0.0530)	(0.0182)
Shanghai Jinling Co Ltd	12/92-8/94	(0.0130)	0.3301	0.9735	(0.0393)	(0.0133)
Shanghai Jiabao Industry and Commerce Co Ltd	12/92-8/94	(0.0084)	0.3646	1.0431	(0.0231)	(0.0081)
Shanghai Tyre and Rubber Co Ltd	12/92-8/94	(0.0376)	0.3075	0.9255	(0.1223)	(0.0406)
Shanghai Forward Group Ltd	1/93-8/94	(0.0245)	0.3003	0.8888	(0.0815)	(0.0275)
Shanghai Naicissus Electric Appliances Ind Co Ltd	1/93-8/94	(0.0243)	0.3251	1.0006	(0.0746)	(0.0242)
Shanghai Shenda Textile and Garments Co Ltd	1/93-8/94	(0.0338)	0.3453	1.0404	(0.0980)	(0.0325)
Shanghai Electric Apparatus Co Ltd	1/93-8/94	(0.0574)	0.3215	0.9605	(0.1785)	(0.0597)
Shanghai New World Trading Co Ltd	1/93-8/94	0.0611	0.6741	1.1840	0.0906	0.0516
Shanghai Linguang Industrial Co Ltd	2/93-8/94	(0.0154)	0.3477	1.0453	(0.0442)	(0.0147)
Shanghai Dragon Head Co Ltd	2/93-8/94	(0.0538)	0.3554	1.0557	(0.1513)	(0.0510)
Shanghai No. 1 Department Store Co Ltd	2/93-8/94	(0.0908)	0.2791	0.8032	(0.3252)	(0.1130)
Shanghai Hualian Corporation	2/93-8/94	(0.0904)	0.3005	0.8886	(0.3008)	(0.1017)
Shanghai Shuanglu Electric Appliance Shareholding Co Ltd	3/93-8/94	(0.0260)	0.3513	1.0637	(0.0741)	(0.0245)
Shanghai Alfatronic Co Ltd	3/93-8/94	(0.0175)	0.3386	1.0045	(0.0516)	(0.0174)
Shanghai Putong Dazhong Taxi Co Ltd	3/93-8/94	0.0072	0.3724	1.0981	0.0192	0.0065
Shanghai 3F New Materials Co Ltd	3/93-8/94	(0.0061)	1.1108	3.1452	(0.0055)	(0.0019)
Shanghai Video & Audio Electronics Co Ltd	3/93-8/94	(0.0399)	0.2965	0.8884	(0.1346)	(0.0449)
Shanghai Huangpu Real Estate Co Ltd	3/93-8/94	(0.0304)	0.3708	1.1327	(0.0821)	(0.0269)

	Sample Period	Mean Return	Standard Deviation	Beta	Ratio 1	Ratio 2
Shanghai Jinqiao Export Processing Zone Development Co Ltd	3/93-8/94	0.0363	0.4265	1.2359	0.0851	0.0293
Shanghai Guomai Industrial Co Ltd	4/93-8/94	(0.0702)	0.3133	0.9427	(0.2240)	(0.0744)
Shanghai Zhong Cheng Enterprises Co Ltd	4/93-8/94	(0.0555)	0.3602	1.1580	(0.1541)	(0.0479)
Shanghai Energy Co Ltd	4/93-8/94	(0.0769)	0.2908	0.8128	(0.2645)	(0.0946)
Shanghai AJ Corporation	4/93-8/94	(0.0794)	0.3189	1.0414	(0.2489)	(0.0762)
Leshan Electric Power Co Ltd	4/93-8/94	(0.0959)	0.3477	1.0927	(0.2757)	(0.0877)
Shanghai Wang Chun Flower Industry Co Ltd	5/93-8/94	(0.0290)	0.2887	0.8786	(0.1004)	(0.0330)
Shanghai CITIC-Jiading Industrial Co Ltd	5/93-8/94	(0.0368)	0.3299	0.9894	(0.1117)	(0.0372)
Shanghai New Asia Fast Food Co Ltd	5/93-8/94	(0.0551)	0.4072	1.1199	(0.1353)	(0.0492)
Shanghai Outer Gaoqiao Free Trade Zone Development Co Ltd	5/93-8/94	(0.0035)	0.2500	0.8039	(0.0142)	(0.0044)
Shanghai Raw Water Supply Co Ltd	5/93-8/94	(0.0637)	0.3278	0.7251	(0.1942)	(0.0878)
Shanghai Jinjiang Tower Co Ltd	6/93-8/94	(0.0450)	0.3582	1.1409	(0.1257)	(0.0395)
Shanghai Fello Acoustics Co Ltd	8/92-8/94	(0.0354)	0.4524	1.0454	(0.0782)	(0.0338)
Shanghai ACE Electonics Equipment Co Ltd	8/92-8/94	(0.0441)	0.4995	1.1317	(0.0883)	(0.0390)
Shanghai Shenhua Electronics Union Co Ltd	8/92-8/94	(0.0381)	0.3809	1.1020	(0.0999)	(0.0345)
Shanghai Fello Shareholding Co Ltd	8/92-8/94	(0.0051)	0.3951	1.1754	(0.0128)	(0.0043)
Shanghai Yuyuan Tourist Super Bazar Co Ltd	8/92-8/94	(0.0059)	0.3534	1.0580	(0.0168)	(0.0056)
Zhejiang Phoenix Chemical Co Ltd	9/92-8/94	(0.0554)	0.6932	0.4574	(0.0799)	(0.1211)
Beijing Tian Qiao Department Store Co Ltd	5/93-8/94	(0.0540)	0.3012	0.8484	(0.1794)	(0.0637)

Table 11.1A (continued)

	Sample Period	Mean Return	Standard Deviation	Beta	Ratio 1	Ratio 2
Beijing Tian Long Co Ltd	5/93–8/94	(0.0426)	0.3296	0.8171	(0.1291)	(0.0521)
Fujian Fulian Co Ltd	5/93–8/94	(0.0359)	0.3661	1.0973	(0.0979)	(0.0327)
Fujian Yaohua Glass Industry Co Ltd	6/93–8/94	(0.0668)	0.3522	1.1013	(0.1896)	(0.0606)
Shanghai Nanyang International Industrial Co Ltd	6/93–8/94	(0.0594)	0.3405	1.0968	(0.1746)	(0.0542)
Shanghai Pudong Qiangshan Taxi Co Ltd	6/93–8/94	(0.0246)	0.3883	1.1456	(0.0633)	(0.0214)
Shanghai Lujiazui Finance & Trade Zone Development Stock Co Ltd	6/93–8/94	0.0191	0.3659	1.1816	0.0522	0.0162
Harbin Pharmaceutical Share Holdings Co Ltd	6/93–8/94	(0.0876)	0.3210	0.9708	(0.2729)	(0.0903)
Shanghai Huchang Special Steel Co Ltd	7/93–8/94	(0.0540)	0.3704	1.0963	(0.1459)	(0.0493)
Southwest Pharmaceutical Co Ltd	7/93–8/94	(0.0076)	0.4700	1.0195	(0.0161)	(0.0074)
Wuxi Taiji Industry Co Ltd	7/93–8/94	(0.0585)	0.3136	0.9962	(0.1865)	(0.0587)
Zhejiang Jianfeng Group Co Ltd	7/93–8/94	(0.0815)	0.3805	1.1416	(0.2142)	(0.0714)
Anshan Co-operation (Group) Co Ltd	8/93–8/94	(0.0844)	0.3845	1.0834	(0.2195)	(0.0779)
North East Hualian Co Ltd	8/93–8/94	(0.0953)	0.3590	0.9156	(0.2654)	(0.1041)
Hangzhou Tian Mu Shan Pharmaceutical Co Ltd	8/93–8/94	(0.0488)	0.4154	1.2175	(0.1174)	(0.0400)
Sichuan Guanghua Chemical Fibre Co Ltd	9/93–8/94	(0.0625)	0.3691	1.0479	(0.1694)	(0.0597)
Chengdu Measuring & Cutting Tools Co Ltd	9/93–8/94	(0.0876)	0.3925	1.0596	(0.2232)	(0.0827)
Emei Ferro-Alloy Holdings (Group) Co Ltd	9/93–8/94	(0.0758)	0.4079	1.1139	(0.1859)	(0.0681)
China Enterprise Stock Co Ltd	9/93–8/94	(0.0099)	0.3534	1.0474	(0.0281)	(0.0095)
Shanghai Iron & Steel Transportation Co Ltd	9/93–8/94	(0.0144)	0.3868	1.1351	(0.0372)	(0.0127)

Company	Sample Period	Mean Return	Standard Deviation	Beta	Ratio 1	Ratio 2
Zhejiang Zhonghui (Group) Co Ltd	9/93-8/94	(0.0541)	0.3851	1.0480	(0.1404)	(0.0516)
Sichuan Golden Summit (Group) Co Ltd	10/93-8/94	(0.1135)	0.2763	0.5082	(0.4108)	(0.2233)
Shanghai Phoenix Bicycle Co Ltd	10/93-8/94	(0.0330)	0.3210	0.8944	(0.1027)	(0.0368)
Shanghai Posts & Telecommunications Equipment Co Ltd	10/93-8/94	0.0054	0.3978	1.1080	0.0136	0.0049
Wuhan Besun (Group) Co Ltd	10/93-8/94	(0.0284)	0.3621	0.9614	(0.0783)	(0.0295)
Nanjing Xinjiekou Department Store Co Ltd	10/93-8/94	(0.0343)	0.3807	1.0138	(0.0902)	(0.0339)
Ningbo Hualian Group Co Ltd	11/93-8/94	(0.0865)	0.4049	1.0150	(0.2137)	(0.0852)
Guangzhou Pearl River Industrial Development Enterprises Co Ltd	11/93-8/94	(0.0632)	0.4295	1.1117	(0.1472)	(0.0569)
Guangzhou Shipyard International Co Ltd	11/93-8/94	(0.0278)	0.3768	0.9802	(0.0737)	(0.0283)
Xiamen Motor Co Ltd	11/93-8/94	(0.0873)	0.3325	0.8351	(0.2626)	(0.1046)
Xiamen International Trading Titan Co Ltd	11/93-8/94	(0.0476)	0.2660	0.6705	(0.1791)	(0.0711)
Shanghai Petro-chemical Co Ltd	11/93-8/94	(0.0612)	0.3612	0.9356	(0.1693)	(0.0654)
Shanghai Sanmao Textiles Co Ltd	11/93-8/94	(0.0332)	0.4232	1.1583	(0.0785)	(0.0287)
Qingdao Haier Regrigerator Co Ltd	11/93-8/94	(0.0740)	0.3826	0.9867	(0.1935)	(0.0750)
Dongxin Electrical Carbon Co Ltd	11/93-8/94	(0.0536)	0.3706	0.9828	(0.1446)	(0.0545)
Shanghai Yatong Co Ltd	11/93-8/94	(0.0088)	0.3887	1.0612	(0.0227)	(0.0083)
Fuzhou Dong Jie Kou Department Store Trading Co Ltd	11/93-8/94	(0.0919)	0.3862	1.0414	(0.2378)	(0.0882)
Dalian Department Store Co Ltd	11/93-8/94	(0.0775)	0.4424	1.0634	(0.1751)	(0.0728)
Shanghai Dajiang (Group) Stock Co Ltd	11/93-8/94	(0.0270)	0.3756	1.0198	(0.0719)	(0.0265)

Table 11.1A (continued)

	Sample Period	Mean Return	Standard Deviation	Beta	Ratio 1	Ratio 2
Hawson (Fujian) Ltd	12/93-8/94	(0.0802)	0.4540	1.1003	(0.1767)	(0.0729)
Changchun Automobiles Town Department Store Co Ltd	12/93-8/94	(0.0247)	0.4087	1.0437	(0.0603)	(0.0236)
JInan Qingqi Motorcycle Co Ltd	12/93-8/94	(0.0330)	0.3206	0.8321	(0.1030)	(0.0397)
Liaoyuan Deheng Co Ltd	12/93-8/94	0.0258	0.1785	0.1422	0.1445	0.1813
Tianjin Global Magnetic Card Co Ltd	12/93-8/94	(0.0124)	0.3938	1.0182	(0.0314)	(0.0121)
Huaxin Cement Co Ltd	1/94-8/94	(0.0440)	0.3877	0.9223	(0.1135)	(0.0477)
Fujian Cement Stock Co Ltd	1/94-8/94	(0.0330)	0.3918	0.9667	(0.0842)	(0.0341)
Hebei Weiyuan Industry Co Ltd	1/94-8/94	0.0005	0.3359	0.8265	0.0016	0.0007
Chengdu Gong Yi Metallurgy Co Ltd	1/94-8/94	(0.0131)	0.4333	1.0224	(0.0301)	(0.0128)
Jiangsu Yueda Co Ltd	1/94-8/94	0.0067	0.2656	0.6412	0.0254	0.0105
Kunming Machine Tool Co Ltd	1/94-8/94	0.0006	0.4025	0.9774	0.0015	0.0006
Jinan Department Store Stock Co Ltd	1/94-8/94	(0.0083)	0.4683	1.0810	(0.0178)	(0.0077)
Manshan Iron & Steel Co Ltd	1/94-8/94	(0.0222)	0.4158	1.0155	(0.0534)	(0.0219)
Shanxi Xinghuacun Fenjiu Distillery Co Ltd	1/94-8/94	(0.0041)	0.3642	0.8991	(0.0111)	(0.0045)
Shenma Industry Co Ltd	1/94-8/94	(0.0090)	0.1908	0.3907	(0.0471)	(0.0230)
Orient Inc. Co Ltd	1/94-8/94	(0.0029)	0.4142	1.0042	(0.0069)	(0.0028)
North China Pharmaceutical Ltd	1/94-8/94	0.0247	0.5145	1.1606	0.0479	0.0212
Anshan No. 1 Construction Machinery Co Ltd	1/94-8/94	(0.0280)	0.3353	0.8100	(0.0834)	(0.0345)
Hangzhou Jiefang Road Department Store Co Ltd	1/94-8/94	(0.0405)	0.3740	0.8739	(0.1083)	(0.0463)
Xiamen Engineering Machinery Co Ltd	1/94-8/94	(0.0741)	0.4601	1.0675	(0.1611)	(0.0694)

	Sample Period	Mean Return	Standard Deviation	Beta	Ratio 1	Ratio 2
Anshan Trust & Investment Co Ltd	1/94-8/94	0.0504	0.3936	0.8957	0.1282	0.0563
Shanghai Lianghua Industry Co Ltd	1/94-8/94	(0.0361)	0.4604	1.1205	(0.0784)	(0.0322)
Shanghai Forever Bicycle Co Ltd	1/94-8/94	(0.0120)	0.2902	0.6843	(0.0415)	(0.0176)
Shanghai Yaohua Pilkington Glass Co Ltd	1/94-8/94	(0.0079)	0.2922	0.7084	(0.0272)	(0.0112)
Shanghai Tunnel Engineering Co Ltd	1/94-8/94	0.0286	0.4764	1.1775	0.0601	0.0243
Tianjin Quanye Bazaar Co Ltd	1/94-8/94	(0.0183)	0.4015	0.9693	(0.0455)	(0.0188)
Shanghai Goods & Materials Trade Centre Co Ltd	2/94-8/94	(0.0501)	0.4497	1.0115	(0.1115)	(0.0495)
Shanghai Wan Xiang (Group) Co Ltd	2/94-8/94	0.0195	0.4215	0.9226	0.0462	0.0211
Shanghai Yimin Department Store Co Ltd	2/94-8/94	0.0104	0.2764	0.5663	0.0377	0.0184
Shanghai Fashion Inc	2/94-8/94	0.0047	0.4944	1.0709	0.0095	0.0044
Shanghai Lansheng Corporation	2/94-8/94	(0.0271)	0.4831	1.1063	(0.0561)	(0.0245)
Shanghai Friendship Overseas Chinese Co Ltd	2/94-8/94	0.0143	0.4944	1.1359	0.0288	0.0125
Chengdu People's Department Store Co Ltd	2/94-8/94	0.0320	0.3636	0.8170	0.0880	0.0392
Harbin Swan Industry Co Ltd	2/94-8/94	0.0145	0.3406	0.7522	0.0426	0.0193
Ningbo Cheng Huang Miao Industry Co Ltd	2/94-8/94	0.0424	0.4806	0.6856	0.0882	0.0618
Huanghe Machinery and Electronics Co Ltd	2/94-8/94	(0.0491)	0.3862	0.8879	(0.1272)	(0.0553)
Shanghai Oriental Pearl Co Ltd	2/94-8/94	(0.0228)	0.5326	1.1666	(0.0428)	(0.0196)
Shanghai Commercial Real Estate Development Industry Co Ltd	2/94-8/94	(0.0698)	0.4776	1.0095	(0.1461)	(0.0691)
Shanghai Lingqiao Tapewater Co Ltd	2/94-8/94	0.0383	0.4410	1.0150	0.0869	0.0378
Shanghai Shangling Electric Appliances Co Ltd	2/94-8/94	0.0369	0.3838	0.8526	0.0960	0.0432

Table 11.1A (continued)

	Sample Period	Mean Return	Standard Deviation	Beta	Ratio 1	Ratio 2
Shanghai Jielong Industry Co Ltd	2/94-8/94	0.1086	0.2132	0.2046	0.5093	0.5305
SAIC Multiple Trading Co Ltd	2/94-8/94	(0.0336)	0.4383	0.9782	(0.0766)	(0.0343)
Shanghai No. 9 Department Store Co Ltd	2/94-8/94	(0.0103)	0.4318	0.9861	(0.0240)	(0.0105)
Sichuan Changhong Electric Co Ltd	3/94-8/94	(0.0004)	0.4012	0.7910	(0.0010)	(0.0005)
Shaoxing Department Store Co Ltd	3/94-8/94	(0.0134)	0.5119	1.0265	(0.0261)	(0.0130)
Shanghai Diesel Engine Co Ltd	3/94-8/94	0.0017	0.4945	1.0281	0.0034	0.0017
Shanghai Zhongxi Pharmaceutical Co Ltd	3/94-8/94	(0.0387)	0.4965	1.0443	(0.0780)	(0.0371)
Shanghai Industrial Sewing Machine Co Ltd	3/94-8/94	(0.0146)	0.4990	1.0462	(0.0292)	(0.0139)
Shanghai Hero Co Ltd	3/94-8/94	(0.0200)	0.4776	0.9949	(0.0419)	(0.0201)
Shanghai Steel Tube Co Ltd	3/94-8/94	(0.0219)	0.5761	1.2080	(0.0380)	(0.0181)
Shanghai Tongji Science & Technology Industries Co Ltd	3/94-8/94	(0.0451)	0.4570	0.9537	(0.0988)	(0.0473)
Chongqing Wanli Storage Battery Co Ltd	3/94-8/94	(0.0170)	0.3757	0.7006	(0.0452)	(0.0243)
Shanghai Automation Instrumentation Co Ltd	3/94-8/94	(0.0724)	0.4700	0.9809	(0.1540)	(0.0738)
Shanghai Fourth Pharmaceuticals Co Ltd	3/94-8/94	(0.0384)	0.4992	1.0495	(0.0769)	(0.0366)
Shanghai East-China Computer Co Ltd	3/94-8/94	(0.0514)	0.5356	1.1235	(0.0959)	(0.0457)
Shanghai Haixin Co Ltd	4/94-8/94	(0.0065)	0.4006	0.7661	(0.0161)	(0.0084)
China Sichuan International Cooperation Co Ltd	4/94-8/94	0.0835	0.6181	1.1880	0.1351	0.0703
Beiman Special Steel Co Ltd	4/94-8/94	0.0730	0.4682	0.8952	0.1560	0.0816
Jiangsu Chunlan Refregerating Equipment Stock Co Ltd	4/94-8/94	0.0734	0.4159	0.7933	0.1764	0.0925
Beijing Lightbus Co Ltd	4/94-8/94	(0.0276)	0.5014	0.9623	(0.0550)	(0.0286)

	Sample Period	Mean Return	Standard Deviation	Beta	Ratio 1	Ratio 2
Changchun Department Store Co Ltd	4/94-8/94	0.0072	0.5062	0.9731	0.0142	0.0074
Ningbo Zhongbai Co Ltd	4/94-8/94	(0.0203)	0.2268	0.3979	(0.0896)	(0.0511)
Shandong Buohai Group Co Ltd	5/94-8/94	0.1746	0.7090	1.1910	0.2463	0.1466
Beijing Wanfujing Department Store Builing (Group) Co Ltd	5/94-8/94	0.0299	0.3291	0.5246	0.0908	0.0569
Beiren Printing Machinery Holdings Ltd	5/94-8/94	0.0500	0.5034	0.8557	0.0993	0.0584
Beijing Urban & Rural Trading Centre Co Ltd	5/94-8/94	0.0061	0.4634	0.7901	0.0132	0.0077
Nantong Machine Tool Co. Ltd (Group)	5/94-8/94	0.0688	0.6793	1.1602	0.1013	0.0593
Inner Mongolia Mengdran Huaneng Thermal Power Co Ltd	5/94-8/94	0.1861	0.6710	1.1444	0.2773	0.1626

Table 11.1B
Risk and Return of Shanghai B-Shares

	Sample Period	Mean Return	Standard Deviation	Beta	Ratio 1	Ratio 2
Shanghai Vacuum Electron Devices Co Ltd	8/92-8/94	(0.0408)	0.1417	0.7185	(0.2878)	(0.0567)
Shanghai Erfangji Co Ltd	8/92-8/94	(0.0172)	0.2306	1.4428	(0.0746)	(0.0119)
Shanghai Dazhong Taxi Co Ltd	8/92-8/94	0.0193	0.2100	1.2167	0.0918	0.0158
Shanghai Wingsung Stationery Co Ltd	8/92-8/94	(0.0326)	0.1412	0.8146	(0.2307)	(0.0400)
China First Pencil Co Ltd	8/92-8/94	(0.0210)	0.1613	0.8493	(0.1305)	(0.0248)
China Textile Machinery Stock Co Ltd	8/92-8/94	(0.0360)	0.1680	1.0483	(0.2145)	(0.0344)
Shanghai Rubber Belt Co Ltd	8/92-8/94	(0.0398)	0.1539	0.8952	(0.2586)	(0.0445)
Shanghai Chlor-Alkal Chemical Co Ltd	8/92-8/94	(0.0327)	0.1659	0.9771	(0.1969)	(0.0334)
Shanghai Tyre and Rubber Co Ltd	8/92-8/94	(0.0247)	0.1929	1.3173	(0.1280)	(0.0188)
Shanghai Refrigerator Compressor Co Ltd	1/93-8/94	(0.0117)	0.1795	0.7539	(0.0654)	(0.0156)
Shanghai Jinqiao Export Processing Zone Development Co Ltd	6/93-8/94	0.0594	0.2398	1.5447	0.2478	0.0385
Shanghai Outer Gaoqiao Free Trade Zone Development Co Ltd	7/93-8/94	0.0553	0.2268	1.4427	0.2437	0.0383
Shanghai Lian Hua Fibre Corporation Ltd	10/93-8/94	(0.0052)	0.0882	0.4436	(0.0593)	(0.0118)
Shanghai Jinjiang Tower Co Ltd	11/93-8/94	0.0050	0.4021	1.0379	0.0124	0.0048
Shanghai Forever Bicycle Co Ltd	11/93-8/94	(0.0429)	0.1877	1.0833	(0.2283)	(0.0396)
Shanghai Phoenix Bicycle Co Ltd	11/93-8/94	0.0038	0.1559	1.1484	0.0245	0.0033
Shanghai Haixin Co Ltd	12/93-8/94	(0.0098)	0.0983	0.8329	(0.1000)	(0.0118)
Shanghai Yaohua Pilkington Glass Co Ltd	12/93-8/94	(0.0110)	0.1341	1.1301	(0.0821)	(0.0097)
Shanghai Dajiang (Group) Stock Co Ltd	12/93-8/94	(0.0167)	0.0902	0.5872	(0.1851)	(0.0284)
Shanghai Diesel Engine Co Ltd	12/93-8/94	0.0292	0.1088	0.7213	0.2684	0.0405

Table 11.1B (Continued)

	Sample Period	Mean Return	Standard Deviation	Beta	Ratio 1	Ratio 2
Shanghai Hero Co Ltd	12/93-8/94	(0.0185)	0.1166	1.0309	(0.1583)	(0.0179)
Shanghai Sanmao Textiles Co Ltd	12/93-8/94	(0.0069)	0.0997	0.7225	(0.0694)	(0.0096)
Shanghai Friendship Overseas Chinese Co Ltd	1/94-8/94	(0.0210)	0.0861	0.7247	(0.2435)	(0.0289)
Shanghai Industrial Sewing Machine Co Ltd	1/94-8/94	(0.0011)	0.0906	0.5534	(0.0119)	(0.0020)
Shanghai Shangling Electric Appliances Co Ltd	1/94-8/94	0.0120	0.4127	0.0703	0.0292	0.1715
Shanghai Steel Tube Co Ltd	3/94-8/94	0.0653	0.0856	0.1668	0.7627	0.3915
Shanghai Goods & Materials Trade Centre Co Ltd	3/94-8/94	0.0475	0.1060	1.6164	0.4481	0.0294
Shanghai Automation Instrumentation Co Ltd	4/94-8/94	0.0079	0.1492	2.2593	0.0528	0.0035

Table 11.1C
Risk and Return of Shenzhen A-Shares

	Sample Period	Mean Return	Standard Deviation	Beta	Ratio 1	Ratio 2
Shenzhen Development Bank Ltd	8/92-8/94	(0.0497)	0.2146	0.8738	(0.2318)	(0.0569)
China Vanke Co Ltd	8/92-8/94	(0.0537)	0.1807	0.6807	(0.2974)	(0.0789)
Shenzhen Gintian Industry Co Ltd	8/92-8/94	(0.0644)	0.2007	0.7857	(0.3208)	(0.0819)
Shenzhen Shekou Anda Industry Co Ltd	8/92-8/94	(0.0556)	0.2013	0.8629	(0.2764)	(0.0645)
Shenzhen Fountain Corporation	1/94-8/94	(0.0035)	0.5139	1.7677	(0.0068)	(0.0020)
Shenzhen Zhenye Co Ltd	8/92-8/94	(0.0659)	0.2438	1.0216	(0.2701)	(0.0645)
Shenzhen Seg. Dasheng Co Ltd	8/92-8/94	(0.0646)	0.2245	1.0497	(0.2875)	(0.0615)
Shenzhen Jinxing Co Ltd	8/92-8/94	(0.0517)	0.2450	1.2017	(0.2110)	(0.0430)
China Baoan Group Co Ltd	8/92-8/94	(0.0606)	0.1891	0.7387	(0.3205)	(0.0820)
Shenzhen Properties & Resources Development (Group) Ltd	8/92-8/94	(0.0553)	0.1556	0.6863	(0.3555)	(0.0806)
China Southern Glass Co Ltd	8/92-8/94	(0.0419)	0.2107	0.9633	(0.1988)	(0.0435)
Shenzhen PetroChemical Industrial Holdings Co Ltd	8/92-8/94	(0.0610)	0.2010	0.9449	(0.3037)	(0.0646)
Shenzhen Hua Yuan Industrial Co Ltd	8/92-8/94	(0.0398)	0.2339	1.0422	(0.1703)	(0.0382)
Shenzhen Zhonghao (Group) Ltd	8/92-8/94	(0.0571)	0.2152	0.9784	(0.2652)	(0.0583)
Shenzhen Konka Electronic (Group) Ltd	8/92-8/94	(0.0456)	0.1889	0.8292	(0.2415)	(0.0550)
Shenzhen China Bicycles Company (Holdings) Ltd	8/92-8/94	(0.0532)	0.1848	0.8018	(0.2877)	(0.0663)
Victor Onward Textile Co Ltd	8/92-8/94	(0.0453)	0.2475	1.1929	(0.1828)	(0.0379)
Shenzhen Shenbao Industrial Co Ltd	10/92-8/94	(0.0561)	0.2047	0.9795	(0.2743)	(0.0573)
Shenzhen Huafa Electronics Co Ltd	8/92-8/94	(0.0542)	0.2146	1.0270	(0.2526)	(0.0528)
Shenzhen Kaifa Technology Ltd	2/94-8/94	(0.1192)	0.3111	0.9977	(0.3830)	(0.1194)

	Sample Period	Mean Return	Standard Deviation	Beta	Ratio 1	Ratio 2
Shenzhen Chiwan Wharf Holdings Ltd	5/93-8/94	(0.0601)	0.2184	1.0232	(0.2751)	(0.0587)
Shenzhen Universe Industrial Stock Co Ltd	5/93-8/94	(0.0645)	0.2543	1.1752	(0.2535)	(0.0549)
Shekou Zhao Shang Harbour Service Holdings Co Ltd	6/93-8/94	(0.0509)	0.2267	1.0178	(0.2246)	(0.0500)
Shenzhen Tellus Machinery & Electronics Co Ltd	8/93-8/94	(0.0807)	0.2317	0.9702	(0.3484)	(0.0832)
Shenzhen Fiyta Holdings Limited	6/93-8/94	(0.0305)	0.2488	1.0185	(0.1224)	(0.0299)
Shenzhen Energy Resources Investment Co Ltd	1/94-8/94	(0.0398)	0.2634	0.8516	(0.1510)	(0.0467)
Shenzhen Yili Mineral Waters Co Ltd	8/93-8/94	(0.0847)	0.2681	1.1172	(0.3160)	(0.0758)
Shenzhen SEZ Real Estate & Properties (Group) Co Ltd	1/94-8/94	(0.0355)	0.1933	0.6199	(0.1834)	(0.0572)
Shenzhen Lionda Holdings Co Ltd	1/94-8/94	(0.0659)	0.3068	1.0448	(0.2148)	(0.0631)
Shenzhen Baoheng (Group) Shareholding Co Ltd	1/94-8/94	(0.0299)	0.3471	1.2010	(0.0862)	(0.0249)
Shenzhen Sed Industry Co Ltd	1/94-8/94	(0.0642)	0.3321	1.1287	(0.1935)	(0.0569)
Shenzhen Century Plaza Hotel Co Ltd	1/94-8/94	(0.0617)	0.2402	0.8294	(0.2570)	(0.0744)
Shenzhen Wabo Group Co Ltd	5/94-8/94	(0.0010)	0.4291	1.0432	(0.0023)	(0.0009)
China Keijian Co Ltd	1/94-8/94	(0.0688)	0.2580	0.6269	(0.2666)	(0.1097)
Shenzhen Wellzong Chemical Fibre & Industry Co Ltd	6/94-8/94	0.0549	0.3933		0.1397	
Shenzhen Nanshan Power Station Co Ltd	7/94-8/94	0.5798				
China International Marine Container Co Ltd	1/94-8/94	0.0067	0.3187	1.0600	0.0210	0.0063
Wuhan Department Store Co Ltd (Group)	11/92-8/94	(0.0399)	0.2841	1.1760	(0.1405)	(0.0339)
Hainan New Energy Co Ltd	11/92-8/94	(0.0686)	0.2587	0.8513	(0.2652)	(0.0806)
Hainan Chemical Fibre Industrial Co Ltd	11/92-8/94	(0.0606)	0.3894	1.0915	(0.1555)	(0.0555)

Table 11.1C (continued)

	Sample Period	Mean Return	Standard Deviation	Beta	Ratio 1	Ratio 2
Hainan Hong Kong & Macao Industrial Co Ltd	12/92-8/94	(0.0682)	0.3111	0.9833	(0.2192)	(0.0694)
Hainan Pearl River Enterprises Co Ltd	12/92-8/94	(0.0480)	0.3832	1.2670	(0.1253)	(0.0379)
Sichuan Emeishan Salt & Chemical Industry (Group) Co Ltd	5/93-8/94	(0.0888)	0.3050	1.0049	(0.2912)	(0.0884)
Fuhua Group Co Ltd Zuhai SEZ	5/93-8/94	(0.0897)	0.2898	1.2091	(0.3094)	(0.0742)
Hainan Minyuan Modern Agriculture Development Co Ltd	5/93-8/94	(0.0693)	0.2968	1.0346	(0.2335)	(0.0670)
Sichuan Tiange Light Industry (Group) Co Ltd	5/93-8/94	(0.0661)	0.2346	0.9555	(0.2817)	(0.0692)
Sichuan Jinlo Co Ltd	5/93-8/94	(0.0684)	0.2867	0.9654	(0.2386)	(0.0709)
Shenyang Goods & Materials Development Co Ltd	5/93-8/94	(0.0805)	0.2759	1.1275	(0.2916)	(0.0714)
Zhuhai Special Economic Zone Lizhu Pharmaceutical Group Inc	1/94-8/94	0.0333	0.3280	0.8186	0.1015	0.0407
Chongqing Real Estate Development Co Ltd	8/93-8/94	(0.0838)	0.3434	1.3532	(0.2439)	(0.0619)
Chongqing Titanium White Co Ltd	8/93-8/94	(0.0846)	0.3309	1.1683	(0.2557)	(0.0724)
Xian Jiefang Department Store Co Ltd	8/93-8/94	(0.0840)	0.2533	1.0749	(0.3316)	(0.0781)
Ningbo Zhong Yuan Machine & Tube Co Ltd	8/93-8/94	(0.1028)	0.2508	0.8282	(0.4097)	(0.1241)
Jiangsu Sanshan Industry & Commerce Co Ltd	1/94-8/94	(0.1438)	0.3889	1.1627	(0.3697)	(0.1237)
Chengdu Engine Fittings Joine-Stock Co Ltd	1/94-8/94	(0.1206)	0.1699	0.4396	(0.7095)	(0.2743)
Wuhan Phoenex Company Limited	1/94-8/94	(0.1428)	0.4594	1.1506	(0.3108)	(0.1241)
Hefei Mesan Company Limited	1/94-8/94	(0.0592)	0.2999	0.8493	(0.1974)	(0.0697)
Guangzhou Bai Yun Shan Pharmaceutical	1/94-8/94	(0.1215)	0.2972	0.4771	(0.4086)	(0.2546)
Lonkey Industrial Co Ltd Guangzhou	1/94-8/94	(0.0224)	0.3362	0.5909	(0.0667)	(0.0380)
Guangzhou Dongfang Hotel Co Ltd	1/94-8/94	(0.0472)	0.2982	0.8827	(0.1583)	(0.0535)

	Sample Period	Mean Return	Standard Deviation	Beta	Ratio 1	Ratio 2
Nanjing Tianlong Co Ltd	1/94-8/94	(0.2421)	0.5100	1.2292	(0.4747)	(0.1970)
Xiamen Ocean Fishery Development Co Ltd	1/94-8/94	(0.1230)	0.3988	1.3446	(0.3084)	(0.0915)
MD Holdings Co Ltd	1/94-8/94	(0.1526)	0.3217	0.7367	(0.4745)	(0.2072)
Guangxi Liugong Machinery Co Ltd	1/94-8/94	(0.0437)	0.3123	0.5718	(0.1400)	(0.0765)
Guangdong Meiya Stock Co Ltd	1/94-8/94	(0.0295)	0.2483	0.7226	(0.1189)	(0.0409)
Dalian Refrigeration Equipment Co Ltd	1/94-8/94	(0.1318)	0.4854	1.2090	(0.2716)	(0.1090)
Hengyan Heat & Power Co Ltd	1/94-8/94	(0.0873)	0.3350	0.7116	(0.2607)	(0.1227)
Zhuhai Huadian Co Ltd	1/94-8/94	(0.0825)	0.3819	1.1677	(0.2161)	(0.0707)
Guangdong Macro Co Ltd	1/94-8/94	(0.0997)	0.2813	0.8733	(0.3543)	(0.1142)
Shantou Electric Power Development Co Ltd	1/94-8/94	(0.0176)	0.2095	0.6754	(0.0840)	(0.0261)
Monkey King Co Ltd	1/94-8/94	0.0078	0.3853	0.7601	0.0202	0.0103
Mindong Electric Group Co Ltd	1/94-8/94	(0.0648)	0.2654	0.8850	(0.2441)	(0.0732)
Tianjin Leader International Market Co Ltd	1/94-8/94	(0.1868)	0.4010	1.2415	(0.4658)	(0.1505)
Yunnan Baiyao Industries Co Ltd	2/94-8/94	(0.0411)	0.4405	1.4399	(0.0932)	(0.0285)
Guangdong Electric Poer Development Co Ltd	1/94-8/94	(0.1651)	0.4095	0.7191	(0.4032)	(0.2296)
Guiyang Zhongtian (Group) Co Ltd	1/94-8/94	(0.1452)	0.4361	1.0839	(0.3330)	(0.1340)
Foshan Lighting & Electrical Corporation	1/94-8/94	0.1126	0.5075	0.4214	0.2219	0.2673
Huizhou TCL Communication Equipment Share Co Ltd	1/94-8/94	(0.0044)	0.2197	0.7379	(0.0200)	(0.0060)
Wen Energy Co Ltd	1/94-8/94	(0.0014)	0.2273	0.7588	(0.0060)	(0.0018)
Zhengzhou White Dove Group Co Ltd	1/94-8/94	(0.0219)	0.3500	0.9511	(0.0625)	(0.0230)

Table 11.1C (continued)

	Sample Period	Mean Return	Standard Deviation	Beta	Ratio 1	Ratio 2
Jilin Pharmaceutical Stock Co Ltd	1/94-8/94	(0.0738)	0.2843	0.9363	(0.2596)	(0.0788)
Jinlin Light Industrial Co Ltd	1/94-8/94	(0.0438)	0.3458	1.1761	(0.1268)	(0.0373)
Fujian Fufa Co Ltd	1/94-8/94	(0.0155)	0.3824	1.1681	(0.0405)	(0.0133)
Changsha Zhongyi Electrical Appliance Co Ltd	1/94-8/94	(0.0552)	0.3192	1.0679	(0.1728)	(0.0517)
Zhuzhou Torch Spark Plug Co Ltd	1/94-8/94	(0.0960)	0.3828	1.0861	(0.2507)	(0.0884)
Jiang Ling Motors Corporation Co Ltd	1/94-8/94	(0.0553)	0.2729	0.9253	(0.2027)	(0.0598)
Suzhou Goods Group Co Ltd	1/94-8/94	(0.0239)	0.2496	0.7461	(0.0958)	(0.0320)
Gansu Changfeng Baoan Industry Co Ltd	1/94-8/94	(0.0774)	0.2885	0.9732	(0.2683)	(0.0795)
Hubei Sanonda Co Ltd	1/94-8/94	(0.0603)	0.2226	0.6454	(0.2709)	(0.0935)
Shandong Taishan Petro-Chemical Co Ltd	2/94-8/94	(0.0525)	0.3314	1.0447	(0.1586)	(0.0503)
Guizhou Kaidi Co Ltd	2/94-8/94	(0.1146)	0.3268	1.0564	(0.3509)	(0.1085)
Hainan Nanyang Shipping Industrial Co Ltd	5/94-8/94	(0.0696)	0.5621	1.3567	(0.1238)	(0.0513)
Yin Chuan Industry Co Ltd	6/94-8/94	0.0649	0.4452		0.1459	
Shenyang Fangtian Co Ltd	5/94-8/94	(0.0060)	0.5243	1.2732	(0.0114)	(0.0047)
Wan Xiang Qian Chao Co Ltd	1/94-8/94	(0.0562)	0.3988	1.3670	(0.1411)	(0.0411)
Kunming Department Store (Group) Co Ltd	1/94-8/94	(0.0879)	0.3521	1.2068	(0.2496)	(0.0728)
Chongling (Group) Co Ltd	5/94-8/94	0.0149	0.4676	1.1370	0.0319	0.0131
Xinjiang Hongyuan Trust & Investment Co Ltd	4/94-8/94	0.0644	0.5316	1.4743	0.1212	0.0437
Shaanxi International Trust & Investment Co Ltd	4/94-8/94	0.0208	0.5165	1.4323	0.0403	0.0145
Xian Minsheng Department Store Co Ltd	4/94-8/94	0.0012	0.4154	1.1516	0.0028	0.0010

	Sample Period	Mean Return	Standard Deviation	Beta	Ratio 1	Ratio 2
Chongqing Shanxia Paints Co Ltd	4/94-8/94	(0.0305)	0.4230	1.1622	(0.0720)	(0.0262)
Hainan Haiyao Industrial Co Ltd	5/94-8/94	(0.0374)	0.5350	1.2783	(0.0699)	(0.0292)
Hainan Haide Textile Industrial Co Ltd	5/94-8/94	(0.0643)	0.6388	1.5244	(0.1006)	(0.0422)
Luzhou Old-Celler Co Ltd	5/94-8/94	0.1159	0.4887	1.1849	0.2372	0.0978
Changcheng Special Steel Co Ltd	4/94-8/94	0.0415	0.4006	1.1037	0.1036	0.0376
Changchai Co Ltd	7/94-8/94	0.8040				
Hainan New Continent Motorcycle Stock Co Ltd	5/94-8/94	(0.0562)	0.6139	1.4457	(0.0916)	(0.0389)

Table 11.1D
Risk and Return of Shenzhen B-Shares

	Sample Period	Mean Return	Standard Deviation	Beta	Ratio 1	Ratio 2
China Vanke Co Ltd	6/93-8/94	(0.1335)	0.1348	1.0989	(0.9906)	(0.1215)
Shenzhen Gintian Industry Co Ltd	8/93-8/94	(0.4426)	0.1778	1.8494	(2.4896)	(0.2394)
Shenzhen Properties & Resources Development (Group) Ltd	8/92-8/94	(1.2403)	0.1767	1.0900	(7.0204)	(1.1379)
China Southern Glass Co Ltd	8/92-8/94	(0.1497)	0.1928	1.1533	(0.7761)	(0.1298)
Shenzhen PetroChemical Industrial Holdings Co Ltd	8/92-8/94	(1.1340)	0.1706	1.1331	(6.6489)	(1.0008)
Shenzhen Zhonghao (Group) Ltd	8/92-8/94	(1.3863)	0.1721	1.0108	(8.0546)	(1.3715)
Shenzhen Konka Electronic (Group) Ltd	8/92-8/94	(0.6306)	0.1746	1.1068	(3.6128)	(0.5698)
Shenzhen China Bicycles Company (Holdings) Ltd	8/92-8/94	(0.5033)	0.1386	0.6789	(3.6324)	(0.7413)
Victor Onward Textile Co Ltd	8/92-8/94	(1.2040)	0.1541	0.8687	(7.8132)	(1.3860)
Shenzhen Shenbao Industrial Co Ltd	10/92-8/94	(0.8267)	0.1841	1.1113	(4.4912)	(0.7439)
Shenzhen Huafa Electronics Co Ltd	8/92-8/94	(1.2993)	0.1694	0.5530	(7.6687)	(2.3494)
Shenzhen Chiwan Wharf Holdings Ltd	5/93-8/94	0.3032	0.1840	1.3138	1.6480	0.2308
Shekou Zhao Shang Harbour Service Holdings Co Ltd	6/93-8/94	0.6381	0.2024	1.4383	3.1523	0.4437
Shenzhen Tellus Machinery & Electronics Co Ltd	8/93-8/94	(0.2584)	0.0952	0.7092	(2.7130)	(0.3643)
Shenzhen Fiyta Holdings Limited	8/93-8/94	(0.0671)	0.2304	1.7585	(0.2914)	(0.0382)
Shenzhen Yili Mineral Waters Co Ltd	1/94-8/94	(0.3423)	0.0503	0.0015	(6.8025)	(224.6836)
Shenzhen SEZ Real Estate & Properties (Group) Co Ltd	1/94-8/94	(0.1798)	0.1025	1.0551	(1.7545)	(0.1704)
Shenzhen Lionda Holdings Co Ltd	1/94-8/94	(0.3994)	0.1162	0.7351	(3.4363)	(0.5433)
China International Marine Container Co Ltd	3/94-8/94	0.1431	0.0708	0.7318	2.0200	0.1955
Shenzhen Benelus Enterprise Co Ltd	5/94-8/94	(0.0727)	0.1946	(1.5334)	(0.3735)	0.0474
Tsam Kuen (China) Enterprise Co Ltd	1/94-8/94	(0.1165)	0.0870	0.9916	(1.3391)	(0.1175)
Zhuhai Special Economic Zone Lizhu Pharmaceutical Group Inc	1/94-8/94	(0.2461)	0.0261	0.2516	(9.4365)	(0.9784)

$$Ratio\ 1 = \frac{E(R_j)}{\beta_j} \qquad (4)$$

$$Ratio\ 2 = \frac{E(R_j)}{SD(R_j)} \qquad (5)$$

According to the respective rankings of actual return, ratio 1, and ratio 2, we identify top-five stocks ranking in each of the four segments. The ranking considers only those stocks with positive returns in the sample period. Those outstanding stocks are shown in Table 11.2. If they can keep their outstanding risk-return performance in the future, these stocks would be the optimal choices for investors. The data are gathered from two sources: *Jinrong Shi Bao* (Financial Times) and *Securities Market Weekly*, both published in Beijing.

COMPARISONS OF RETURNS

We define the market return of a segment $(R_{m,t})$ as an equal-weighted mean of all stock returns in the segment. We then test whether these segments have significantly different mean returns and standard deviations in a pairwise manner. For a pair of segments, say "segment a" and "segment b," we test their difference in the mean return by calculating a t-statistic as follows:

$$t = \frac{E(R_a) - E(R_b)}{\dfrac{\sqrt{Var(R_a) + Var(R_b)}}{n}} \qquad (6)$$

For testing their difference in the standard deviation, we use the F-statistic:

$$F = \frac{SD(R_a)^2}{SD(R_b)^2} \qquad (7)$$

The findings show that A-shares are riskier than B-shares; SZ and SZ-A are riskier than SH and SH-A; SH-B is riskier than SZ-B. Also, SZ-B has a better mean return than SZ-A; SH and SH-A have better mean returns than

Table 11.2
Top Five Stocks in Terms of Actual Returns and Risk-Adjusted Returns

	Shanghai A-shares	Shanghai B-shares
Ranking by Actual Return		
1st	Inner Mongolia Mengdran Huaneng Thermal Power Co Ltd	Shanghai Steel Tube Co Ltd
2nd	Shandong Buohai Group Co Ltd	Shanghai Jinqiao Export Processing Zone Development Co Ltd
3rd	Shanghai Jielong Industry Co Ltd	Shanghai Outer Gaoqiao Free Trade Zone Development Co Ltd
4th	China Sichuan International Cooperation Co Ltd	Shanghai Goods & Materials Trade Centre Co Ltd
5th	Jiangsu Chunlan Refregerating Equipment Stock Co Ltd	Shanghai Diesel Engine Co Ltd
Ranking by Ratio 1		
1st	Shanghai Jielong Industry Co Ltd	Shanghai Steel Tube Co Ltd
2nd	Inner Mongolia Mengdran Huaneng Thermal Power Co Ltd	Shanghai Goods & Materials Trade Centre Co Ltd
3rd	Shandong Buohai Group Co Ltd	Shanghai Diesel Engine Co Ltd
4th	Jiangsu Chunlan Refregerating Equipment Stock Co Ltd	Shanghai Jinqiao Export Processing Zone Development Co Ltd
5th	Beiman Special Steel Co Ltd	Shanghai Outer Gaoqiao Free Trade Zone Development Co Ltd
Ranking by Ratio 2		
1st	Shanghai Jielong Industry Co Ltd	Shanghai Steel Tube Co Ltd
2nd	Liaoyuan Deheng Co Ltd	Shanghai Shangling Electric Appliances Co Ltd
3rd	Inner Mongolia Mengdran Huaneng Thermal Power Co Ltd	Shanghai Diesel Engine Co Ltd
4th	Shandong Buohai Group Co Ltd	Shanghai Jinqiao Export Processing Zone Development Co Ltd
5th	Jiangsu Chunlan Refregerating Equipment Stock Co Ltd	Shanghai Outer Gaoqiao Free Trade Zone Development Co Ltd

Shenzhen A-shares

Ranking by Actual Return
1st   Changchai Co Ltd
2nd   Shenzhen Nanshan Power Station Co Ltd
3rd   Luzhou Old-Celler Co Ltd
4th   Foshan Lighting & Electrical Corporation
5th   Yin Chuan Industry Co Ltd

Ranking by Ratio 1
1st   Luzhou Old-Celler Co Ltd
2nd   Foshan Lighting & Electrical Corporation
3rd   Yin Chuan Industry Co Ltd
4th   Shenzhen Wellzong Chemical Fibre & Industry Co Ltd
5th   Xinjiang Hongyuan Trust & Investment Co Ltd

Ranking by Ratio 2
1st   Foshan Lighting & Electrical Corporation
2nd   Luzhou Old-Celler Co Ltd
3rd   Xinjiang Hongyuan Trust & Investment Co Ltd
4th   Zhuhai Special Economic Zone Lizhu Pharmaceutical Group Inc
5th   Changcheng Special Steel Co Ltd

Shenzhen B-shares

Shekou Zhao Shang Harbour Service Holdings Co Ltd
Shenzhen Chiwan Wharf Holdings Ltd
China International Marine Container Co Ltd
Shenzhen Fiyta Holdings Limited
Shenzhen Benelus Enterprise Co Ltd

Shekou Zhao Shang Harbour Service Holdings Co Ltd
China International Marine Container Co Ltd
Shenzhen Chiwan Wharf Holdings Ltd
Shenzhen Fiyta Holdings Limited
Shenzhen Benelus Enterprise Co Ltd

Shekou Zhao Shang Harbour Service Holdings Co Ltd
Shenzhen Chiwan Wharf Holdings Ltd
China International Marine Container Co Ltd
Shenzhen Benelus Enterprise Co Ltd
Shenzhen Fiyta Holdings Limited

SZ and SZ-A. These results indicate that different segments of China stocks have different risk-return properties. Finance theorists accept that stocks of higher risk will have good performance in a bull market but poor performance in a bear market. Our sample represents a bear market of the China stocks since most stocks have negative mean returns. It is obvious that riskier segments in the sample tend to have poor mean returns.

COMPARISONS BETWEEN "WITH-B" AND "WITHOUT-B" COMPANIES

Listed companies which issue both A- and B-shares ("with-B" companies) can have a different risk-return performance from those which issue only A-shares ("without-B" companies). This is probably because "with-B" companies have a better management, and these companies have extensively been studied by foreign brokers and investment banks. To test the difference between "with-B" and "without-B" companies in their A-shares, this section formulates two portfolios: "without-B" portfolio and "with-B" portfolio. The former is an equally weighted index of all "without-B" shares and the latter is an equally weighted index of all "with-B" shares. To test whether "without-B" and "with-B" portfolios are different in return and risk, we follow the previous procedures to calculate the *t*-statistic and the *F*-statistic. We find that "without-B" and "with-B" portfolios (in the Shanghai, the Shenzhen, and the entire China markets) do not have any significant difference in their mean returns. However, "with-B" portfolios have significantly smaller standard deviations than "without-B" portfolios. When investors are concerned about both risk and return and want to hold some A-shares in China, investing in those A-shares of "with-B" companies appears to be a more desirable decision. This is because "with-B" portfolios have similar returns as "without-B" portfolios but are less risky (i.e., have smaller standard deviations). The lower risk of the A-shares of the "with-B" companies suggests that such listed companies are better, for example, in management quality, than other companies. Or, the lower risk can be due to the lower uncertainty of the "with-B" companies because of the availability of information or research studies.

STOCK MARKET EFFICIENCY

An efficient stock market means that stock prices adjust quickly to all information about the intrinsic value of a company. Fama's (1965) efficient market hypothesis (EMH) has attracted the attention of many finance theorists. Operationally, this hypothesis is categorized into three forms: weak-form EMH, semi-strong-form EMH, and strong-form EMH. The weak-form EMH suggests that stock prices reflect all information, including historical information available in the market, such as price history, trading volume, financial statements, and so on. The semi-strong-form EMH argues that market prices adjust rapidly to all information, including new information released. The empirical results on this hypothesis are mixed. On the one hand, event studies on stock splits, initial public offerings, and accounting changes support the semi-strong-form EMH. On the other hand, other studies find that the P/E ratios, company size, neglected stocks, price-to-book-value ratios, and unexpected earnings can help to predict stock returns, and the semi-strong-form EMH is not supported. The strong-form EMH asserts that market prices reflect all information from both public and private sources. It implies that nobody can earn above-average profit. Studies find that corporate insiders can earn above-average profits after their trading, while other studies on the performance of professional fund managers conclude that they do not outperform a simple buy-and-hold policy.[1]

Most of the previous tests on EMH were done with U.S. data. Some recent studies on emerging markets find that these markets are not as efficient as the U.S. market. China can be regarded as an emerging stock market in the world and currently has attracted international attention. Therefore, it is worthwhile to investigate whether the EMH holds in the Chinese market.

Data

There are four stock indexes in our sample, namely Shanghai A-share Index (SH-A), Shanghai B-share Index (SH-B), Shenzhen A-share Index (SZ-A), and Shenzhen B-share Index (SZ-B). They are value-weighted indexes. The A-share indexes are quoted in Rmb and the B-share indexes are quoted in U.S. dollars (SHSE) and H.K. dollars (SZSE), respectively. The sample period is from October 6, 1992 to March 24, 1995. There are 644 daily observations. Daily index return $R_{j,t}$ is calculated by $\Delta \ln P_{j,t} = \ln P_{j,t} - \ln P_{j,t-1}$.

Step 1: Autocorrelations Tests

In order to investigate whether the four index returns are independent, we begin by first estimating the first-order autocorrelation (β_1) with the following model:

$$R_{j,t} = \alpha + \beta_1 R_{j,t-1} + u_t \tag{8}$$

A high first-order autocorrelation implies that the previous day's stock returns can help to predict today's returns. Tests are based on White's (1982) heteroscedasticity-consistent standard errors. Next, we use the following model to capture the day-of-the-week effect on the first-order autocorrelation:

$$R_{j,t} = \alpha + (\Sigma \beta_{1,i} D_i) R_{j,t-1} + u_t \tag{9}$$

where D_i is a dummy on the day in a week. $D_i = 1$ if the observation is on the ith day of the week (Monday, Tuesday, . . . , and Friday); otherwise, $D_i = 0$. Furthermore, we estimate the autocorrelation of other lags (lag 2 to lag 10) with Equation (1) by replacing $\beta_1 R_{j,t-1}$ with $\beta_k R_{j,t-k}$ for $k = 2, . . . , 10$, respectively.

Step 2: Cointegration and Causality

Whether the four indexes are interdependent can be seen from their cointegration and causality tests. We begin by looking at the stationarity of $\ln P_{j,t}$ and $R_{j,t}$ with the unit root Dickey and Fuller (DF) and Augmented Dickey and Fuller (ADF) tests (Dickey and Fuller, 1979, 1981). If they belong to same order of integration, we then apply the residual-based cointegration test of Engle and Granger (1987) with the following pairwise model:

$$\ln P_{j,t} = \alpha + \beta \ln P_{i,t} + e_{j,i,t} \tag{10}$$

The pairs of indexes $(P_{j,t}, P_{i,t})$ are divided into:
  Group A (A-B-share combinations):
    (SH-A, SH-B), (SH-B, SH-A), (SZ-A, SZ-B), (SZ-B, SZ-A); and
  Group B (Shanghai-Shenzhen combinations):
    (SH-A, SZ-A), (SZ-A, SH-A), (SH-B, SZ-B), (SZ-B, SH-B).
We use Ordinary Least Squares (OLS) for the estimation and then test the stationarity of the residual, $e_{j,i,t}$. Critical values are based on those used by MacKinnon (1990). If the residuals are stationary, the pairs of indexes are said to be cointegrated, and a long-term relationship is established between them.

For noncointegrated pairs of indexes, we apply the traditional causality test of Granger (1980), i.e.,

$$\Delta \ln P_{j,t} = \alpha + \Sigma \Theta_k \Delta \ln P_{j,t-k} + \Sigma \tau_k \Delta \ln P_{i,t-k} + u_t \qquad (11)$$

For cointegrated pairs of indexes, we apply the modified causality test of Engle and Granger (1987), i.e.,

$$\Delta \ln P_{j,t} = \alpha + \Sigma \Theta_k \Delta \ln P_{j,t-k} + \Sigma \tau_k \Delta \ln P_{i,t-k} + \delta_{j,i} e_{j,i,t-1} + u_t \qquad (12)$$

In both Equations (11) and (12), u_t is the error term and k denotes the lag number. If a variable, X, is said to "Granger-cause" another variable, Y, it simply means that Y can be predicted with better accuracy by the past values of X. Hence, a Granger causality can be a result of either a causal relationship, a lead-lag relationship, or both.

To check the robustness of the test results to the choice of k, we try $k = 2, 4, 6, 8,$ and 10 respectively. We use F-statistic to test whether all τ_k are jointly zero (that is, $\Delta \ln P_{i,t}$ does not Granger-cause $\Delta \ln P_{j,t}$). If it is rejected, it suggests that $\Delta \ln P_{i,t}$ Granger-causes $\Delta \ln P_{j,t}$. The $e_{j,i,t-1}$ in Equation (12) comes from Equation (10) and the $\delta_{j,i}$ measures the single-period response of the dependent variable to departures from the long-term relationship between $\ln P_{j,t}$ and $\ln P_{i,t}$. A significantly negative $\delta_{j,i}$ indicates that $\ln P_{j,t}$ adjusts to correct departures from the long-term relationship.

Step 3: Whole-Sample and Subsample Results

Since the exchange rate in China was highly volatile before the new exchange system was launched on January 1, 1994, the tests on cointegration between the A-share and B-share market can be biased by the exchange-rate volatility. Therefore, we repeat the above cointegration and causality analyses with the sample period between January 2, 1994 and March 24, 1995. The exchange rate was more stable in this subsample period. Then we compare these results with the whole-sample results.

EMPIRICAL RESULTS

Autocorrelations

Table 11.3 presents the summary statistics of the daily index return, $R_{j,t}$. All four index returns are not significantly different from 0, and the A-share markets appear to be more volatile than the B-share markets as suggested by their standard deviations of returns. Table 11.4 displays the estimates of Equation (8) and (9) for the first-order autocorrelations. It shows that the value of ß is not significant in the A-share markets, while it is significantly positive in the B-share markets. The two explained R^2 for the B-share markets are rather large (up to fifteen percent). SH-B's $R^2(1)$ and $R^2(2)$ are 10.26 percent and 10.81 percent, respectively. SZ-B's are 9.26 percent and 15.53 percent, respectively. This means that the previous day's stock returns can account for nine percent to fifteen percent of the variability of today's stock returns in China's stock markets. The results of autocorrelations of other orders, β_2 to β_{10}, are shown in Table 11.5. For SH-A, β_3, β_8, and β_9 are significant. For SZ-A, β_4, β_6, and β_{10} are significant.

Table 11.3
Summary Statistics for the Daily Stock Returns of the A- and B-Shares

Statistics	Shanghai A	Shanhgai B	Shenzhen A	Shenzhen B
Mean	-0.041%	-0.029%	-0.118%	-0.108%
Median	-0.304%	-0.110%	-0.382%	-0.146%
min	-14.600%	-8.242%	-14.777%	-7.700%
Max	30.852%	9.526%	29.571%	13.799%
SD	4.438%	1.905%	3.706%	1.514%
Skewness	1.536	0.525	1.250	2.064
Kurtosis	9.361	4.111	8.722	21.821
Shapiro-Wilk Statistic	0.887	0.936	0.937	0.819
p-value	0.000	0.000	0.000	0.000

Source: Datastream International Limited, United Kingdom.

Table 11.4
The First Autocorrelation of the Daily Returns

$$r_{t+1} = \alpha + \beta r_t \qquad (1)$$
$$r_{t+1} = \alpha + (\Sigma \beta_i D_i) r_t \qquad (2)$$

Series	β (*t*-value)	R^2 (1)	R^2 (2)
Shanghai A	-0.0106 (-0.22)	0.0001	0.0102
Shanghai B	0.3203 (4.59)	0.1026	0.1100
Shenzhen A	-0.0114 (-0.23)	0.0001	0.0062
Shenzhen B	0.3102 (2.66)	0.0962	0.1576

Table 11.5
Autocorrelation for the Daily Returns Series

$$r_{t+1} = \alpha + \beta_i r_t$$

Lag	Shanghai A			Shenzhen A		
	β_i	t-statistics	p-value	β_i	t-statistics	p-value
1	-0.0106	-0.22	0.828	-0.0114	-0.23	0.815
2	0.0436	0.58	0.562	0.0477	0.66	0.508
3	0.1467	2.95	0.003	0.0357	0.70	0.482
4	0.0664	1.21	0.228	0.1077	1.92	0.056
5	0.0326	0.82	0.413	0.0290	0.55	0.582
6	0.0542	0.85	0.397	-0.0871	-1.76	0.079
7	0.0037	0.08	0.936	-0.0167	-0.29	0.769
8	-0.0901	-2.24	0.025	-0.0108	-0.26	0.799
9	0.1140	2.31	0.021	0.0512	1.47	0.141
10	-0.0269	-0.51	0.608	-0.1026	-2.43	0.016
	Shanghai A			Shenzhen B		
1	0.3203	4.46	0.000	0.3102	2.66	0.008
2	0.0521	0.83	0.410	0.1950	2.12	0.034
3	-0.0128	-0.22	0.828	0.0939	1.26	0.207
4	0.0398	0.80	0.424	0.1339	2.04	0.042
5	0.0315	0.69	0.493	0.0575	1.34	0.182
6	0.0050	0.11	0.912	0.0387	1.02	0.306
7	0.0554	1.53	0.127	0.0300	0.76	0.448
8	0.0339	0.83	0.409	0.0246	0.60	0.547
9	0.0388	1.01	0.314	0.0393	1.00	0.319
10	0.0240	0.62	0.536	0.0232	0.67	0.501

Note: t-statistics and p-value are calculated by the heteroscedasticity-consistent standard errors of White (1980).

Combining these results, we conclude that the China stock returns do not follow a random walk and past returns can help to predict future returns. In other words, the China stock markets are inefficient in the weak form. Positive first-order autocorrelation is very pronounced only in the B-share markets. Although this may be due to positive feedback trading (DeLong, Shleifer, Summers, and Waldman 1990; Culter, Poterba, and Summers 1990), the problem of infrequent trading (Scholes and Williams, 1977; Atchinson, Butler, and Simonds, 1987; Lo and MacKinlay, 1988) is a better explanation. Since only a small portion of listed companies issued B-shares and they are solely traded among foreigners, the liquidity would be lower in the B-share markets than in the A-share markets, and the reactions of foreigners to Chinese news would be slower than those of China nationals. This would result in a positive first-order autocorrelation.

Cointegration and Causality

Table 11.6 summarizes the results of unit root tests with and without a trend. With respect to the DF and ADF(1) to ADF(4) results, we find that all four $\ln P_{j,t}$ are nonstationary but all four $R_{j,t}$ are stationary, suggesting that the four $\ln P_{j,t}$ have the same order of integration, i.e., $I(1)$. These results are robust across the tests with and without a trend.

Table 11.7 displays the test results of cointegration. The SH-B and SZ-B are cointegrated, but the A-share and B-share markets are not. The cointegration tests on SH-A and SZ-A show a mixed result. Only the test with SH-A as dependent variable shows the two A-share markets are cointegrated.

Table 11.8 presents the test results of Equations (11) and (12). For the noncointegrated pairs of indexes, we find that SZ-A Granger-causes SZ-B as suggested by the significant *F*-statistics. This result is robust to all five lags. It can be attributed to the infrequent trading problem in the B-share market. For the cointegrated series, we find that SH-B Granger-causes SZ-B. This result is robust to four of the five lags. This suggests that past returns of SH-B can help to predict future returns of SZ-B.

With regard to the $\delta_{j,i}$ in Equation (12), it is significantly negative in all four pairs of indexes studied, except the pair (SZ-A, SH-A). This suggests that the pairs of the indexes, (SH-A, SZ-A) and (SH-B, SZ-B) have long-term relationships.

Subsample Results

For the subsample period after the new exchange rate system from January 1994, we find that none of the pairs of indexes are cointegrated. Table 11.9 presents the results of causality tests (for noncointegrated series) of the subsample period. It can be seen that SZ-A Granger-causes SH-A (robust to four of the five lags), SH-B Granger-causes SZ-B (robust to four of the five lags), SH-B Granger-causes SH-A (robust to three of the five lags), and SZ-A Granger-causes SZ-B (robust to all five lags). To a certain extent, they are consistent with the results for the whole-sample period.

Table 11.6
Augmented Dickey and Fuller Unit Root Test

$$\Delta X_t = \alpha_0 + \alpha_1 t + \beta X_{t-1} + \sum \gamma_j \sum X_{t-j} + \varepsilon_t$$

Price Index Level

	DF		ADF1		ADF2		ADF3		ADF4	
	WT	WOT	WT	WOT	WT	WOT	WT	WOT	WT	WOT
SH-A	-2.20	-1,77	-2.20	-1.75	-2.34	-1.86	-2.59	-2.13	-2.66	-2.23
SH-B	-1.50	-1.30	-2.04	-1.86	-1.89	-1.70	-2.18	-2.00	-2.19	-2.02
SZ-A	-2.30	-1.16	-2.30	-1.17	-2.45	-1.27	-2.49	-1.31	-2.65	-1.42
SZ-B	-0.67	-0.17	-1.27	-0.80	-1.50	-1.01	-1.51	-0.98	-.1.76	-1.22

First Difference*

	DF		ADF1		ADF2		ADF3		ADF4	
	WC	WOC	WC	WOC	WC	WOC	WC	WOC	WC	WOC
SH-A	-23.87	-24.89	-16.66	-16.67	-12.03	-12.04	-10.29	-10.29	-9.03	-9.04
SH-B	-19.14	-19.15	-16.21	-16.22	-11.97	-11.98	-10.70	-10.71	-10.10	-10.11
SZ-A	-24.58	-24.58	-16.33	-16.32	-13.32	-13.31	-10.99	-10.97	-9.56	-9.55
SZ-B	-17.77	-17.72	-12.88	-12.83	-11.21	-11.17	-9.14	-9.10	-9.03	-9.00

Note: WT = with trend. WOT = without trend. WC = with constant. WOC = without constant. * = one percent level of significance.

Table 11.7
Cointegration Test

Dependent Variable	Independent Variable	*t*-statistics
Within an Exchange		
Shanghai A	Shanghai B	-2.0628
Shanghai B	Shanghai A	01.6677
Shanghai A	Shenzhen B	01.7517
Shenzhen B	Shanghai A	01.0942
Within the Same Type of Investors		
Shanghai A	Shenzhen A	-3.1422*
Shenzhen A	Shanghai A	-2.8342
Shanghai B	Shenzhen B	-4.0185†
Shenzhen B	Shanghai B	-3.6826‡

Note: *, †, ‡ = 10 percent, 5 percent, and 1 percent level of significance, respectively.

CONCLUSION

This chapter has shown the risk-return properties of China stock in the period from September 1992 to August 1994, and finds that the China stock market was a bear market since most stocks had negative mean monthly returns. We have also compared the risk and return of different segments of China stocks. Briefly, A-shares are riskier than B-shares and Shanghai stocks are riskier than Shenzhen stocks. In our sample period, the riskier segments have already demonstrated a poor mean return. This is consistent with the general agreement of finance theorists that riskier stocks tend to have better returns in bull markets and poor returns in bear markets.

Furthermore, we have compared the performance of "without-B" companies and "with-B" companies in their A-shares. Our results indicate clearly that A-shares of "with-B" companies are less risky than those of "without-B" companies, although these two types of companies have similar returns in their A-shares. This is due to a better quality or better information flow of companies with B-shares. This can be very useful for investors who want to hold A-shares in China. Their first choices should be those companies that issue both A-shares and B-shares since these companies will likely have similar returns as other companies but are less risky.

Table 11.8
Tests of Granger Causality Between Markets and Investors

Not Granger-caused	Error term	Not Granger-caused	Error term
Lag 2			
Market			
SH-A ⇐ SH-B		SH-B ⇐ SH-A	
SZ-A ⇐ SZ-B*		SZ-B ⇐ SZ-A‡	
Investors			
SH-A ⇐ SZ-A	-0.024†	SZ-A ⇐ SH-A*	-0.010
SH-B ⇐ SZ-B†	-0.025‡	SZ-B ⇐ SH-B‡	-0.020‡
Lag 4			
Market			
SH-A ⇐ SH-B		SH-B ⇐ SH-A	
SZ-A ⇐ SZ-B		SZ-B ⇐ SZ-A‡	
Investors			
SH-A ⇐ SZ-A	-0.028†	SZ-A ⇐ SH-A	-0.009
SH-B ⇐ SZ-B	-0.031‡	SZ-B ⇐ SH-B‡	-0.017‡
Lag 6			
Market			
SH-A ⇐ SH-B		SH-B ⇐ SH-A*	
SZ-A ⇐ SZ-B		SZ-B ⇐ SZ-A‡	
Investors			
SH-A ⇐ SZ-A	-0.031‡	SZ-A ⇐ SH-A	-0.009
SH-B ⇐ SZ-B	-0.030‡	SZ-B ⇐ SH-B‡	-0.015‡
Lag 8			
Market			
SH-A ⇐ SH-B		SH-B ⇐ SH-A	
SZ-A ⇐ SZ-B		SZ-B ⇐ SZ-A‡	
Investors			
SH-A ⇐ SZ-A	-0.029†	SZ-A ⇐ SH-A	-0.008
SH-B ⇐ SZ-B	-0.034‡	SZ-B ⇐ SH-B‡	-0.011*
Lag 10			
Market			
SH-A ⇐ SH-B		SH-B ⇐ SH-A	
SZ-A ⇐ SZ-B		SZ-B ⇐ SZ-A‡	
Investors			
SH-A ⇐ SZ-A	-0.035‡	SZ-A ⇐ SH-A†	-0.006
SH-B ⇐ SZ-B	-0.037‡	SZ-B ⇐ SH-B‡	-0.011*

Note: SH, SZ = Shanghai and Shenzhen, respectively. A, B = A and B shares, respectively.
*, †, ‡ = 10 percent, 5 percent, and 1 percent level of significance, respectively.

Table 11.9
Tests of Granger Causality Between Markets and Investors: Subperiod Results

Not Granger-caused	Not Granger-caused
Lag 2	
Market	
SH-A ⇐ SH-B†	SH-B ⇐ SH-A
SZ-A ⇐ SZ-B*	SZ-B ⇐ SZ-A‡
Investors	
SH-A ⇐ SZ-A*	SZ-A ⇐ SH-A
SH-B ⇐ SZ-B†	SZ-B ⇐ SH-B*
Lag 4	
Market	
SH-A ⇐ SH-B*	SH-B ⇐ SH-A
SZ-A ⇐ SZ-B	SZ-B ⇐ SZ-A‡
Investors	
SH-A ⇐ SZ-A	SZ-A ⇐ SH-A
SH-B ⇐ SZ-B	SZ-B ⇐ SH-B
Lag 6	
Market	
SH-A ⇐ SH-B*	SH-B ⇐ SH-A
SZ-A ⇐ SZ-B	SZ-B ⇐ SZ-A‡
Investors	
SH-A ⇐ SZ-A*	SZ-A ⇐ SH-A
SH-B ⇐ SZ-B	SZ-B ⇐ SH-B†
Lag 8	
Market	
SH-A ⇐ SH-B	SH-B ⇐ SH-A
SZ-A ⇐ SZ-B	SZ-B ⇐ SZ-A†
Investors	
SH-A ⇐ SZ-A*	SZ-A ⇐ SH-A
SH-B ⇐ SZ-B	SZ-B ⇐ SH-B†
Lag 10	
Market	
SH-A ⇐ SH-B	SH-B ⇐ SH-A
SZ-A ⇐ SZ-B	SZ-B ⇐ SZ-A†
Investors	
SH-A ⇐ SZ-A*	SZ-A ⇐ SH-A
SH-B ⇐ SZ-B	SZ-B ⇐ SH-B*

Note: Same as Table 11.8.

In investigating the price linkage between the Shanghai and Shenzhen stock markets, we find that the daily returns in the China stock markets do not follow random walks. Also, there is no convincing evidence that the four index series, SH-A, SH-B, SZ-A, and SZ-B, are cointegrated. The absence of cointegration between A-share and B-share markets can be the result of the exchange-rate volatility. The absence of cointegration between the Shanghai and Shenzhen markets can be attributed to the rapid development of the two stock markets. Many newly listed companies were continuously added to the index series. These companies belong to different businesses and have different levels of riskiness. Some of them issue B-shares while others do not. Such a dynamic market structure should generate an unstable long-term relationship between the index series.

On the other hand, there is strong evidence that SZ-A Granger-causes SH-A and SH-B Granger-causes SZ-B. This suggests that Shenzhen has a faster information flow than Shanghai in the A-share market, while Shanghai has a faster information flow than Shenzhen in the B-share market. The faster reaction of the local investors in Shenzhen can be attributed to their better access to news reported by international news agencies. This is because Shenzhen is geographically closer to Hong Kong and local investors in Shenzhen can obtain news directly from Hong Kong. The fact that foreign investors react faster in Shanghai can be attributed to their more active participation in the Shanghai market. Both the market value of B-shares and the number of companies having B-shares are larger in Shanghai than in Shenzhen. The China stock markets appear to grow rapidly along with the economic growth of China. These causalities, however, disappear when there are improvements in communication facilities for local investors, changes in the dynamic structure of the market indexes, and advancements in investment knowledge.

NOTE

1. For a summary on EMH and the various tests, see Reilly (1994, pp. 194–239).

REFERENCES

Atchinson, Michael D., Kirt C. Bulter, and Richard R. Simonds, 1987, "Nonsynchronous Security Trading and Market Index Autocorrelation," *Journal of Finance*, 42: 111–118.

Culter, David M., James M. Poterba, and Lawrence H. Summers, 1990, "Speculative Dynamics and the Role of Feedback Traders," *American Economic Review*, 80(2) May: 63–68.

DeLong, J. Bradford, Andrei Shleifer, Lawrence H. Summers, and Robert J. Waldman, 1990, "Positive Feedback Investment Strategies and Destabilizing Rational Speculation," *Journal of Finance*, 45: 379–395.

Dickey, David A., and Wayne A. Fuller, 1979, "Distribution of the Estimators for Autoregressive Time Series with a Unit Root," *Journal of American Statistical Association*, 74: 427–431.

————, 1981, "The Likelihood Ratio Statistics for Autoregressive Time Series with a Unit Root," *Econometrica*, 49: 1057–72.

Engle, Robert T., and Clive W. J. Granger, 1987, "Cointegration and Error Correction: Representation, Estimation and Testing," *Econometrica*, 55: 1057–1072.

Fama, Eugene F., 1965, "The Behaviour of Stock Market Prices," *Journal of Business*, 38: 34–105.

Granger, Clive W. J., 1980, "Testing for Causality: A Personal Viewpoint," *Journal of Economic Dynamics and Control*, 2 November: 329–352.

Lo, Andrew W. and A. Craig MacKinlay, 1988, "Stock Market Prices Do Not Follow Random Walks: Evidence from a Simple Specification Test," *Review of Financial Studies*, 1: 41–66.

MacKinnon, James G., 1990, *Critical Values for Cointegration Tests*, Discussion Paper 90–4, University of San Diego.

Reilly, Frank K., 1994, *Investment Analysis and Portfolio Management*, New York: Dryden Press.

Scholes, Myron, and Joseph Williams, 1977, "Estimating Betas from Nonsynchronous Data," *Journal of Financial Economics*, 5(3) December: 309–328.

Sharpe, William, and Gordon Alexander, 1990, *Investments* (4th edition). Prentice-Hall International, Inc.

White, Halbert, J. 1980, "A Heteroskedasticity Consistent Covariance Matrix Estimator and a Direct Test of Heteroskedasticity," *Econometrica*, 48: 817–838.

Index

About the Editor and Contributors

BARANDIARAN, Edgardo, Resident Mission in China, The World Bank, Washington, D.C., USA.

CHAI, Pangshun, China Desk, Swiss Volksbank, Hong Kong.

CHEN, Pochih, Department of Economics, National Taiwan University, Taipei, Taiwan.

JIANG, Wei, Department of Economics, University of Chicago, USA.

JUN, Kwang W., International Finance Division, The World Bank, Washington, D.C., USA.

KAN, Chak-Yuen, Department of Economics and Finance, City University of Hong Kong, Hong Kong.

KATADA, Saori N., School of International Relations, University of South California, Los Angeles, USA.

KINOSHITA, Toshihiko, Research Institute for International Investment and Development, The Export-Import Bank of Japan, Tokyo, Japan.

KWOK, Raymond H. F., Daiwa Institute of Research (H.K.) Limited, Hong Kong.

LEUNG, Winson S. C., Waverley International Limited, Hong Kong.

LI, Kui-Wai, Department of Economics and Finance, City University of Hong Kong, Hong Kong.

LO, Kenneth W. K., Department of Economics and Finance, City University of Hong Kong, Hong Kong.

NYAW, Mee-Kau, Lingnan College, Hong Kong.

TANG, Xu, The Graduate School, People's Bank of China, Beijing, People's Republic of China.

WALL, David, School of African and Asian Studies, University of Sussex, England.

WONG, Clement Yuk-pang, Department of Economics and Finance, City University of Hong Kong, Hong Kong.

WONG, Kwok-Fai, Department of Economics and Finance, City University of Hong Kong, Hong Kong.

WONG, Michael C. S., Department of Economics and Finance, City University of Hong Kong, Hong Kong.